About This Book

Why is this topic important?

Exploring and developing emotional intelligence not only makes us happier and more successful, but it helps us motivate ourselves, manage stress more eff⋯ ⋯ ⋯olve conflict with others. It gives us the skills to be able t⋯ ⋯nd confront different kinds of people appropriately in di⋯ ⋯ effectively we express our emotions within the cultural c⋯ ⋯e, and our community. It determines how well people list⋯ ⋯.

What can you achieve with this book?

As an easy-to-use informational reference to the key components of emotional intelligence, this book is unsurpassed. The sixty-five cross-referenced exercises serve as an invaluable resource for trainers, coaches, facilitators, HR professionals, managers, and anyone who needs to build emotional intelligence competencies in their work with individuals, teams, or groups.

Several books are available that discuss this topic, but very few provide exercises and learning scenarios to help build emotional intelligence skills. This book breaks new ground in providing a cross-reference matrix that maps the exercises to four of the leading emotional intelligence models—the EQ-i2.0® or EQ360®, TESI® and TESI® Short, the MSCEIT™, and EISA—making it easy to use with all the models.

How is this book organized?

This book is organized into three parts. Part One provides an overview of using emotional intelligence to create real change. It includes sections on why emotional intelligence is important and how to best use this book. It also contains the cross-reference table that maps the exercises to four leading emotional intelligence models. Last, it discusses the integral connection between thinking and emotions. Part Two gives a synopsis of sixteen components of emotional intelligence. Part Three features sixty-five exercises to help build effective emotional skills. Each exercise includes a purpose statement, summary, description of the outcome/desired results, estimated time, intended audience, skill level needed by facilitator, step-by-step instructions, and reproducible handout sheets for participants where applicable.

About Pfeiffer

Pfeiffer serves the professional development and hands-on resource needs of training and human resource practitioners and gives them products to do their jobs better. We deliver proven ideas and solutions from experts in HR development and HR management, and we offer effective and customizable tools to improve workplace performance. From novice to seasoned professional, Pfeiffer is the source you can trust to make yourself and your organization more successful.

Essential Knowledge Pfeiffer produces insightful, practical, and comprehensive materials on topics that matter the most to training and HR professionals. Our Essential Knowledge resources translate the expertise of seasoned professionals into practical, how-to guidance on critical workplace issues and problems. These resources are supported by case studies, worksheets, and job aids and are frequently supplemented with CD-ROMs, websites, and other means of making the content easier to read, understand, and use.

Essential Tools Pfeiffer's Essential Tools resources save time and expense by offering proven, ready-to-use materials—including exercises, activities, games, instruments, and assessments—for use during a training or team-learning event. These resources are frequently offered in looseleaf or CD-ROM format to facilitate copying and customization of the material.

Pfeiffer also recognizes the remarkable power of new technologies in expanding the reach and effectiveness of training. While e-hype has often created whizbang solutions in search of a problem, we are dedicated to bringing convenience and enhancements to proven training solutions. All our e-tools comply with rigorous functionality standards. The most appropriate technology wrapped around essential content yields the perfect solution for today's on-the-go trainers and human resource professionals.

Essential resources for training and HR professionals

This book is dedicated to all those who help others enhance the quality of life by developing deeper, more profound business and personal relationships. Their actions, which add richness, strength, and meaning to life, resonate throughout the world and transform our lives.

Emotional Intelligence in Action

Training and Coaching Activities for Leaders, Managers, and Teams

SECOND EDITION

MARCIA HUGHES

JAMES BRADFORD TERRELL

Pfeiffer

A Wiley Imprint
www.pfeiffer.com

Published by Pfeiffer
An Imprint of Wiley
One Montgomery Street, Suite 1200, San Francisco, CA 94104-4594
www.pfeiffer.com

For additional copies/bulk purchases of this book in the U.S. please contact 800-274-4434.

Pfeiffer books and products are available through most bookstores. To contact Pfeiffer directly call our Customer Care Department within the U.S. at 800-274-4434, outside the U.S. at 317-572-3985, fax 317-572-4002, or visit www.pfeiffer.com.

Pfeiffer publishes in a variety of print and electronic formats and by print-on-demand. Some material included with standard print versions of this book may not be included in e-books or in print-on-demand. If this book refers to media such as a CD or DVD that is not included in the version you purchased, you may download this material at http://booksupport.wiley.com. For more information about Wiley products, visit www.wiley.com.

Library of Congress Cataloging-in-Publication Data

Hughes, Marcia.
    Emotional intelligence in action : training and coaching activities for leaders, managers, and teams / Marcia Hughes, James Bradford Terrell.—2nd ed.
        p. cm.
    Includes bibliographical references and index.
    ISBN 978-1-118-12804-6 (pbk.); 978-1-118-17126-4 (ebk.); 978-1-118-17127-1 (ebk.); 978-1-118-17128-8 (ebk.)
        1. Executives—Training of—Handbooks, manuals, etc. 2. Leadership—Study and teaching—Handbooks, manuals, etc. 3. Executive coaching—Handbooks, manuals, etc. 4. Counselors—Training of—Handbooks, manuals, etc. 5. Group facilitation—Handbooks, manuals, etc. 6. Personnel departments—Employees—Training of—Handbooks, manuals, etc. 7. Emotional intelligence—Handbooks, manuals, etc. 8. Active learning—Handbooks, manuals, etc. I. Terrell, James Bradford, 1951- II. Title.
    HD30.4.H824 2012
    658.4'071245—dc23
                                                                                                    2011041420

Acquiring Editor: Holly Allen

Director of Development: Kathleen Dolan Davies

Developmental Editor: Susan Rachmeler

Production Editor: Michael Kay

Printed in the United States of America

Editor: Rebecca Taff

Editorial Assistant: Michael Zelenko

Manufacturing Supervisor: Becky Morgan

PB Printing   10 9 8 7 6 5 4 3 2 1

Contents

Contents

5 Assertiveness

6 Independence

7 Interpersonal Relationships

8 Empathy

On the Web

From the Internet, you can download for free the handouts that are part of the various exercises. To obtain these handouts electronically, please access the following web address:

www.pfeiffer.com/go/EIAction2
password: training

Below is a list of the handouts posted on the website.

Self-Regard

- Lighten Up with Self-Compassion
- Of Thine Own Self Be Aware
- Reconciliation
- Aspect and Roles

Self-Actualization

- Leverage Your Time with a 2% Solution
- Your 2% Solution
- The Scavenger Hunt
- Becoming All That You Can Be
- Applying Inspiration

Emotional Self-Awareness

- Expanding Your Uncommon Awareness
- Are You in Touch?
- It Just Bubbles Up
- Moving Toward and Moving Away

Emotional Expression

- Expressing Resistance
- Say It Nonverbally!
- Expressing Emotions in Social Media

Assertiveness

- Developing Appropriate Assertiveness Within Your Team
- Ramp It Up
- Dial It Back
- Getting Your Point Across

Independence

- Virtual Decision Making
- Cut the Apron Strings
- Solitary Effort
- Going Along with the Group—Or Not

Interpersonal Relationships

- You've Got Good News
- Making New Friends

Empathy

- Mixed Emotions
- Do as the Empathic Do

Social Responsibility

- Reflect the Best
- Who Do I Work for?

Problem Solving

- When Problems Become Conflicts
- Emotions Affect Decision Making
- MasterSolve Model© for Teams
- Win-Win Negotiating
- Let's Cover Our Bases

Reality Testing

- Feel, Hear, See—Is it Reality?
- Visit Their Reality
- Using All Three of Your Minds

Impulse Control

- Putting on the Brakes
- *King Lear*, Act 1, Scene 1
- To Impulse or Not to Impulse
- The Urge to Splurge
- Hot Buttons

Flexibility

- The Highly Flexible Team
- No More Shutdowns
- Yes, No, Maybe So

Stress Tolerance

- EZ Stress Buster
- Personality Quiz
- 'Cause You've Got Personality
- Deep Center Breathing

Optimism

- Optimistic Self-Talk and Behavior
- Be Solution-Focused
- The Optimistic Explanation

Happiness/Well-Being

- Beyond Personal Silos
- Growing My Happiness

Acknowledgments

The authors wish to acknowledge and thank:

Steve Stein, James Buchanan, Derek Mann, and the MHS team; Diana Durek, for her astute leadership and guidance in working with EI; Reuven Bar-On, Peter Salovey, John D. Mayer, David R. Caruso, Daniel Goleman, Richard E. Boyatzis, Cary Cherniss, and Marilyn K. Gowing, for their pioneering emotional intelligence work; Robert Carkhuff for his substantial contribution to the field of interpersonal communication.

Martin Delahoussaye, editor of the first edition, for being there to welcome us in and guide us with such good cheer; and current editor Holly Allen, Susan Rachmeler, Kathleen Dolan Davies, Michael Zelenko, Rebecca Taff, Michael Kay, Denise Sullivan, and Tolu Babalola at Pfeiffer and Wiley for guiding us with gentle insistence to the quality we most desired to achieve. A big thanks to L. Bonita Patterson for all her excellent work on the first edition of this book.

Michael Snell, our agent, for creating an excellent interface with our publisher, orchestrating a win-win process, and continuing down the publishing path with us.

All of our parents, families, teachers, mentors, clients, and adversaries, and the grace and pluck that have gotten us each this far along the crazy paths we call our lives.

Introduction

Getting the Most from This Resource

PURPOSE

Emotional intelligence research and experience validate its importance as a critical factor in personal and business success. The Consortium for Research on Emotional Intelligence in Organizations provides a business case for emotional intelligence that lists success stories that resulted from developing or expanding emotional intelligence skills. They note:

> "Optimism is an emotional competence that leads to increased productivity. New salesmen at Met Life who scored high on a test of 'learned optimism' sold 37 percent more life insurance in their first two years than did pessimists." (www.eiconsortium.org)

The need for emotional intelligence increases with higher levels of responsibility, such as management or parenthood, and becomes even more important with groups, such as work teams. Recognizing the importance of emotional intelligence is a great starting place, but how do we develop competencies in the actual skills that empower us to function more effectively at work, at home, and in the community? The Guidelines for Best Practices for training and development in EI created by the EI Consortium emphasize the critical need for experiential practice to learn and enhance EI competencies. This book addresses that need by providing experiential learning scenarios drawn from real life to enhance emotional intelligence skills and competencies.

AUDIENCE

This book is designed for coaches, trainers, facilitators, HR professionals, managers, and anyone who wants to help others improve their emotional intelligence. The in-depth description of key elements of emotional intelligence is supported by easy, practical, and impactful exercises.

For individual coaching, the primary audiences are leaders, managers, supervisors, and employees whose job success requires improved interpersonal skills. The exercises will also be useful in clinical applications with clients who need to develop emotional intelligence to achieve therapeutic goals.

For group development, the primary audiences are management teams, intact teams at any level, and cross-functional teams. The exercises will also be an important resource for those providing public workshops for people interested in developing competencies in social and emotional intelligence, improving relationships, and expanding their career development opportunities.

ASSESSMENTS

The exercises contained in Part Three of this book may be used with or without assessments. For those who use assessments, we urge you to consider using multiple assessments whenever possible. No one measure can tell everything about a person or a team. Multiple data sets provide the opportunity to corroborate results, to better understand the feedback, and to understand the interrelationships among multiple factors. Dr. Cary Cherniss, professor, author of pivotal books on EI, and co-founder of the EI Consortium, stated in his presentation at Collaborative Growth's EQ Symposium that many organizations are increasingly requesting the use of multiple assessment tools and finding more validity in results when they do so.

Assessments one might consider using in accompaniment with any of the four EQ measures discussed in this book include the Myers-Briggs Type Indicator® (MBTI), Emergenetics®, FIRO-B®, the Center for Creative Leadership's Benchmarks, the DiSC®, and the Campbell Interest and Skills Inventory. One interesting explanation of the combination of assessment benefits is found in Pearman (2009), where he discusses MBTI and emotional intelligence.

HOW THIS BOOK IS ORGANIZED

This book is organized into three parts. Part One, Using Emotional Intelligence to Create Real Change, explains the rationale for developing emotional intelligence (EI) and highlights four key EI measures. The first section outlines the case for emotional intelligence. It explains why EI has such a powerful impact on personal effectiveness. The next section introduces the four most significant emotional intelligence measures and presents a matrix for cross-referencing the individual exercises in this book with the specific competencies for which each measure provides instruction. If you are working with one of the four EI measures—the EQ-i$^{2.0®}$ or EQ360®, TESI®, the MSCEIT™, or EISA—you can look up your measure of choice in the cross-reference matrix and find the exercises that apply. These exercises will help you develop the competencies important to you for whichever measure you use.

Perhaps the best part is that you don't have to be working with a measure at all! You can use these exercises independently to strengthen any competency that is needed. For example, if you wanted to work with a team or individual to help him or her develop flexibility, you would look in Part Two for the in-depth description of the competency and then go to Part Three, where, under the heading Flexibility, you would find four choices—Exercises 13.1, 13.2, 13.3, and 13.4. Just choose the one that is best suited to your situation.

Part Two, Exploring Emotional Intelligence and Well-Being Skills, provides an in-depth description of each of sixteen emotional skills to help you and your clients become thoroughly familiar with the dimensions of each skill.

Part Three, Emotional Intelligence Exercises to Build Effective Skills, contains exercises, all framed as experiential learning scenarios. The first three sections of each exercise—Purpose, Thumbnail, and Outcome—explain the following: Purpose answers WHY you would have the people do this exercise; Thumbnail tells you HOW participants will engage with the instructional material to generate the learning experience; and Outcome explains WHAT your target is—the desired results that can be achieved. The exercises contain reproducible handouts (also available at www.pfeiffer.com/go/Hughes/EIAction2) that you may copy for your participants.

The book closes with a list of resources for finding additional useful information.

Note to coaches and facilitators: Most of the exercises can be used in individual coaching situations as well as with intact teams and groups. The thumbnail summaries and instructions usually are written for the team and group experience. If you are coaching an individual, simply reframe the instructions for the one-on-one environment and the exercises will be effective for you and your client.

KEY TERMS

EI is an acronym for emotional intelligence.

EQ (emotional quotient) is a measure of the degree of emotional intelligence development, similar to IQ. The term was coined by Dr. Reuven Bar-On.

ICONS

We have developed a set of icons to highlight specific parts of each chapter to which you may want to give special attention. They are meant to be fun and informative landmarks that help you navigate the material efficiently and make the best use of it.

The treasure chest icon is the first one you will encounter. It appears in the in-depth description of each specific competency, where it highlights a helpful tip or insight about that skill, how to develop it, qualities that make it important, or how applying it effectively can make a difference in the quality of your life.

The star performer icon indicates a biographical note about someone in real life who is an excellent model of that specific competency. Martin Luther King, Gandhi, Maya Angelo, and Meryl Streep are among the examples you will find.

There are many excellent examples of emotionally intelligent behavior in the movies, so we have done our best to utilize some of the more popular films to illustrate each of the competencies. You will find *The King's Speech, The Hurt Locker, Jack Goes Boating, Precious, Lilies of the Field, Remember the Titans,* and *The Wizard of Oz* among our favorites.

The purpose of the thumbnail is to let the coach or trainer quickly know how long he or she will need to allow for the exercise and what sort of an experience he or she will be facilitating.

The website for the book has easily downloadable copies of all handouts associated with the exercises. These can be printed out, which supports you in your preparation for using each exercise in coaching or training.

FACILITATOR COMPETENCIES

This section is designed to show the coach or trainer how skillful he or she will have to be in order to successfully conduct each exercise. There is generally also a significant relationship with how sophisticated the learning experience will be for the participants. If participants' skills tend to be less developed in an area, then starting with an easier exercise will provide better results.

Three levels of facilitator skills are identified as:

○ EASY

◐ MODERATE

● ADVANCED

FACILITATOR GUIDELINES

Preparation
- Review this section, "Introduction: Getting the Most from This Resource," section to familiarize yourself with the icons used in this book.
- Review the appropriate section in "Part Two—Exploring Emotional Intelligence and Well-Being Skills" to better understand the emotional intelligence aspect on which you will be working.

- Read applicable material from the Resources list and the References at the back of the book if you are seeking supplemental information.
- Ensure the room size and table arrangements are conducive to the type of exercise you will be leading.
- Make sufficient copies of the reproducible participant handouts that are included in the exercises (and available on the website) and gather other needed materials.
- Consider playing music during the reflective phases of the exercises when participants are asked to think about their behaviors and responses. We recommend calming instrumental music that is played at a soft volume. (If you do use music, be sure to abide by any copyright restrictions.)

Materials
- The "Materials" section of each exercise contains a list of materials you will need.
- Reproducible participant handouts are included in most exercises.
- Full-size printable versions of the handouts are available at www.pfeiffer .com/go/Hughes/EIAction2.

Debriefing and Reflection
- Debriefing is one of the most important phases of each exercise. It gives participants a chance to reflect on and synthesize their experiences and to share what they have learned. It provides one of the best opportunities for introverts to be heard.
- Ask questions that help the participants uncover what they learned and surface any "a-ha's." Your mission is to lead them on a journey of self-discovery. The learning is more powerful when they recognize for themselves how they benefited from the exercise, versus having you tell them what they learned.

Selection
- Refer to the cross-reference matrix in Chapter 2 of this book to identify the exercise(s) you want to use.
- Look up the potential exercises you identified from the cross-reference matrix, and refer to the purpose, thumbnail, outcome, audience, estimated time, and facilitator competency information to help you identify the best exercise(s) for your situation.

Using Emotional Intelligence to Create Real Change

In Part One we explain the rationale for developing emotional intelligence (EI) and highlight four key EQ measures. In the first section we outline the case for emotional intelligence and explain why EI has such a powerful impact on effectiveness. In the next section we introduce four of the most significant emotional intelligence measures and present a matrix for cross-referencing the individual exercises in this book with the specific skills in which each measure provides instruction.

If you are working with one of these four major measures—the EQ-i$^{2.0}$ or EQ360, TESI®, the MSCEIT®, or EISA—you can look up your measure of choice in the cross-reference matrix and find the exercises that apply. These exercises will help you develop the competencies important to you for whichever measure you use.

Perhaps the best part is that you don't have to be working with a measure at all! You can use these exercises independently to strengthen any competency that is needed. For example, if empathy is your focus, go to Exercises, 8.1, 8.2, 8.3, and 8.4 and choose the one that is best suited to your situation.

CHAPTER 1

The Case for Emotional Intelligence

Would you like to be more effective in your work and in your personal life? Would you like to be able to better understand what you are feeling and why? Would you like to be able to participate more consciously in what you feel and how you respond, rather than just reacting in the same old patterns that you always have? Would you like to have more friends or be able to be closer and more open with the friends you have now? Would you like to be able to better monitor and motivate your progress toward your short- and long-term goals? Then you'll *love* exploring the world of emotional intelligence!

Exploring and developing our emotional intelligence not only makes us happier, but it makes us able to motivate ourselves, manage stress in our lives, and resolve conflict with others. It gives us the skills to be able to encourage, comfort, discipline, and confront different kinds of people appropriately in different situations. It determines how effectively we express our emotions within the cultural contexts of our family, our workplace, and our community. It determines how well people listen to us and how well we are heard.

EMOTIONS: WHAT ARE THEY?

To effectively introduce the topic of emotional intelligence we need to start by talking a little bit about emotions and what they are. We like to say that emotions are about what we touch...not just what we touch with our fingers or our skin, but what we touch with our eyes and ears, what we touch with our taste buds and the olfactory nerves in our noses. Emotions are how we feel about what we touch with our imagination, from the dread of a loud scary noise in the dark to those fifteen minutes of fame when you know you're at the top of your game and everyone else gets to see. Emotions are what move us and motivate us. All three of these words—*emotion, move,* and *motivate*—share the Latin root *emovare,* which means *to move.* Emotions are what sustain us through our struggles and crown us in our victories. In fact, when you really think about why we do anything that we do, there is always a feeling involved—something that we are avoiding and moving away from or something that we want and are moving toward. Fear and desire are two of our strongest emotions and have long been considered the most powerful motivators in the animal kingdom.

Research at the National Institute of Mental Health by Candace Pert has shown that emotions are very closely associated with neuropeptides, long chain protein molecules that circulate throughout the organs of the body and act like "messenger molecules," conveying information about what is happening in one part of the body throughout the entire system. In her book, *Molecules of Emotion* (1997), Pert considers emotions to be a transformative link between mind and body, the mysterious quantum mechanical interface where information turns into matter and our bodies synthesize the chemicals of consciousness.

Recognizing that our feeling responses are grounded in our biochemistry is an important understanding. Emotional states such as anger, sorrow, depression, and joy can be influenced and even directed by us, but this does not mean they can be turned on and off like a light bulb. It takes our body time to metabolize these chemical components—such as the adrenaline that is released when we feel frightened. The chemistry of emotions can help us change our viewpoint and see the world through different attitudinal lenses depending on how we are feeling. When we create and maintain positive thoughts about ourselves and our world through our self-talk, we support positive emotional states such as resourcefulness, optimism, and motivation.

A good way to imagine emotions is as an invisible link that connects people with each other and to some extent with all living creatures—they constitute a field of specific information that we sense and decode using the ancient instinctual languages of facial expression, smell, body posture, and the whole realm of nonverbal language. On top of all that, human beings are able to add another layer of sophisticated interpretation. Through our use of cognitive intelligence and semantic language, we are able to label our feelings and give them a wide variety of symbolic meanings with subtle degrees of texture and nuance.

Intelligence

Early in the 20th century psychologists began to devise tests for measuring cognitive ability and intellect in human beings. The eventual result was what we know today as the standardized IQ test. As research into human intelligence continued along these lines, it began to appear as if it was an inherited capacity and was not greatly influenced by any amount of educational effort. Adults did not necessarily have higher IQ scores than children, and over the course of their lifetimes they didn't seem to develop more. The view that intelligence was what was measured by IQ tests and that it was controlled by genetics generally prevailed into the 1970s. Yet when Weschler developed the IQ measure, he stated that there are other forms of intelligence besides the IQ he addressed.

Other scientists agreed with Weschler and were not satisfied with a static, one-dimensional definition of intelligence or the way in which it was measured. In the 1980s Howard Gardner published research that validated his work on "multiple intelligences," demonstrating the importance of expanding that definition, and Reuven Bar-On coined the term "emotional quotient" in an attempt to differentiate emotional competencies from intellect. Leading research by John Mayer and Peter Salovey was instrumental in developing a theory of emotional intelligence that consists of four domains: *perceiving emotions, facilitating thought, understanding emotions*, and *managing emotions*. They were joined in their efforts by David Caruso and together developed the MSCEIT (Mayer-Salovey-Caruso Emotional Intelligence Test), a reliable, valid, ability-based assessment of emotional intelligence with a normative database of five thousand people.

Their definition of emotional intelligence emphasizes "intelligence" and differs significantly enough from others that we will include it here:

> "'Emotions' refer to the feelings a person has in a relationship. For example, if a person has a good relationship with someone else, that individual is happy; if the person is threatened, he or she is afraid. Intelligence, on the other hand, refers to the ability to reason with or about something. For example, one reasons with language in the case of verbal intelligence, or reasons about how objects fit together in the case of spatial intelligence. In the case of emotional intelligence, one reasons with emotions, or emotions assist one's thinking. That is, emotional intelligence, as measured by the MSCEIT™, refers to the capacity to reason with emotions and emotional signals, and to the capacity of emotion to enhance thought." (Mayer, Salovey, & Caruso, 2001, p. 2)

For more information on their description of intelligence within the concept of emotional intelligence, see the discussion of the "concept of an intelligence that processes and benefits from emotions" in Mayer, Salovey, and Caruso (2000, p. 105).

The idea of having an ability-based emotional intelligence test with right and wrong answers may seem foreign to those who think emotions are too subjective to be quantified, but here is a simple explanation of how it works:

> "Emotional skills can also be measured in an objective way through the use of ability, performance, or knowledge tests. Such tests would ask a series of questions like these:
>
> - What is the cause of sadness?
> - What is an effective strategy for calming an angry customer?

The MSCEIT™ (pronounced mess-keet) asks people to solve emotional problems, and the correctness of the answers is evaluated. In turn, a person's scores are compared to a large, normative database to compute a sort of emotional intelligence quotient, or EI score" (Caruso & Salovey, 2004, p. 75).

The Brain

Processing emotion is a non-conscious event. It is something we do intuitively that allows us to anticipate others' behaviors in a more direct, immediate fashion than language can. Emotional intelligence is all about immediacy. The circuitry in our brains is set up to process emotional responses without having to consider them rationally. How am I feeling right now? How are you feeling right now? How are our feelings affecting each other and the actions we are choosing to take in this moment? These are the kind of critical comparisons that the limbic system, or emotional brain, is making for us constantly, most of it below the threshold of conscious awareness.

When sensory input enters our brain, it first is processed in the thalamus, which scans information for familiar patterns that may have been especially significant to us in the past. Such patterns are then forwarded to the hippocampus, which further screens them for threatening content before the amygdala's final decision as to whether it should trigger the fight-or-flight response. If it turns out there is no precedent for fear, the information is then passed along to the neocortex, which is able to analyze it for meaning in a rational process.

The emotional circuits in the brain also regulate the balance of two critical hormones throughout the body, cortisol and DHEA. Cortisol plays many positive roles in bodily functions; however, it is often known as the "stress hormone" because stressful situations cause it to be secreted in excess, and then it can have very negative effects on many aspects of our health. DHEA, on the other hand, is sometimes known as the "anti-aging hormone" because it counteracts the negative effects of cortisol that tend to wear the body out and cause it to age.

The Heart

But the brain is not alone in governing our emotional intelligence. In fact, recent research at the Institute of HeartMath (Childre & Martin, 1999) has revealed the heart to be a major player in the process of understanding and responding to our world. Our heart communicates chemically to the rest of our body by producing mood-enhancing hormones. Perhaps even more remarkably, the electromagnetic signal it sends to the brain (and every other cell as well) is the most powerful signal in the entire body! It produces an electromagnetic field that can be detected several feet away from the body in all directions. The heart also communicates mechanically with the rest of the body through pressure waves that are conducted through the vascular system. What is it sending in all these different channels of communication? It is giving the entire body feedback about how the whole system is functioning.

Research by Antonio Damasio (2003) has determined that human beings cannot make any cognitive decisions without also processing emotional information that incorporates how we feel about the situation. It turns out that emotional intelligence is actually the synthesis of both heart and brain functions, weaving together thought and feeling into the marvelously rich fabric of human experience.

EMOTIONS AND IDENTITY

Emotional intelligence also plays a critical role in conflict resolution. In their fundamental book, *Getting to Yes,* Fisher and Ury (1981) characterize the process of resolving conflict as one of helping people move from "No" to "Yes." What makes this difficult is that we tend to identify with our positions, so in order for us to change them there has to be a change in our identity. In other words, if we think that we are the ones who deserve the promotion and the corner office because of our length and quality of service, we will have to change our sense of who we are and what those rewards mean to us symbolically in order to be able to accept another (equally good) solution. That change in identity may also come from the process of working through a deep disappointment and discovering that our competencies in flexibility and reality testing can truly help us transform.

Emotions play a critical role in identifying ourselves—in knowing who we are in the world and distinguishing "self" from "other." In addition to governing the fight-or-flight process, the limbic system also manages our immune system. The critical task of the immune system is to be able to distinguish what is part of us and what is foreign. Even the process of understanding who we are once again turns out to be grounded in our biochemistry. Our cells have self-receptors that are "read" by immune cells to determine whether or not they are part of the self or invaders that pose a threat to the health, wholeness, and integrity of our systems.

My very sense of "I-ness" comes from recognizing familiar sensory patterns in the environment and experiencing the same emotional responses that were originally generated throughout my body/mind and recorded in my memory. After enough memories have been stored (generally around age two), this sense of familiarity undergoes a profound transformation. The billions of bits of data crystallize and initiate the advent of self, the recognition that it is "I" who is having this experience—"I" who is hungry and wants to eat; "I" who feel safe, or threatened, or curious; "I" who is powerful and can make things happen in the world!

Over time, sophisticated menus of preference and aversion come to be developed through this same process of associational memory. "I" discover that I know what I like and dislike and, depending on my level of confidence, am able to express that effectively to the people whom I depend on for survival. If I have lived in a cooperative environment, family, or culture that requires me to obtain the approval of others for my decisions and actions at every level, then my need for interdependence will tend to overshadow my need for independence. If I have lived in a competitive environment in which I am only able to satisfy my desires through continuously creating and asserting new behavioral strategies which satisfy but the letter of the law, my need for independence will tend to overshadow my need for interdependence.

My ability to remodel, update, and even upgrade my identity, to resolve problems and conflicts, and consequently my ability to move myself and others from "No" to "Yes," will be dependent on how consciously or unconsciously I process my emotions. If I am unconsciously embedded in the automatic sequence of stimulus-response conditioning, I will tend to be a creature of habit and be liable to perceive myself as a victim of the world. If, through self-reflective processes, I have been able to lengthen the amount of time between stimulus and response, in other words to make myself more conscious of the processes that determine my behavior, then I will be more flexible and tolerant and have available to me a more robust repertoire of behaviors and be able to generate better decisions and more creative solutions to the problems I encounter in my daily life. This is perhaps the truest measure of our emotional intelligence.

EMOTIONAL POWER

So as you begin the adventure of exploring new ways to develop your own emotional competence, as well as that of your clients, through the "exercises" in this book, we urge you to learn the distinctions and relationships among the skills defined in the EQ-i$^{2.0}$. They combine to provide a tremendously powerful lens through which human behavior and motivation can be seen and understood as never before. Significant examples of this can be found in the work of Geetu Orme (2001), who exposes some of the popular myths about emotional intelligence and then develops the three strategic components that are critical for building quality in our relationships: tuning in, understanding, and taking action.

It is because our culture has conditioned us to perceive the world and measure the quality of life in terms of objective acquisition that we misunderstand our interpersonal relationships and fail to value them appropriately. Consequently, we need all the help we can get in learning how to develop, enhance, and care for our connectedness in ways that counteract this fragmentation. Fortunately, the methods for developing emotional intelligence have arrived on the scene in the nick of time and begun to re-weave the fraying strands of postmodern civilization. Whether we avail ourselves of such healing or not, the world will continue to grow more and more complex, and the quality of our lives will be impacted more deeply on a daily basis by the feelings and decisions of people we have never met or even seen before.

In a way, we each live at our own center of the World Wide Web, and in order to make all the connections in our network as secure and beneficial as possible, we have to be very skillful in the way we generate and broadcast our emotional power—too much and people avoid us or set up defenses that block communication; too little and they take advantage of us or we never break through the barriers to intimacy or develop enough energy to achieve the very dreams that give our lives their meaning.

CHAPTER 2

How Everyone Can Use the Exercises

Cross-Reference Matrix

Emotional intelligence is well established as a critical aspect of successful leadership. The greater the leadership responsibility, the more important our emotional intelligence competencies. Of the many emotional intelligence models and assessment instruments, four that have risen to prominence because of their validity, reliability, and market acceptance are reviewed here—each uses a different approach, but all seek to foster skill development along the lines addressed by the exercises in this book. The four are

- EQ-i$^{2.0}$ and EQ360
- Team Emotional and Social Intelligence Survey® (TESI®)
- MSCEIT™
- Emotional Intelligence Skills Assessment (EISA)

In this chapter we discuss each model's unique approach to emotional intelligence and present a matrix that cross-references the exercises to all four models. The matrix enables you to quickly identify exercises relevant to the model you are using. It helps increase your awareness of the emotional intelligence field by providing a perspective on the interrelationships among the different models. The bottom-line positive intention of the authors for each of the four models was to create a useful instrument for facilitating greater awareness, thus leading to positive change. The exercises in this book were developed to provide specific learning experiences for each of the basic emotional skills and can be used to support whichever instruments you are using to assist your clients in developing their emotional intelligence. It can also be very helpful, even if no assessments are given.

The following discussions are brief overviews of the models. We strongly encourage you to gain even more information about any specific model you are using by reviewing the materials distributed by the publisher of the model and its authors.

EMOTIONAL QUOTIENT INVENTORY® (EQ-I²·⁰ AND EQ360)

The EQ-i²·⁰ is a well-researched self-report measure of social and emotional intelligence capabilities developed over the course of over twenty years. The EQ-i was originally developed by Dr. Reuven Bar-On and has recently been updated and supported by development of a new comprehensive normative data base by MHS. The updated report is known as the EQ-i²·⁰. The EQ360® is a multi-rater format, also supported by the new normative research. The EQ-i²·⁰ and EQ360 utilize a 1–5–15 method of scoring in which there is a single overall emotional intelligence score called the "Total EQ." This is broken down into the five composite scales: Self-Perception, Self-Expression, Interpersonal, Decision Making, Stress Management. These five scales are each made up of three specific skills, for a total of fifteen competencies. Additionally a Happiness score is reflected as a part of a Well-Being Indicator and is treated as the sixteenth skill in this book. It is these sixteen skills that give the user the real "meat." Following are the five scales, fifteen skills, and the happiness/well-being indicator:

Self-Perception
- Self-Regard
- Self-Actualization
- Emotional Self-Awareness

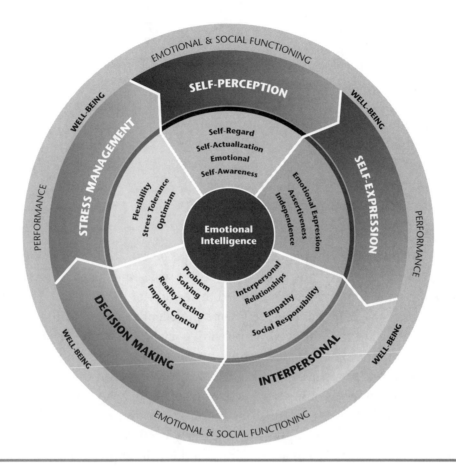

Figure 1.2.1. EQ-i Model

Self-Expression
- Emotional Expression
- Assertiveness
- Independence

Interpersonal
- Interpersonal Relations
- Empathy
- Social Responsibility

Decision Making
- Problem Solving
- Reality Testing
- Impulse Control

Stress Management
- Flexibility
- Stress Tolerance
- Optimism

Happiness/Well-Being

Each individual who completes the measure receives a report showing how strong his or her scores are in each of the subscales and usually receives a debriefing with someone who is certified to administer the measure. A skilled interpreter of the EQ-i$^{2.0}$ and EQ360 helps the client understand the relative meaning of each score, as well as providing insight into the relationships between the scores. For instance, it might turn out that a person with a very high score in reality testing and a significantly low score in optimism might want to explore how his or her perspective on life might change if he or she did not automatically devote so much attention to making critical evaluations. Might the person feel more optimistic? Similarly, can you imagine what might happen if someone is high in assertiveness and low in impulse control?

The Self-Perception composite includes the following subscales: Self-Regard, Self-Actualization, and Emotional Self-Awareness. These are the capabilities that are necessary to develop, maintain, and understand one's self effectively.

The Self-Expression composite includes Emotional Expression, Assertiveness, and Independence, all of which contribute to the ability to express one's self so that others have better understanding and will facilitate interaction.

The Interpersonal scale looks at how effectively we interface and engage within the social milieu. It is composed of Interpersonal Relationships, Empathy, and Social Responsibility.

The Decision Making composite includes Problem Solving, Reality Testing, and Impulse Control. These help us integrate our emotional responses and awareness with the ways we engage and make decisions.

The Stress Management scale measures how well we feel we do at coping with the tension, disappointment, and pain that come from living in a less-than-perfect world. It is that discrepancy between what we desire and what we are able to obtain that constitutes the essence of stress. Stress Management includes Flexibility, Stress Tolerance, and Optimism. Optimism shows us how hopeful we are about the quality of the future we expect, and Flexibility and Stress Tolerance help us act in accord with our hopefulness.

Happiness/Well-Being, which is listed as a separate piece of information, shows how satisfied we feel in the present moment and is tied to the relevant skills of Self-Regard, Optimism, Interpersonal Relationships, and Self-Actualization as these particularly influence our experience of being happy.

Our descriptions of these skills are merely summaries; we suggest you refer to *The EQ Edge* (Stein & Book, 2011) and the reports themselves for more detailed information. The elegance of the EQ-i$^{2.0}$ and EQ360 is that the simple, straightforward presentation belies the rigor of its design. Developmental strategies for improving results are included in the individual report. After six months, the assessment can be retaken to assess progress in specific areas and the overall development of emotional intelligence.

TEAM EMOTIONAL AND SOCIAL INTELLIGENCE SURVEY® (TESI®)

The Team Emotional and Social Intelligence (TESI) assessment, developed in 2006 by Marcia Hughes and James Terrell, identifies and measures seven competencies most critical for effective team functioning: Team Identity, Motivation, Emotional Awareness, Communication, Stress Tolerance, Conflict Resolution, and Positive Mood. It also specifies the four results that teams will enjoy as they build these competencies—Empathy, Trust, Loyalty, and Better Decisions—which lead to the two benefits of long-term success, Sustainable Productivity and Emotional and Social Well-Being for the team (Hughes & Terrell, 2007, 2009).

Each of the seven skills for team success influences the others; skills in one area flow into and build an influence in each of the others. In addition, synergistic results are achieved when a team strengthens competencies in most or all of these core areas. Their success becomes greater than the simple

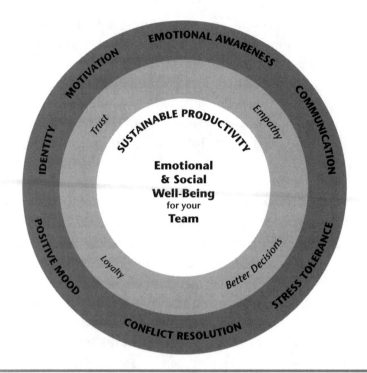

Figure 1.2.2. The TESI Model

combination of each independent skill, building what Hughes and Terrell term Collaborative Intelligence™ (Hughes & Terrell, 2009).

There are two assessment formats available. The TESI Short is an abbreviated, twenty-one-item version of this assessment and is published by Pfeiffer. The short version works well when teams want to take a quick look at their functioning. It's available in a self-scoring format that creates the flexibility of not having to administer it in advance of a team engagement or workshop. A longer version of the TESI with demographic and other breakouts is available from Collaborative Growth®. Each team member is asked to rate the team's skills—from his or her individual perspective—in the seven team behaviors of success. An individual report is created, as well as a full team report and many optional demographic reports can be assessed. This serves to create a team 360-degree assessment of all team members' views on team functioning. From this report, participants better understand the team's functioning and take steps to build upon their strengths and develop areas needing enhancement. More information about each of the skills is provided in Part Two of this book. In addition, the *TESI Facilitator's Guide* (Hughes & Terrell, 2009) is a valuable resource for more information on this assessment.

THE MSCEIT™

The Mayer-Salovey-Caruso Emotional Intelligence Test, known as the MSCEIT (mes-keet), is unique in that it undertakes to measure actual intelligence rather than the behavioral competencies and social skills that are associated with individual workplace success. The authors define emotional intelligence as the "ability to perceive emotions, to access and generate emotions so as to assist thought, to understand emotions and emotional knowledge, and to regulate emotions so as to promote emotional and intellectual growth" (Mayer, Salovey, & Caruso, 2002, p. 17). Their test is designed as an ability measure with objective "right and wrong" answers, in contrast with the more subjective competency measures that rely on self-report.

Some examples of the abilities that the MSCEIT undertakes to measure include the ability to label emotions and understand the relationships between words and feelings, the ability to distinguish between authentic emotional expressions and those that are inauthentic or feigned, and the ability to manage emotions by strengthening positive ones and reducing negative ones. Although not all the abilities they seek to measure correspond with specific emotional skills, one can easily see that those listed above have significant correlations with such competencies as emotional self-awareness, empathy, optimism, and impulse control.

As shown in Figure 1.2.1, the authors group these abilities in a $1 - 2 - 4 - 8$ hierarchy so the individual taking the test receives fifteen different scores in the report. The first score is a total emotional intelligence score and is composed of two area scores for Experiential and Strategic emotional intelligence. Experiential refers to the basic human ability to respond emotionally—feeling, processing, recognizing, and classifying emotions. Strategic refers to the higher-level, more conscious processing of emotions, reasoning about them, understanding how they originate and develop over time, and how human beings can manage them to enhance social relationships.

Figure 1.2.3. Abilities Hierarchy

Each of the area scores is composed of two branch scores. Experiential includes the scores of Perceiving Emotion and Facilitating Thought. Perceiving Emotion measures the ability to recognize what you and others are feeling. This entails accurately detecting, decoding, and responding to the emotional signals of our own internal states, as well as our nonverbal communication, most of which is unconscious. Facilitating Thought is the ability to engage the feeling content of our experience on behalf of improved reasoning, decision making, and problem solving. This is the ability to emotionally activate cognitive processes and creatively utilize the variety of viewpoints that we experience as our moods change.

The Strategic score is also composed of two branch scores, Understanding Emotion and Managing Emotions. Understanding Emotion measures the ability to label emotions appropriately and reason with them in an understandable and effective manner. This includes our ability to recognize how our emotions combine and change over time and how well we are able to symbolically represent this complex process. Managing Emotions is the ability to remain open to emotional information when it will enhance our experience and the ability to limit and control that information when it might cause us to react impulsively. Managing emotions is the ability to appropriately balance their significance in our intellectual outlook and behavior, our general ability to cope with life in an emotionally effective manner.

Each of these four branch scores is composed of two task scores that measure eight specific emotional intelligence abilities, such as reading emotion accurately in faces and pictures, understanding how basic emotions combine to produce more complex feelings, and understanding the sequence that emotions go through as they change from one to another. These scores are to be used more hypothetically than predicatively (that is, for developmental suggestions), inasmuch as the reliability for some of the eight task scores is lower than that of the composite scores to which they give rise (Mayer, Salovey, & Caruso, 2002).

EMOTIONAL INTELLIGENCE SKILLS ASSESSMENT

The Emotional Intelligence Skills Assessment (EISA), developed by Steven Stein, Derek Mann, and Peter Papadogiannis (2009), identifies and measures five core factors of emotional intelligence in adults: Perceiving, Managing,

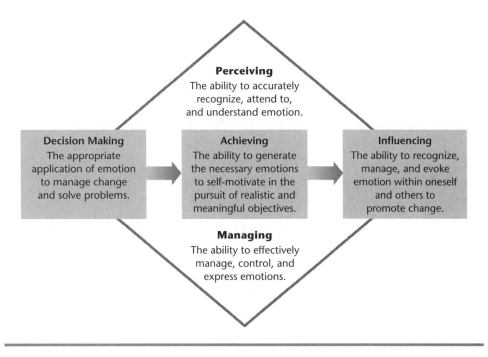

Figure 1.2.4. EISA Model

Decision Making, Achieving, and Influencing. While all five factors are important, the first two—Perceiving and Managing—are considered foundational to emotional intelligence, as without the ability to accurately perceive and manage one's own emotions, it is more difficult to respond appropriately to situations requiring effective Decision Making, Achieving, and Influencing.

The EISA asks each individual to respond to fifty emotional and behavioral statements; both self and 360 versions of the assessment are available. Individuals receive detailed information about each of the five factors and an indication of their areas of emotional strength and opportunities for growth. Respondents are also encouraged to create a plan that will help them further develop those emotional and social skills needed for improved success.

More information about each of the five factors, Perceiving, Managing, Decision Making, Achieving, and Influencing, is provided in Part Two of this book. In addition, the *EISA Facilitator's Guide* (Stein, Mann, & Papadogiannis, 2010) is a valuable resource for more information on this assessment.

CROSS-REFERENCE MATRIX

The following matrix has been designed for easily cross-referencing the exercises found in Part Three of this book to the relevant content areas for each of the four assessments.

Table 1.2.1. Cross-Reference Matrix

Exercise	Page	Title	EQ-i²·⁰® and EQ360® (MHS) Skill	TESI® and TESI® Short (Hughes, Terrell) Skill	MSCEIT™ (Mayer, Salovey, Caruso) Scale	EISA (Stein, Mann, Papadogiannis) Skill
1.1	123	Lighten Up with Self-Compassion	Self-Regard	Emotional Awareness	Understanding Emotions	Perceiving, Managing
1.2	127	Of Thine Own Self Be Aware	Self-Regard	Emotional Awareness	Understanding Emotions	Perceiving
1.3	131	Reconciliation	Self-Regard	Conflict Resolution	Managing Emotions	Influencing
1.4	137	Toot Your Horn and Scratch Your Back	Self-Regard	Positive Mood	Managing Emotions	Decision Making
2.1	141	Leverage Your Time with a 2% Solution	Self-Actualization	Motivation	Understanding Emotions, Facilitating Thought, Managing Emotions	Achieving
2.2	147	The Scavenger Hunt	Self-Actualization	Team Identity, Motivation	Facilitating Thought	Achieving
2.3	157	Becoming All That You Can Be	Self-Actualization	Motivation	Understanding Emotion	Managing
2.4	165	Applying Inspiration	Self-Actualization	Stress Tolerance, Positive Mood	Perceiving Emotions, Managing Emotions	Influencing, Achieving

(*Continued*)

Table 1.2.1. (Continued)

Exercise	Page	Title	EQ-i2.0® and EQ360® (MHS) Skill	TESI® and TESI® Short (Hughes, Terrell) Skill	MSCEIT™ (Mayer, Salovey, Caruso) Scale	EISA (Stein, Mann, Papadogiannis) Skill
3.1	173	Expanding Your Uncommon Awareness	Emotional Self-Awareness	Emotional Awareness	Perceiving Emotions, Understanding	Decision Making
3.2	177	Are You In Touch?	Emotional Self-Awareness	Emotional Awareness	Perceiving Emotions, Managing Emotions	Achieving
3.3	183	It Just Bubbles Up	Emotional Self-Awareness	Emotional Awareness	Perceiving Emotions, Understanding Emotions	Perceiving
3.4	189	Moving Toward, Moving Away	Emotional Self-Awareness	Communications, Emotional Awareness	Perceiving Emotions, Understanding Emotions	Managing, Decision Making
4.1	197	Expressing Resistance	Emotional Expression	Communications	Perceiving Emotions Managing Emotions	Achieving
4.2	201	Say It Non-verbally!	Emotional Expression	Communications	Perceiving Emotions, Managing Emotions	Perceiving
4.3	205	Tell a Story	Emotional Expression	Communications, Team Identity	Facilitating Thought	Perceiving, Managing
4.4	209	Expressing Emotions in Social Media	Emotional Expression	Communications, Team Identity	Understanding Emotions	Managing

5.1	213	Developing Appropriate Assertiveness Within Your Team	Assertiveness	Communications, Conflict Resolution	Understanding Emotions, Managing Emotions	Influencing
5.2	219	Ramp It up	Assertiveness	Communications, Conflict Resolution	Facilitating Thought, Managing Emotions	Influencing
5.3	225	Dial It Back	Assertiveness	Communications, Conflict Resolution	Managing Emotions	Influencing
5.4	229	Getting Your Point Across	Assertiveness	Communications, Conflict Resolution	Facilitating Thought, Understanding Emotions	Influencing
6.1	233	Virtual Decision Making	Independence	Communications	Managing Emotions	Decision Making
6.2	239	Cut the Apron Strings	Independence	Emotional Awareness, Communications	Facilitating Thought, Managing Emotions	Decision Making
6.3	243	Solitary Effort	Independence	Motivation	Facilitating Thought, Managing Emotions	Decision Making
6.4	247	Going Along with the Group—Or Not	Independence	Positive Mood	Understanding Emotions, Facilitating Thought	Decision Making
7.1	251	Investment in Friends	Interpersonal Relationships	Positive Mood	Understanding Emotions, Managing Emotions	Perceiving

(Continued)

29

Table 1.2.1. *(Continued)*

Exercise	Page	Title	EQ-i2.0® and EQ360® (MHS) Skill	TESI® and TESI® Short (Hughes, Terrell) Skill	MSCEIT™ (Mayer, Salovey, Caruso) Scale	EISA (Stein, Mann, Papadogiannis) Skill
7.2	255	You've Got Good News	Interpersonal Relationships	Motivation, Positive Mood	Facilitating Thought	Perceiving
7.3	261	Making New Friends	Interpersonal Relationships	Positive Mood	Perceiving Emotions, Managing Emotions	Perceiving
7.4	267	Fun and Meaningful Relationships	Interpersonal Relationships	Positive Mood	Facilitating Thought, Understanding Emotions	Perceiving
8.1	271	Recipe for Influence: Curiosity and Compassion	Empathy	Emotional Awareness, Communications	Perceiving Emotions, Managing Emotions	Perceiving
8.2	275	Connect Feeling with Meaning	Empathy	Emotional Awareness, Communications	Facilitating Thought	Perceiving
8.3	279	Mixed Emotions	Empathy	Emotional Awareness, Communications	Perceiving Emotions, Understanding Emotions, Facilitating Thought	Perceiving
8.4	287	Do as the Empathic Do	Empathy	Emotional Awareness, Communications	Facilitating Thought, Understanding Emotions, Managing Emotions	Perceiving

9.1	291	Focus on Something Bigger Than Yourself	Social Responsibility	Team Identity, Positive Mood	Perceiving Emotions	Managing
9.2	295	Reflect the Best	Social Responsibility	Team Identity	Facilitating Thought, Understanding Emotions, Managing Emotions	Decision Making
9.3	301	Who Do I Work for?	Social Responsibility	Team Identity, Emotional Awareness	Facilitating Thought, Understanding Emotions	Influencing
9.4	307	The Value of Volunteering	Social Responsibility	Motivation, Emotional Awareness	Facilitating Thought, Understanding Emotions, Perceiving Emotions, Managing Emotions	Perceiving
10.1	311	When Problems Become Conflicts	Problem Solving	Communication, Conflict Resolution	Facilitating	Decision Making
10.2	319	Emotions Affect Decision Making	Problem Solving	Emotional Awareness, Communication	Perceiving	Decision Making
10.3	325	Using the MasterSolve Model for Teams	Problem Solving	Communication, Conflict Resolution	Facilitating	Decision Making

(Continued)

Table 1.2.1. (Continued)

Exercise	Page	Title	EQ-i²·⁰® and EQ360® (MHS) Skill	TESI® and TESI® Short (Hughes, Terrell) Skill	MSCEIT™ (Mayer, Salovey, Caruso) Scale	EISA (Stein, Mann, Papadogiannis) Skill
10.4	333	Win-Win Negotiating	Problem Solving	Conflict Resolution, Team Identity	Understanding Emotions, Managing Emotions	Influencing
10.5	337	Let's Cover Our Bases	Problem Solving	Communication, Team Identity	Managing Emotions, Facilitating Thought	Influencing
11.1	343	Political Savvy	Reality Testing	Emotional Awareness, Communication	Managing	Managing
11.2	347	Feel, Hear, See—Is It Reality?	Reality Testing	Stress Tolerance, Communication	Facilitating Thought Perceiving Emotions	Perceiving
11.3	351	Visit Their Reality	Reality Testing	Emotional Awareness, Communication	Understanding Emotions	Perceiving
11.4	357	Using All Three of Your Minds	Reality Testing	Stress Tolerance, Emotional Awareness	Facilitating Thought, Perceiving Emotions	Decision Making
12.1	363	Putting on the Brakes	Impulse Control	Stress Tolerance	Understanding Emotions, Facilitating Thought, Managing Emotions	Managing

12.2	367	To Impulse or Not to Impulse	Impulse Control	Stress Tolerance	Facilitating Thought, Understanding Emotions	Decision Making
12.3	379	The Urge to Splurge	Impulse Control	Motivation, Stress Tolerance	Perceiving Emotions, Managing Emotions, Understanding Emotions	Decision Making
12.4	385	Hot Buttons	Impulse Control	Emotional Awareness, Stress Tolerance	Perceiving Emotions, Managing Emotions	Perceiving
13.1	389	The Highly Flexible Team	Flexibility	Team Identity, Communication	Perceiving Emotions, Managing Emotions	Managing
13.2	393	No More Shutdowns	Flexibility	Stress Tolerance, Communication	Facilitating Thought, Managing Emotions	Managing
13.3	399	Yes, No, Maybe So	Flexibility	Stress Tolerance, Communication	Facilitating Thought, Managing Emotions, Understanding Emotions	Achieving
13.4	403	Flex Time	Flexibility	Positive Mood, Stress Tolerance	Managing Emotions, Understanding Emotions	Managing
14.1	407	The EZ Stress Buster	Stress Tolerance	Stress Tolerance	Perceiving Emotions, Managing Emotions	Managing
14.2	413	'Cause You've Got Personality	Stress Tolerance	Stress Tolerance, Emotional Awareness	Perceiving Emotions, Managing Emotions	Decision Making
14.3	423	Water Off a Duck's Back	Stress Tolerance	Stress Tolerance, Motivation	Perceiving Emotions, Managing Emotions	Decision Making

(Continued)

Table 1.2.1. (Continued)

Exercise	Page	Title	EQ-i2.0® and EQ360® (MHS) Skill	TESI® and TESI® Short (Hughes, Terrell) Skill	MSCEIT™ (Mayer, Salovey, Caruso) Scale	EISA (Stein, Mann, Papadogiannis) Skill
14.4	427	Deep Center Breathing	Stress Tolerance	Stress Tolerance, Positive Mood	Perceiving Emotions, Managing Emotions	Perceiving
15.1	433	Optimistic Self-Talk and Behavior	Optimism	Positive Mood	Perceiving Emotions, Managing Emotions	Influencing
15.2	439	Be Solution-Focused	Optimism	Motivation, Positive Mood	Facilitating Thought, Understanding Emotions	Influencing
15.3	443	See a Positive Resolution	Optimism	Communication, Positive Mood	Facilitating Thought, Managing Emotions	Influencing
15.4	447	The Optimistic Explanation	Optimism	Conflict Resolution, Positive Mood	Facilitating Thought, Understanding Emotions	Achieving
16.1	455	Beyond Personal Silos	Happiness	Positive Mood	Perceiving Emotions, Managing Emotions	Perceiving
16.2	461	Growing My Happiness	Happiness	Emotional Awareness, Positive Mood	Perceiving Emotions, Managing Emotions	Decision Making
16.3	465	Pay It Forward with Gratitude	Happiness	Team Identity, Positive Mood	Facilitating Thought, Understanding Emotions	Managing
16.4	469	Attitude of Gratitude	Happiness	Motivation, Positive Mood	Facilitating Thought, Understanding Emotions	Managing

TWO

Exploring Emotional Intelligence and Well-Being Skills

Part Two provides a description of each of the sixteen emotional skills that combine to make up social and emotional intelligence according to the EQ-i$^{2.0}$ model (the other models have similarities in their depiction of emotional intelligence, and their list of skills can be found in the Cross-Reference Matrix in Chapter 2).

The descriptions of each skill begin with a section entitled What Is It?, in which we define the skill. Following that is a section called Why Should We Care About It? Here we point out both the advantages that strength in this skill gives and the disadvantages we may experience if it is a weaker area. Next we provide a section called How Can We Build It? This starts with a tip to help develop the skill or appreciate what makes it valuable and provides the specific instruction necessary for increasing skillfulness in this area. In the section called Transformational Benefits, we discuss how building this particular competency into a strength can transform one's experience of life, increasing the level of satisfaction and effectiveness.

STARS AND MOVIES

One of the best ways to learn is by looking for role models who practice a skill, so for each skill, we have a section naming a Star Performer and a section labeled Reel Performer, in which we list a movie that demonstrates the concept. All are listed in Table 2.1. Have fun and think of your own stars and movies!

Table 2.1. Stars and Movies

EI SKILL	STAR	MOVIE
Self-Regard	Doris Lessing	*The Good Girl*
Self-Actualization	Viktor Frankl	*It's a Wonderful Life*
Emotional Self-Awareness	Maya Angelou	*Frost/Nixon*
Emotional Expression	T.S. Eliot	*Jack Goes Boating*
Assertiveness	Dr. Martin Luther King, Jr.	*12 Angry Men*
Independence	Mahatma Ghandi	*The Matrix; Norma Rae*
Interpersonal Relations	Dalai Lama	*Something's Got to Give*
Empathy	Mother Teresa	*Terms of Endearment*
Social Responsibility	Jimmy Carter	*Remember the Titans*
Problem Solving	William Ury	*The King's Speech*
Reality Testing	Hillary Rodham Clinton	*The Hurt Locker*
Impulse Control	Georgia O'Keefe	*To Kill a Mockingbird*
Flexibility	Meryl Streep	*Lilies of the Field*
Stress Tolerance	Tom Hanks	*Precious*
Optimism	Nelson Mandela	*The Wizard of Oz*
Happiness/Well-Being	Dame Julia Elizabeth Andrews	*Happythankyoumoreplease*

Self-Regard

WHAT IS IT?

Simply defined, self-regard indicates how good we feel about ourselves. It also reflects our ability to accept ourselves warts and all. *Webster's* (1993) dictionary defines self-regard as "consideration of oneself or one's own interests." In contrast, it defines self-esteem as "a confidence and satisfaction in one's self: self-respect."

Self-regard is demonstrated when we like ourselves, can accept our good parts and more challenging parts, and present ourselves with dignity. "Feeling sure of oneself is dependent on self-respect and self-esteem, which are based on a fairly well developed sense of identity. A person with good self-regard feels fulfilled and satisfied with himself/herself. At the opposite end of the continuum are feelings of personal inadequacy and inferiority" (Bar-On, 2002, p. 15).

WHY SHOULD WE CARE ABOUT SELF-REGARD?

This is obviously a bit like asking, "Why should I care about myself?" Self-regard is a critical competency because, without a well-integrated identity that allows you to know and respect yourself, there is no way you can ever participate authentically in life, be truly reliable in work or love, or fully express all the gifts you have to give. A lack of self-regard often indicates feelings of uncertainty and insecurity, an unwillingness to venture out into one's own world and explore it with appropriate reality testing.

In his research, Bar-On (2000, p. 374) found that self-regard emerged "as one of the most powerful predictors of competent behavior."

HOW CAN WE BUILD SELF-REGARD?

Stand in front of the mirror. Look deep in your eyes. Call your name out loud with authority three times, then be silent and feel yourself show up! Now clap wildly and bow.

How worthy or unworthy you feel about receiving good in your life results from a blend of ingredients that includes your experiences, values, attitudes, behaviors, and expectations. You will perceive these conditions more or less accurately, depending on how honest and self-aware you are.

Where emotional self-awareness reflects how well you know your feelings, think of self-regard as how well you know, and like, the whole constellation of features that combine to make up who you are. This is determined to a large degree by how congruently you express your values and desires through your external behavior. Because much of your motivation to move toward some things and away from others is unconscious, building healthy self-regard must include a process of ongoing self-exploration so that you can continue to discover more of your full self and give more complete expression to the whole you.

The overlap with emotional self-awareness demonstrates the deep integration of all sixteen factors of the EQ-i$^{2.0®}$. Other examples that illustrate this deep interconnectedness between skills include the way in which self-regard relates to problem solving and assertiveness. It is not possible to hold oneself in the highest regard if one is unsuccessful in solving problems in one's life or unable to assert one's desires with sufficient strength to satisfy them. Reciprocally, as one strengthens his or her self-regard, his or her problem-solving and assertiveness skills may also strengthen.

TRANSFORMATIONAL BENEFITS

As self-regard is one of the most powerful predictors of competent behavior, then the benefits of its development will include an expanding knowledge of identity that is richer, more flexible, more confident, and more secure. As we continue to build increasingly positive self-regard, we expand our capacity to enjoy our lives and be of service to others.

STAR PERFORMER

Doris Lessing is a self-educated writer who was born to British parents in what is now Iran. She was raised in colonial Rhodesia, now Zimbabwe, and lives in London. She is a writer extraordinaire and winner of the Nobel Prize for literature in 2007 as well as numerous other prizes. She's considered an African writer, a women's writer, and has been described by Irving Howe as "the archaeologist of human relations." In announcing the award in Stockholm in October 2007, the Swedish Academy called her an "epicist of the female experience, who with skepticism, fire, and visionary power has subjected a divided civilization to scrutiny."

She is highly regarded as one of the most important English-language post-World War II writers. Her novels, short stories, and essays have focused on a wide range of issues, from the politics of race that she confronted in her early novels set in Africa, to the politics of gender, which has led to her adoption by the feminist movement, especially for her novel *The Golden Notebook*, to the role of the family and the individual in society, explored in her space fiction of the late 1970s and early 1980s.

Lessing helps us take a look at ourselves both as individuals and in relationship with one another. Her unflinching willingness to observe and report often cost her in many ways, including as a woman writer when that frankness was often disapproved. Yet, her powerful courage and commitment to tell the truth as she saw it has made us better people. Her healthy self-regard is at the core of her ability to share her skills and we are grateful.

▣ REEL PERFORMER

Jennifer Aniston in *The Good Girl* presents a remarkable example of the development of self-regard. As a young high school graduate, she's married and working in a chain discount store. Her life is predictable and boring. She undertakes self-exploration in part by developing a relationship with a young man who is very "out there" for this conservative small town. Through challenges, including her pregnancy and the young man's suicide, she begins to come into herself, becoming much more alive and whole. She becomes more aware and accepting of herself.

Self-Actualization

WHAT IS IT?

Bar-On presents the following definition: "Self-actualization is the process of striving to actualize one's potential capacity, abilities, and talents. It requires the ability and drive to set and achieve goals. It is characterized by being involved in and feeling committed to various interests and pursuits. Self-actualization is a life-long effort leading to the enrichment of life" (2001, p. 89).

Psychologist Abraham Maslow was probably the first to identify the skill of self-actualization. Remember his hierarchy of needs? Writing in the middle of the 20th century, Maslow (1970) identified a hierarchy of core needs, each of which must be adequately addressed before the next step can be fully taken. The hierarchy proceeds from physiological (food, shelter, water) to safety (security, order, law) to belongingness and love needs (giving and receiving affection) to esteem needs (self-respect and the esteem of others) and finally to self-actualization.

Maslow emphasized that we must live up to our potential or we will feel dissatisfied. Self-actualization is the process of being true to our own nature and fully committed to developing our capabilities. It includes the concepts of growth, motivation, and meeting our "being" needs. Maslow later redefined self-actualization as a function of peak experiences, and it is from this aspect of the definition that some people associate self-actualization with mystical experiences. While those fortunate ones who do have mystical experiences surely are on the track of self-actualization, there are many other more common expressions of this skill to be found in daily life.

In accord with Maslow, Bar-On (2001) writes that self-actualization "is most likely the next and ultimate step after EI in the complex process of personal development. While emotional intelligence relates to being effective, self-actualization relates to doing the best you can possibly do. Or, put another way, when we are self-actualized, we have gone beyond EI to achieve a higher level of human effectiveness" (p. 85).

In this 2001 article, Bar-On reports that "the best predictors of self-actualization are the following eight EI factors, listed in order of importance:

Happiness
Optimism
Self-regard
Independence
Problem solving
Social responsibility
Assertiveness
Emotional self-awareness" (p. 92)

What a profound example of the importance of building all parts of our emotional intelligence! Self-actualization reflects how successful we feel at achieving the goals that make life meaningful for us individually. This ability to construct meaning from the challenging and even violent aspects of human experience demonstrate the amazing resilience of the human spirit. Inspiring stories of people who were able to demonstrate this skill under the very worst of conditions can be found in *Man's Search for Meaning* by Viktor Frankl.

In this work, we are focusing on the aspects of self-motivation, which, when combined with strengths in happiness and optimism as well as the other six skills, helps us live an energized and fully engaged life. Self-actualization is a journey, not a destination. It is the place where our "doing" and our "being" modes can be joined.

Thus the key questions are

- How am I doing on this journey?
- How am I being on this journey?

- Am I happy about where am I now?
- Am I pacing myself on this journey?
- Am I motivated to be the best I can be?

WHY SHOULD WE CARE ABOUT SELF-ACTUALIZATION?

We all have a deep inner calling to be all that we can be. For some of us this is a loud and insistent holler, while for others it may be a quiet whisper. Our current state of happiness, optimism, and the other six factors that are the underpinnings of self-actualization will influence our desire to grow this skill and our sense that it is possible. If we are inclined to be pessimistic, we limit our sense of possibility and miss many opportunities. Perhaps even the pessimist can say to him- or herself, "Well, *IF* it were possible, I would like to be...." This is the path to actualizing our dreams, what makes our lives meaningful—one day at a time.

Self-actualization is critical for today's successful businesses. Millions of dollars are spent annually in working with teams and in developing employees to help grow their motivation to be the best they can be. In this very practical sense, self-actualization is at the heart of organizational success. In fact, when Stein and Book (2011) wrote *The EQ Edge*, they conducted research using the EQ-i on nearly five thousand working people in many different occupations. They found that the first of the top five factors of overall success is self-actualization. Thus, it is one of the most important factors for organizations to highlight for employee development.

HOW CAN WE BUILD SELF-ACTUALIZATION?

> Remember that self-actualization is an evolutionary journey. Be motivated to be the best you can be today. Don't get depressed that you haven't accomplished everything by today, and watch success unfold!

Pay attention to your longings and the deep messages you give yourself. Are you longing to be an artist, but you're a banker—or vice versa? This

EI skill builds on eight other skills, so it's not an area of solo perfection. It's an integrated part of who one is. Use the exercises in Part Three of this book to identify your own or your client's capacities in the eight identified skill areas. It is important to notice which skills support us the most and which can be improved to help increase our self-actualization.

Pace yourself and teach your client(s) to do the same! This isn't a race; it's evolutionary. If you will intentionally move forward on a regular basis, one step at a time, keeping the vision as a possibility, you'll be able to listen to the wisdom within and enjoy much more growth than if you are always feeling bad because you "should do more." After all, the "should's" are out—they went with the last century. This is the time of possibility.

TRANSFORMATIONAL BENEFITS

Are you kidding? This is it, baby! Self-actualization can rocket a person right off the planet! The potential as one grows this skill is unlimited. Welcome the surprises.

Individually, we are much more comfortable, resilient, and fun to be with when we know we are on the right path. For most organizations, motivating employees is a key goal. Developing self-actualization is central to inspiring employees and helps everyone clarify which motivational strategies are most effective for him or her.

STAR PERFORMER

Viktor Frankl, M.D., Ph.D., the author of *Man's Search for Meaning* (2000) was a highly inspirational psychiatrist and a professor of neurology and psychiatry at the University of Vienna Medical School. He was interned for three years at Auschwitz, Dachau, and other concentration camps. During that time he began his study of what guides us as humans. He noticed that the same horrendous conditions affected all the prisoners in the camps, yet a few were able to survive. His answer to why that occurred focused on people's individual attitudes. His teachings that no one else can ever control one's attitude, and that this is a great personal resource, have been recited across the world to inspire people in all walks of life.

▤ REEL PERFORMER

In *It's a Wonderful Life,* George Bailey (Jimmy Stewart) struggles with wondering whether his hardworking life in Bedford Falls has been worth anything. He gave up travel and other personal desires to save the small town from being taken over by a rich skinflint, Mr. Potter. But his work looks like a failure when his uncle loses $8,000 on Christmas Eve, resulting in Bailey thinking he'll lose the business and go to jail. When wondering whether suicide is a good option, prayers and an angel help him realize how valuable he is to so many. George is able to appreciate the value of his life and his many contributions.

Emotional Self-Awareness

WHAT IS IT?

Understanding what you're feeling and why you are feeling that way is perhaps one of the most critical components of emotionally effective living. It is intimately associated with how well we use our empathy by understanding what other people are feeling and *why* they feel the way they do. Together these two skills of emotional awareness and empthy are what enable us to motivate and influence the thoughts and actions of ourselves and others—in short, the skills most necessary to succeed in life.

Consider for a moment the fact that emotions are deeply connected with sensation; in fact, our emotional life begins when we explore our physical world as newborns and infants. Until we are strong enough to at least turn over in bed, we are pretty much subject to the conditions in our environment. If something is poking or constraining us, we can't really locate it and change it. Nonetheless, our bodies reflexively express aversion by contracting their muscles—initially at the point of discomfort, then throughout the limb or trunk, and eventually throughout the whole body if the discomfort is great enough. If all this still provides no relief and we are uncomfortable enough, we cry for help!

If, on the other hand, something pleases us, like a warm bottle or someone rocking us in his or her arms, our muscles tend to generally relax so we can enjoy the experience. Obviously, feeding involves some muscular engagement (also largely reflexive), but more interesting perhaps is the fact that enjoyment itself actually requires a kind of "effort" called awareness. Consciously noticing the sensations we are feeling is rather like pushing the "record" button on our life recorders and making the memories of that sensory experience conscious. In contrast, the sensations of feeding may be recorded unconsciously because of their reflexive nature or consciously if the baby is alert and attending to the sensory experience.

WHY SHOULD WE CARE ABOUT EMOTIONAL SELF-AWARENESS?

Here's the point. Emotions begin as the values we learn to place on our sensory experience, our likes and our dislikes. The conditions surrounding our pleasant and unpleasant sensations give rise to our ability to recognize and express our emotional preferences. All of our sensory life is recorded in us (perhaps even *as* us if Candace Pert (2000) is correct in the thesis of her work *The Body Is Your Subconscious Mind*) and the way in which we recall those emotions—either more consciously and intentionally or more unconsciously and reactively—has everything to do with the level of our emotional self-awareness.

The next stage of development after sensory awareness and emotional awareness is symbolic awareness—we begin to translate our experience into the words and ideas of our native language. This is a hugely rewarding and exciting time in our lives! By now we are also developing the muscular strength and coordination that free us to explore our world (more or less) at the whim of our own interest…and we can *tell* people what we want and need much more specifically.

Unfortunately, the ability to objectify our world through language and operate on it as "other than ourselves" is often overly emphasized and reinforced as we start thinking ahead about our children's future in terms of the goals they will need to accomplish to be successful in our technologically driven postmodern society. As parents, we are busy, our own attention is split in a dozen directions, we are trying to achieve our own measures of success, we are tired. If we do not know how to take the time to consciously model how the emotional world integrates with the symbolic world, our children may end up reacting out of their conditioned emotional preferences rather than responding with emotional intentionality, that is, emotional intelligence.

HOW CAN WE BUILD EMOTIONAL SELF-AWARENESS?

To develop the ability to consciously express emotional self-awareness in our children and in ourselves, we need to connect to parts of our experience—what we're feeling and why we are feeling that way. In a very simple language pattern that Robert Carkhuff introduced in his human relations training in the 1970s, we can discover and share our internal experience by filling in the blanks to: "I feel _____ , because _____." "I feel worried because I can't reach my daughter." "I feel mad because you misled me." "I feel really excited because I've never seen a roller coaster that big before." We have to regularly check in and take our own emotional pulse and then, when appropriate, we may want or need to share what we have discovered with the other people around us.

TRANSFORMATIONAL BENEFITS

Without emotional self-awareness, we will live a life of reaction rather than initiation. It will seem to us as if we are at the effect of life rather than able to influence it effectively on our own behalf and on behalf of those we care for. Reconnecting with our sensory and emotional awareness and using that awareness consciously not only helps us achieve what we want in life, but also enables us to enjoy it much more fully when we do.

STAR PERFORMER

With pride in sharing our humanity with her, we nominate Maya Angelou as the star performer for emotional self-awareness. She's an American author and poet who was active in the Civil Rights movement and supported the work of Martin Luther King. She read one of her powerful poems at the inauguration of President William Jefferson Clinton. Ms. Angelou is well known for her series of autobiographical volumes that focus on her childhood and early adult experiences. The first and most highly recognized is *I Know Why the Caged Bird Sings* (1969). She has been awarded numerous honorary degrees and was nominated for a Pulitzer Prize for her 1971 volume of poetry, *Just Give Me a Cool Drink of Water 'Fore I Diiie*. We quote one powerful stanza from her poem "Still I Rise" from her volume of poetry *And Still I Rise* (1978):

"You may write me down in history
With your bitter, twisted lies,
You may trod me in the very dirt
But still, like dust, I'll rise."

President Barack Obama presented Angelou with the Presidential Medal of Freedom in 2011.

▦ REEL PERFORMER

For this example, we select Michael Sheen playing David Frost in the movie *Frost/Nixon*. This is the story of an amazing game of wits in which the historical stakes are as high as they have ever been. David Frost must get keenly in touch and stay in touch with his emotional self-awareness or be publicly manipulated and stonewalled by former President Richard Nixon; this manipulation would allow Nixon to rewrite history and rehabilitate his reputation while effectively destroying that of the former talk show host.

While his research team is working diligently and trying to school him on the facts, Frost is often preoccupied, traveling to try to raise the $600,000 he needs to pay Nixon. The first three interviews do not go well. Nixon is able to parry the planned questions and successfully indulges in long self-justifying monologues. Four days before the last interview, in a weird twist of fate, a drunken Nixon calls Frost at his hotel and points out that it will be matter of winner take all. This conversation galvanizes Frost's awareness of what he needs to do. He sends one of his researchers to follow up a lead he had previously discounted, and his colleague comes back with gold. Rejuvenated by this positive turn of events, Frost works tirelessly for the next three days and meets Nixon with a new confidence and determination. He can no longer be misled and distracted, but the former president is still a wily adversary until confronted by new evidence from a recording of the conversation with Chuck Colson. Frost is now the master, here pushing hard, then backing up quickly and letting Nixon implicate himself with his self-serving explanations. Without his skillful use of emotional self-awareness, the truth behind the Watergate scandal and Nixon's involvement in it might have remained mired forever in denial and dispute. It was David Frost's ability to adjust to the moment-by-moment shifts in emotional nuance that enabled him to outmaneuver Nixon, who was relying instead on a powerful, presidential rehearsal of the past as he perceived it.

Emotional Expression

WHAT IS IT?

In the earlier version of the EQ-i, the questions that guide exploration of the level of effectiveness in emotional expression were included in the skill of emotional-self awareness. However, they are in fact significantly different skills, and are much better represented in the 2.0 version. Whereas emotional awareness is about how sensitive we are to our emotional energy and how well we can recognize our emotions, emotional expression is a measure of how accurately and effectively we can communicate our feelings to others. In addition to being about as different as listening is from talking, there is also the need for a well-diversified emotional vocabulary that allows us to translate our experience from sensory data into verbal expression.

For instance, when team members rate their team's emotional awareness with the TESI, part of what they are capturing is how well the individuals notice team communication behavior relative to expressing feelings. In order to do this effectively, people need to have enough feeling words at their disposal to be able to accurately differentiate the wide variety of emotional states that constitute team climate. This includes not only major differences such as enthusiasm versus discouragement, but degrees of intensity within a specific feeling as well. Are the people happy to be there or passionately committed to succeed? Are they worried that the beta test might need to be finished a little later, or concerned that the product will never perform as promised?

WHY SHOULD I CARE ABOUT EMOTIONAL EXPRESSIVENESS?

Emotions express values. Our bodies don't go to the trouble of producing an emotional response unless there's something valuable in the environment we need to be aware of. It could be a negative value to be avoided at all costs or a positive value that we really want to take advantage of. It could be something that is blocking us from a goal we are deeply committed to achieve, indicating that we need to supercharge our efforts to overcome the obstruction. It could be an opportunity to give, to help another person or group meet significant challenges they face but are unable to achieve alone.

HOW CAN WE BUILD EMOTIONAL EXPRESSIVENESS?

Increasing our emotional vocabulary is certainly one of the most important steps to increasing our emotional expressiveness. If we lack the words that are able to communicate the nuances of what we are feeling, it will be hard for others to consciously understand specifically what we are feeling. It is critical to recognize, however, that our nonverbal communication is telling them at every level whether we are happy or unhappy, whether we feel threatened or are threatening.

Increasing our emotional expressiveness requires the confidence that comes from self-regard and the courage that is fundamental to assertiveness, so improving those two skills may also be necessary if we are going to express our feelings more openly and authentically.

Expressing emotions effectively also depends on using our nonverbal expressions more intentionally. Our posture, tonality, facial expression, gestures, the volume and rhythm of our voice, and other nonverbals communicate over 90 percent of the messages we send. Words account for only about 7 percent. Because our nonverbal communication is predominantly unconscious, we may unintentionally communicate our own fear, anger, or judgment in ways that make us less influential instead of more effectively engaging the attention and cooperation of those around us.

CARE TO EXPRESS

 When something matters to your clients, suggest they express it with respect rather than stuffing the emotions. Suggest that they:

- Notice how they are feeling and why and silently tell themselves.
- Take a deep breath and become calm.
- Tell others "I feel _____ because _____."
- For a stretch goal, they can then reciprocate and explore how the others involved are feeling and why.

TRANSFORMATIONAL BENEFITS

Desire, fear, anger, and altruism are the four main types of motivations available to us as humans. They are what move us to action. We move toward what we desire in order to *get* it; we move away from what we fear or dislike; we move against the objects, policies, and people who obstruct us from obtaining what we desire. When we are motivated by our altruistic emotions, we move toward the people and situations that we care about in order to *give* the emotional and physical resources we have and wish to share with others. Understanding the relationship between emotions and motivation can help us read others more accurately and send more intentional messages that are more easily understood.

STAR PERFORMER

Although any number of poets could easily have been chosen as star performers in expressing emotion, we chose T.S. Eliot for his eloquent use of emotional expression to communicate vast insight about life's most subtle mysteries through mere words. His artistry in stringing their cognitive, practical, rational meanings together in ways that reveal far more than words were ever commissioned to do is breathtaking. But as he himself ranted in East Coker from the Four Quartets (1943/1971) it is never easy.

But in addition to that patience and determined perseverance, he also knew how to apply the most rigorous self-discipline, also called impulse control in the language of emotional intelligence. Later, from East Coker he writes of the need to wait without hope or love as they would be for the wrong thing, but rather to have faith "so the darkness shall be the light, and the stillness the dancing."

▐▊▌ REEL PERFORMER

Movies show lives of other people that we get to try on if we are brave enough to do so. They give us a front row seat on how others weave fate, relationships, choices, and consequences into the most successful and meaningful lives they can create. We get to peer into them in a voyeuristic manner that is impossible in "real life." Often, it is just sensational, but in *Jack Goes Boating*, it is as healing as it is encouraging and instructive. This is a brilliant fear-defying smorgasbord of lessons in emotional expressiveness. In it, two sensitive adults who deeply long to connect, to know and be known, to love and be loved by another give it their very best shot—even though they have almost none of the skills necessary to do so.

Jack (Philip Seymour Hoffman) and Connie (Amy Ryan) are both the kind of introverts who make us wonder how such socially unskillful people could ever manage to live, let alone stake claim to space on life's canvas and slowly begin filling it with beauty until the boundaries are pushed back to reveal robust and heroic lives. Although awkward and clumsy and plagued with bad timing, they are refreshingly faithful to that fragile spark of love that might, on a very long shot, flame up for them. And in being faithful, they provide critical lessons in courage and honesty to the couple who introduced them and whose own relationship is being torn apart by the unskillful choices that they have made and left uncorrected. No one who is brave enough to love life can watch this without learning a great deal about the most intimate nuances of emotional expressiveness.

Assertiveness

WHAT IS IT?

Assertiveness is the ability to express feelings, beliefs, and thoughts and defend one's rights in a nondestructive manner. Stein and Book (2000, p. 66)[*] present the following definition:

> "Assertiveness is composed of three basic components: (1) the ability to express feelings (for example, to accept and express anger, warmth, and sexual feelings); (2) the ability to express beliefs and thoughts openly (being able to voice opinions, to disagree, and to take a definite stand, even if it is emotionally difficult to do so and even if you have something to lose by doing so); and (3) the ability to stand up for personal rights (not allowing others to bother you or take advantage of you). Assertive people are not over-controlled or shy—they are able to express their feelings (often directly), without being aggressive or abusive."

Assertiveness, which requires directness, finesse, and consideration of others, is described by Weisinger (1998, p. 122) as "the ability to stand up for your rights, opinions, ideas, beliefs, and needs while at the same time respecting those of others."

The concept of negative space can help us understand the difference between assertiveness and aggressiveness. Artists and designers use the concept of negative space to gain clarity about the shape, contour, and contextual meaning of an object. This is accomplished by looking at the space surrounding the object. For example, if you are drawing a pear, shift your eyes slightly away from the pear to see how it blocks and shadows the space or objects around it. This is a helpful tool to use in examining a concept.

To explore a concept's negative space, pay attention to what it is not. This helps minimize false assumptions and faulty conclusions. Assertiveness is not aggressiveness. Aggressiveness moves beyond assertiveness and into obtrusiveness, combativeness, and militancy. The key difference between the two is that aggressiveness leaves no room for the consideration of others' feelings, viewpoints, or objectives. Aggressiveness is about winning at all costs. The metaphor of steamrolling over someone encapsulates aggressiveness.

Assertiveness is an expressive behavior that respects others' dignity and humanity even when conveying something that might be unwelcome or controversial. Bottom line: Assertiveness is the balanced space between being a pushover and a steamroller.

WHY SHOULD I CARE ABOUT ASSERTIVENESS?

Assertiveness is our backbone, spine, spunk, or chutzpah—our ability to interact with our environment and make our voices heard! Assertiveness empowers us and helps us define ourselves to others. It feeds our sense of self-regard because we are caring for ourselves by announcing our desires, feelings, and thoughts and by clearly setting our boundaries.

While assertiveness starts in the inner realm of dealing with our own feelings and responses, it ultimately manifests in how we communicate and behave. To communicate effectively, we are often required to be assertive and to verbalize risky positions. The authors of *Skilled Interpersonal Communication* describe assertive communication in this way: "Assertive responses involve standing up for oneself, yet taking the other person into consideration. The assertive style involves...openly and confidently expressing personal feelings and opinions; valuing oneself equal to others; being prepared to listen to the other's point of view..." (Hargie & Dickson, 2004, p. 300).

Differences of opinion and conflicts are ever-present among people. To be effective in our own lives, whether at work or home, we must appropriately surface issues and deal with differences. In *The Power of a Good Fight*, Lynn Eisaguirre asserts, "We need to move toward embracing conflict as a friendly force to be directed and used, not avoided like the enemy. Leadership involves learning to value conflict" (2002, p. 5).

How much happier and more effective would we be if, in risky situations, we were consistently able to state our positions yet maintain, or even deepen, relationships? Assertiveness enables us to be true to ourselves and to respect others.

HOW CAN WE BUILD ASSERTIVENESS?

Building assertiveness usually means:

- Building it up—from reticence
- Dialing it back—from aggressiveness

First, identify where your client is on the continuum (see Figure 2.5.1). When assertiveness is required, does he or she keep silent or go into overdrive? When he or she is not being appropriately assertive does he or she always go to one end of the continuum or bounce back and forth depending on the situation? Stein and Book (2011, pp. 73–75) include a similar concept in their description of assertiveness.

Empathy and courage are requisites of assertiveness. They help us moderate our behavior at both ends of the continuum. Empathy helps us be more

| Reticence | Assertiveness | Aggressiveness |

Figure 2.5.1. The Assertiveness Continuum.

sensitive to others' viewpoints and helps mitigate our defensiveness. It makes it easier to treat others with respect and dignity. It will also help us consider how the information we are withholding from them could help them grow.

Courage helps us take more risks. It can stoke our spirit when we are feeling meek. It can also help us to open up and leave room for other opinions.

 ## ASSERTIVE NOT PASSIVE

Your client can shift from squirming inside because he or she did not speak up to stating his or her point of view factually and forthrightly and feeling good about it.

ASSERTIVE NOT AGGRESSIVE

Your client should stop trying to overpower or intimidate others into bending to his or her will and move to stating his or her case factually and calmly.

How does it feel to be assertive? Are you more effective when you engage your assertiveness?

TRANSFORMATIONAL BENEFITS

Enhanced assertiveness skills can exponentially increase our value, impact, and well-being. When we employ them elegantly, we behave neither as victims nor as instruments of mass destruction. We do not make ourselves sick from harboring ill thoughts toward others and keeping ugly feelings bottled up inside. Nor do we make others sick by exploding all over them in an offensive and caustic way. The elegant application of assertiveness makes us empowered people who face that which needs to be addressed and who can be relied on for clarity and honesty.

Organizations are more productive when managers and employees are appropriately assertive and openly share information and issues.

STAR PERFORMER

Dr. Martin Luther King, Jr., was a civil rights activist whose concept of "somebodiness" symbolized the celebration of human worth and the conquest of subjugation. He gave black and poor people hope and a sense of dignity. His philosophy of nonviolent, direct action and his strategies for rational and non-destructive social change galvanized the conscience of this nation and reordered its priorities (TheKingCenter.com, 2003, p. 1).

 REEL PERFORMER

Assertiveness is demonstrated with courage and substantial consequences in *12 Angry Men*, where one person on a twelve-person jury is able to raise enough doubt to convince the others that the capital murder case is not as clear as it seemed in court. The jury is deliberating in the first-degree murder trial of a young Latino accused in the stabbing death of his father, and a guilty verdict means the death sentence. Eleven of the jurors immediately vote "guilty"; only Mr. Davis (Juror Number 8) casts a "not guilty" vote. As the deliberations unfold, the story becomes a study of the jurors' complex personalities and their emotional expressions and we learn that the power of assertiveness is often a matter of persistence, not superior force.

Independence

WHAT IS IT?

Independence is the ability to think for oneself and not be unduly influenced by the thoughts, desires, and emotions of others. It does not mean that one is completely insensitive to the needs of other people or to societal mores. It means a person is able to sift through others' input and expectations, access his or her own beliefs and values, then reach conclusions and take actions that make sense for his or her own life.

The degree of independence considered appropriate and how it is expressed are influenced by culture. Eastern societies value group process above individual needs, while Western cultures have a higher tendency toward independence. The timeless American icon, the cowboy, is the quintessential figure of independence.

To highlight the desirability of independence, the *Star Trek: Next Generation* television series created an alien society called the Borg. Each seemingly separate being was neurally connected to all of the others, and they operated with one mind. The concept was called the "hive mind." The power of the Borg archetype was that their complete and utter lack of independence was repulsive to the audience's Western way of thinking. Thus, it reaffirmed the Western commitment to independence.

Independence often requires courage, because a person's actions may set him or her apart from the group and raise visibility. It can be difficult to think and act independently of others. The term "groupthink" conveys the concept of conforming to the values and ethics of others. As the polar opposite of independence, groupthink does not allow for individuality.

Webster's defines independent as "(1) not subject to control by others: not subordinate; not affiliated with or integrated into a larger controlling unit" (1993).

WHY SHOULD WE CARE ABOUT INDEPENDENCE?

Independence is the ability to stand on one's own two feet and trust one's own judgment. It reflects self-confidence and the willingness to take risks. Independence is a key leadership trait that can enhance effectiveness whether one is the leader of a global company, supervisor of a small team, a parent, volunteer with a community organization, or the leader of his or her life.

Independence is important in a team environment, as long as it is expressed with sensitivity to the group process and is applied with a collaborative spirit. One is valued as a team member when he or she is able to take initiative to get things done while including others and contributing to the collective efforts of the group.

HOW CAN WE BUILD INDEPENDENCE?

Notice when and where in your life you are reluctant to exercise your independence. Is it in all situations or in certain circumstances with specific people? Explore what it is that makes you uncomfortable asserting your independence. Are you concerned that people will not think you're "nice"? Will others be angry? Will someone challenge your position or conclusion? Ask these same questions of your client(s).

Assess the risk of acting independently. If there is more to be gained (self-respect, confidence, and improved teamwork) by asserting independence, then map out a step-by-step plan to promote its development. If you stick with the plan, you will find that you are facing your fears about being independent and increasing your capabilities. The same can happen for your client(s) as you guide them in this direction.

THE JOY OF INDEPENDENCE

Remember riding your first two-wheeled bike:

- At first it had training wheels, and then they were removed.
- You were left with just the two wheels and your parent holding the back of your seat while you pedaled.
- Finally, you experienced the freedom of doing it all by yourself. What a rush!!

Share this with your client and ask whether his or her confidence soared after that accomplishment.

TRANSFORMATIONAL BENEFITS

A person who uses independence effectively will have the satisfaction of knowing that he or she acts according to his or her sense of ethics and values and resists the pressure to conform in an unhealthy way. These people are not just puppets on a string. Each time a person stays true to his or her beliefs and intuition, the independence response is fortified. When the tough situations arise, he or she will have the gumption to face the challenges presented.

STAR PERFORMER

Mahatma Gandhi was a British barrister who fought for civil liberties and freedom in South Africa and in his native India. He followed his own sense of ethics and acted independently of societal expectations. His lifelong struggle was against the prejudices of creed, caste, and race. He eschewed violence and rose to prominence in the social arena on a platform of individual resistance and non-cooperation. "Gandhi had a rare combination of readiness to resist wrong and capacity to love his opponents which baffled his enemies and compelled their admiration" (www.MKGandhi.com, 2003). He was the galvanizing force that freed India from British rule.

▓▓ REEL PERFORMER

In *The Matrix* we see a good example of independence in Neo (Keanu Reeves), a software techie by day and computer hacker by night. Morpheus (Laurence Fishburne) reveals the dark truth about the world—humans are the slaves of the machines they created. The humans live in pods, where their energy is harvested to run the machines. They do not resist because the machines have deluded them into thinking they live in a gleaming metropolis, when in reality they live in a virtual world, the matrix.

Neo rebels against the conventional wisdom of the matrix and fights for freedom and truth. The people in the matrix were ignorantly blissful, while the rebels faced the harsh reality. Opting for independence makes his life enormously harder, but it gives Neo a conscious life with real meaning and consequence in place of his former unconscious dream.

In *Norma Rae*, Sally Field plays a young single mother who works in an Alabama textile mill. Distaste for the deplorable conditions of the work environment and exposure to Reuben (Ron Leibman), a dedicated New York lawyer, fuels her campaign to unionize her company. This is a potentially dangerous course of action for her. The safe route is to maintain the status quo, but her fierce independence drives her to improve conditions for herself and her co-workers, even those who oppose her.

Interpersonal Relationships

WHAT ARE THEY?

Interpersonal relationships are the proving ground of emotional intelligence; they are where the rubber meets the road. Our skill in interpersonal relationships governs whether other people in our lives will feel eager to see us again or dread it. Here is where our needs, desires, and expectations are anticipated, acknowledged, appreciated, and treated with respect or where they are thwarted and ignored. The quality of our interpersonal relationships establishes the social and emotional climate in our families, neighborhoods, and workplaces. When our relationships are working well, they provide the common ground where we get to enjoy our own experience of humanness through sharing it with others.

Stein and Book (2011, p. 125) define skill in interpersonal relationships as "the ability to establish and maintain mutually satisfying relationships that are characterized by the ability to both 'give' and 'take' in relationships, and where trust and compassion are openly expressed in words or by behavior." The tricky part is the requirement of mutuality. Developing relationships that truly are mutually satisfying requires surrendering some of our control to another person, or to other people. But out of the natural correspondence between emotional competencies, we discover that kind of surrender is also exactly what it takes to be socially responsible! Nothing will bring our interest and attention to focus faster on the group's needs than when we surrender some of our own self-interest and have, as they say, "some skin in the game."

In order to have an authentically mutual relationship, we have to understand the other people well enough to anticipate their preferences and be able to satisfy them to some extent . . . and *they* get to be the final authority as to whether or not our attempts were successful! To make it even more complicated, there are times when almost everyone is somewhat deceptive about what he or she wants and what he or she is or is not willing to give. For a relationship with real depth, we ultimately need to know the other person well enough to detect when he or she is bluffing and to constructively elicit his or her true perspective when it does matter and recognize when to let it go when it doesn't.

WHY SHOULD WE CARE ABOUT INTERPERSONAL RELATIONSHIPS?

No matter how much we might pretend otherwise, humans *must* care about interpersonal relationships because we are primates, who are by nature highly social creatures. We cannot survive long in isolation. Our ancient biology predisposes us to seek communication with others. Your brain and heart structures and the neurotransmitters that circulate throughout your body are all extensions of millions of years of behavior. You can't escape needing to be touched and held and spoken to. You can't *not* seek reflections of yourself from fellow human beings unless you suffer from some of the more extreme forms of mental dysfunction such as schizophrenia or autism.

As the planet becomes more crowded and more of our resources have to be shared, our ability to make friends and keep them is critical to our ability to progress socially—and perhaps even to survive. Trusting, committed relationships among neighbors and community members were key ingredients in the success of the American Revolution and the settling of the frontier. It has only been as we have grown more and more affluent that we could afford to indulge in the sort of separation and fragmentedness that has now become commonplace. There are serious costs to this alienation. We harbor a vague sense of competition with our neighbors, even suspicion, and the desire not to be bothered by them.

What is surprising to those of us who have been conditioned to believe success comes out of competition and winning is that it not only doesn't cost us anything to reinvest more of our resources and concern in social responsibility, but it actually improves our stress tolerance and makes us happier. Taking a fresh, more honest look at ourselves, we rediscover that we are naturally social creatures.

HOW CAN WE BUILD INTERPERSONAL RELATIONSHIPS?

 "Friendship should be more than biting Time can sever."

T.S. Eliot, *Murder in the Cathedral*

Fortunately, the skills for building durable, mutually beneficial relationships are well-known and easily practiced by those who truly want to improve this skill. It should also be kept in mind that this, of all of the sixteen skills, is most subject to the hereditary constraints of a biological set point. Each of us has a general zone of comfort that governs how reserved and how outgoing we are. We can learn to operate outside of that, but will need to recharge our batteries in order to do so.

The first step is to examine honestly the level of satisfaction you currently experience. Consider the relationships that are central to your life and think about the most and least satisfying aspects. The second step is to recognize that, if you want to make new friends or improve the quality of an existing relationship, it will be *you* who does the changing. . . . It is never a useful goal to set about changing or improving the other person; rather, it is a recipe for certain frustration and failure. The third step is to start working on specific behaviors, such as improving your listening, introducing yourself to others, finding areas of common interest, reading nonverbal cues, and ending conversations in a way that encourages more contact in the future.

Certainly, there are relationships that should be abandoned rather than improved—abusive ones fall in this category. Knowing which relationships to nurture and which to let go is a separate skill, and you can find many resources on that topic. Here we are concerned with ways to start and improve healthy relationships.

TRANSFORMATIONAL BENEFITS

Improving your skills in interpersonal relationships can bring a host of benefits from stress reduction to increased productivity and creativity, as well as an expanded enjoyment of life. Celebrating your accomplishments is a key ingredient in developing happiness. To the extent you can increase the quantity and quality of your interpersonal relationships, you will have more people with whom to enjoy celebrating those achievements! As you assist your clients in building this skill, they are likely to notice more ease and success in achieving the goals that they desire.

STAR PERFORMER

The Dalai Lama is a Buddhist monk as well as the spiritual and political leader of all Tibetan people. His life's work is to enable his people, a large number of whom are living in exile, to maintain the high spiritual, ethical, and artistic values of their ancient culture. He is an excellent model of interpersonal relationships because he is able to humbly reach out and create relationships without judgment across the world. He is able to assert his intelligence and authority effectively in the world without the self-importance that sometimes makes others come off as arrogant and egotistical and through these skills he has brought many more people into relationships.

REEL PERFORMER

In *Something's Got to Give,* Diane Keaton and Jack Nicholson meet when she's in her fifties and he's in his sixties, having his first heart attack. Both are deeply identified with and committed to their singleness, and they defend it with strong protective shields that also "protect" them from the stability of a relationship with a life partner. However, at a deeper level it is as if their souls somehow connect and lead their personalities through a long list of lessons that produce a new and deeply rewarding relationship for both of them. It's not easy, but—wow!—is it worth it!

Empathy

WHAT IS IT?

Empathy is the ability to "understand, be aware of, be sensitive to, and vicariously experience the feelings, thoughts, and experiences of another," according to *Webster's* (1993) dictionary. The key to effectively applying this skill lies in learning how to give others accurate feedback on what they are feeling and why.

Empathy is the ability to "read" others by getting into resonance with them. The first step is to respectfully focus your attention on the person, seeking to truly listen and understand his or her actions and emotions. It requires applying the same level of awareness that you developed in building your emotional self-awareness and following with genuine curiosity the same lines of inquiry about others— What are they feeling now? How strongly? Why do they feel that way?

Our empathic capabilities begin to emerge when we first learn to distinguish between ourselves and others. As humans, we can look in the mirror and recognize ourselves. Most other animals do not have that capacity. In order to exercise our empathic skills, we must be aware of the differences between ourselves and other people. Empathy is not the same as sympathy. In sympathy we lose that critical distance and become so identified with someone else that we automatically feel the same way that he or she is feeling. If he or she is upset, we become similarly upset. If he or she is highly motivated and gung ho, so are we, and though we don't necessarily know why, it's literally because the other person is. This can be very good when we need to respond together to a common challenge, because sympathy is a critical component of loyalty and camaraderie. On the other hand, when it lacks independence, sympathy can degrade into codependency. We lose our objectivity, and with it goes our helpfulness.

Healthy empathy is vital to the ability to develop and maintain deep and lasting interpersonal relationships. It is also at the heart of a well-functioning workplace, community, and family. When we engage empathically, we are motivated to pay attention to other people. We attend to them by noticing their communications from multiple dimensions—by noticing what they are saying verbally as well as tonally and by noticing their non-verbal communications.

Judith Flury and William Ickes (2001, p. 114) state that the "ability to accurately infer the specific content of other people's thoughts and feelings represents the fullest expression of a perceiver's empathic skills."

WHY SHOULD WE CARE ABOUT EMPATHY?

In today's increasingly fast-paced world, empathy becomes more important every day. Paying sufficient attention to other people may take a bit more time up-front, and it definitely takes more commitment and motivation. However, practicing empathy pays off because it leads to dramatically more accurate communications. Productivity is enhanced and conflict is reduced. As Stein and Book state, "When you make an empathic statement, even in the midst of an otherwise tense or antagonistic encounter, you shift the balance. A contentious and uneasy interchange becomes a more collaborative alliance" (2011, p. 112).

Collaborative alliances have resiliency that elevate their strength and productivity. The first step in creating a collaborative climate is empathic interaction. Certainly, it is the beginning of building trust. When you are helping others resolve conflict, your empathic comments will open new lines of communication and bring to the discussion the flexibility that is needed to resolve any concerns. Furthermore, demonstrations of empathy are essential skills you model to the others involved in the conflict.

Scientists are exploring the connection between empathy and our evolution as humans. Natalie Angier reports in the *Denver Post* that researchers were watching the expression of empathy in chimpanzees in zoos. She writes that the "emotion most akin to gravity, the sensation that keep the affairs of humanity on track as surely as the Earth wheels around the Sun, is empathy: the power to recognize the plight of another and to take on that burden as though it were built to order" (1995, p. 2A).

In a world filled with negotiation challenges, we need all the help we can get. One powerful strategy is to use empathy in the communication. Certainly, advice is more persuasive if delivered with empathy.

Each of the emotional intelligence skills we focus on in this book influences the others, and the extent to which our skills in empathy are developed is intimately connected with skills such as emotional self-awareness, self-regard, reality testing, and self-actualization. As Lane (2000) states, "The ability to be aware of one's own emotions probably derives from input from others such as caregivers. Over time the representations of the experiences of the self and others become progressively differentiated from one another. With development, the ability to be accurately attuned to the emotional state of others is probably a function of the ability to draw on one's own emotional experience, which itself is a function of how these emotional experiences were represented and communicated to others in the past" (p. 184).

HOW CAN WE BUILD EMPATHY?

Learn to read body language. Attend to a person's facial expressions, breathing, posture, and tonality; then match his or her physical state in your own body and see how it feels to you! This is an easy way of getting into resonance.

A key factor in increasing our empathy includes forming an intention to pay attention to others. This calls for exercising our motivation to really listen and understand what is being expressed by those seeking to communicate with us, rather than projecting our interpretation of reality on them. This and the other strategies listed below are excellent to use with your coaching or team clients.

- Put yourself in the other person's shoes. This can be a quick interaction as a part of a conversation or you can job share, job shadow, or find another way to experience literally what is happening for the other person.
- Seek to understand the duties of others and the demands they face.
- Inquire. If someone says something that seems way off to you, say, "That's interesting; please tell me more." This can help you correctly understand what the person is seeking to communicate. It might help the other person understand him- or herself better, as well.

TRANSFORMATIONAL BENEFITS

Few of us enjoy fighting, but one of the surest ways we stir up conflict is through misunderstanding what another person intended to say. Of course, we can blame the other person, but the most effective and happiest strategy is for us to take personal responsibility for the effectiveness of the communication. Step one is to listen empathically. Not only will we get a more accurate read on what someone is seeking to tell us, but we will in all likelihood help the person to become clearer about what he or she is seeking to say.

For example, Stephanie is carefully listening to Tom describe a difficult situation with one of his customers. Periodically she gives him feedback by repeating both what she is hearing him say and how he seems to feel about it. "So they ordered two thousand units on Thursday and then called up Tuesday morning after they had shipped, to cut it down to six hundred? Man, you must have felt angry—as well as discouraged."

Tom knew he was feeling angry about this inconsiderate behavior and all the hassles it was going to cause him, but he hadn't yet acknowledged consciously that he felt discouraged because the loss in volume meant he still hadn't made his quota. Stephanie's reflection can help him develop a more effective response to his challenge because it requires different kinds of resources to rebound from discouragement than from anger.

STAR PERFORMER

Mother Teresa, as she is lovingly known around the world, was born Agnes Gonxha Bojaxhiu in Skopje, Macedonia, on August 26, 1910. She felt a deep calling to serve in the ministry of Christ, so at eighteen she joined the Sisters of Loreto, an Irish community of nuns with missions in India. In 1950, Mother Teresa received permission to start her own order, "The Missionaries of Charity," whose primary task was to love and care for those persons nobody was prepared to look after. In 1965 the Society became an International Religious Family by a decree of Pope Paul VI. She was awarded the Nobel Peace Prize in 1979 and is well known for the unquestioning care and compassion she gave to so many in painfully poor circumstances.

REEL PERFORMER

In *Terms of Endearment*, many of the actors worked empathically with the challenge of a young mother dying from cancer. Even Jack Nicholson's character, who was most inclined to be a curmudgeon, became an empathic and helpful neighbor. This greatly expanded his connection with and appreciation for life, as he was able to experience a wider variety of his own feelings more deeply.

Social Responsibility

WHAT IS IT?

Social responsibility entails recognizing and assuming responsibility for the well-being of the larger group and for the other individuals who live and operate within it. That larger group could be a business enterprise, a church congregation, a sports league, a community, and so on. One demonstrates that he or she is a constructive and cooperative member of the social group by contributing to it in a reliable manner. Typically, one would give one's time, effort, participation, money, and allegiance to the group and its individual members in order to help it accomplish its collective purpose in a way that benefits all its members.

WHY SHOULD WE CARE ABOUT SOCIAL RESPONSIBILITY?

Social responsibility is the glue that holds societies and communities together. It is the reciprocal relationship between the individual members and the group that supports them and allows groups to achieve collective goals far beyond what an individual ever could alone.

How do we ever come to identify and know ourselves as a society? We can only gain this wisdom through the reflections we receive from the world around us. In our postmodern electronic global community, those reflections increasingly come through the electronic media. Because the authentic energy of an actual person-to-person connection is not present there, it makes it more difficult for our children to develop social responsibility skills and more essential that we cultivate and model them as adults.

According to Joseph Turow (1997, p. 3), "The U.S. is experiencing a major shift in balance between society-making media and segment-making media. Segment-making media are those that encourage small slices of society to talk to themselves, while society-making media are those that have the potential to get all those segments to talk to each other."

This shift has resulted in much unconscious and conscious jostling for status between newly fragmented groups that perceive all "others" to be different. It makes developing and maintaining social responsibility all the more difficult and all the more imperative!

The cost of allowing our social responsibility to erode is perhaps best captured in the following declaration made by Pastor Martin Niemoller to the Council of the Evangelical Church in Germany, October 18, 1945. There are many versions of his remarks in circulation, but his actual statement can be found at www.christianethicstoday.com (click on #9 for the specific issue).

> "First they came for the Communists, and I did not speak out—because I was not a Communist;
>
> Then they came for the socialists, and I did not speak out—because I was not a socialist;
>
> Then they came for the trade unionists, and I did not speak out—because I was not a trade unionist;
>
> Then they came for the Jews, and I did not speak out—because I was not a Jew;
>
> Then they came for me—and there was no one left to speak out for me."

There are two kinds of human behavior that the pendulum of history has swung between for a very long time, competition and collaboration. *Competitive* behavior produces more content: rapid change and innovation, reduced monetary costs, more efficient manufacturing and distribution of products, and of course, winners and losers. That is because these kinds of goals tend to be linear in nature and are attainable through rational mechanistic processes led by individuals with high IQs.

Collaborative behavior produces more context: slower, system-sensitive change, reduced social and environmental costs, a more integrated and equal distribution of resources, and far fewer winners and losers. That is because these kinds of goals tend to be multidimensional, interdisciplinary in nature, and follow organic, intuitive processes led by teams with high EQ.

Rational intelligence did a great job at solving most of the problems that got our species out of the dark ages and into the 20th century, but since 1900 the number of people sharing this planet and all of its resources has increased by a factor of 3.5, and the unpaid interest on the debts that have accrued from the reductionist worldview leave us with problems too complex for it to understand, let alone resolve. In spite of all the apparent evidence to the contrary, the pendulum accelerates toward collaboration.

HOW CAN WE BUILD SOCIAL RESPONSIBILITY?

As you explore and rededicate your commitment to social responsibility, allow the words of Robert Kennedy to guide you:

"Some men see things as they are and ask 'why?'
I dream things that have never been and ask 'why not?'"

The first step in building social responsibility is to learn to value our social engagements in a new way relative to our self-interest. We must pay a new kind of attention to the cooperative advantage we sustain through communicating honestly and working together toward common goals that will genuinely benefit all of us. The economic advantage we have achieved through technology has served to weaken this awareness. When we look at the human species in comparison with all others, we notice that no other animal has an insatiable "need" for more. All other species, including the great apes, orangutans, chimpanzees, and other higher primates to which we are most biologically similar, observe a natural limit to the amount of food, territory, and so forth that they attempt to control and/or consume. Humans alone do not.

This is perhaps largely due to our ability to think symbolically, the capacity that supposedly makes us more evolved than all other animals. The downside of the "subject-object" schism is that it allows us to perceive ourselves as distinct from everything else. Our liability to this kind of misperception should be recognized for what it is and managed consciously, intelligently, and rigorously; otherwise, we can jeopardize life as we know it on the planet.

Building social responsibility means developing more relationships that explore and express our interdependency and strengthen our appreciation of that connection. In order to act in ways that bind us together rather than fragment us, we must integrate and synthesize an honest agreement about what our real needs, desires, and interests should be.

In order to build these kinds of relationships, we must re-evaluate from where we derive our sense of identity. If we see ourselves as a single isolated human body that might perish any day in an accident, or at best survive eight or nine decades before disappearing into oblivion, it could make sense to live as if "whoever dies with the most toys wins." To build socially responsible relationships we must identify with something larger than ourselves. For eight billion people to share this planet in peace and prosperity, what we value and feel a part of will need to expand to include much more of the Earth's rich diversity. Perhaps someday we will grow to feel socially responsible for all of her environment, all of her resources, all of her people.

TRANSFORMATIONAL BENEFITS

The more responsibility we take for each other and for all life on the planet, the safer we will feel, the more we can achieve, the better we can care for the fragile environment that supports us. Each of us will feel a greater sense of purpose. We will feel more valued and appreciated. We will each feel that our contribution is more meaningful, that we belong and are more fully supported in achieving our life purpose. We experience less stress when we know we are not alone.

STAR PERFORMER

Former President Jimmy Carter smiles and speaks with a serenity and compassion that is unmistakably representative of an internal peace of mind. Through his continued efforts to help resolve conflict around the world, he demonstrates an unquestionable commitment to social responsibility so remarkable that he was awarded the Nobel Peace Prize in 2002 for his work to find peaceful solutions to international conflicts, to advance democracy and human rights, and to promote economic and social development through the carter center. He is also a key figure in Habitat for Humanity.

REEL PERFORMER

In *Remember the Titans*, Denzel Washington plays Herman Boone, a Virginia football coach at a newly integrated high school in the 1970s. He must first help the young men overcome their own racial prejudice enough to bond and function as an effective football team. Then he must protect and continue to nurture their unity in the face of the community's hostility toward the coach and the African-American students. His best demonstration of building social responsibility comes when he runs his players to a Civil War battleground and helps them connect with the human pain and suffering that was common to everyone on both sides. They leave with a commitment to do their personal best to transcend those human foibles in themselves for the sake of what they all hold in common, their love of the game.

Problem Solving

WHAT IS IT?

Problem solving is the social emotional competency that calls into action our sleuthing skills, as it is very much like detective work. However, when we problem solve we don't merely consider objective facts; we have emotional responses to the matter. This skill addresses how we manage and use that emotional information as we solve problems. Problem solving requires that we be alert and observant, noticing as much as possible within the context that surrounds us. Then we must proceed in a manner that uses our logical and our intuitive responses to connect the dots that lead to a sound resolution. This requires disciplined attention, emotional awareness, and perseverance because problems do not necessarily yield to the first attempt at a solution. That is why we call them problems!

Stein and Book (2011, p. 166) define problem solving as "the ability to find solutions to problems in situations where emotions are involved, and to understand how emotions impact decision making."

In the fullest sense, we are working with social *and* emotional intelligence, which requires both left- and right-brain applications. As one works to develop this skill, it is valuable to notice how problems are solved now. You might ask your clients if they tend to use more of a right-brain or left-brain strategy or a hybrid approach. Evaluate a range of problems (from simple to medium complexity) that have been solved in the past and notice what kinds of solutions were achieved and the process for achieving the resolution. This direct feedback will guide your clients in evaluating whether their current strategy works well or could use some fine-tuning. As a part of the process, work with them on how they incorporate emotional data to solve problems well.

WHY SHOULD WE CARE ABOUT PROBLEM SOLVING?

Problem solving is a skill we employ constantly in our lives, from figuring how to get all our materials *and* a hot cup of coffee into the car in a single trip without spilling anything to planning for our children's college and our own retirement. Regardless of the field in which we are employed, we are expected to solve problems and to solve them quickly, economically, and permanently. Our ability to accomplish these types of goals determines our compensation and how much leisure time and discretionary resources we have to enjoy. And guess what? If you think back to your last vacation, you will no doubt recall at least one or two significant problems you had to solve just to be able to enjoy your enjoyment!!

HOW CAN WE BUILD OUR PROBLEM SOLVING COMPETENCIES?

 CREATE A CHECKLIST

Ask yourself whether you have

- Properly defined the issue
- Gathered all the facts
- Incorporated your emotional responses and sorted your emotions to determine which are helpful and which might be holding you back
- Brainstormed all the possibilities, and
- Incorporated all this into a timely solution.

Emotional Intelligence in Action

Probably the most important component to effective problem solving is using a proven method that includes *all* the necessary steps. The Collaborative Growth Master Solve© Problem-Solving Model we use in Exercise 10.3 of this book utilizes ingredients from a variety of sources, one of the most significant being neuro-linguistic programming, a powerful technology in the field of strategic communications.

TRANSFORMATIONAL BENEFITS

Improving your skills in problem solving will add to your value as a team player, make you more productive and effective regardless of the field in which you work, and, perhaps most importantly, it will make life flow more smoothly and more enjoyably.

STAR PERFORMER

William Ury is author of *The Third Side* (2000) and co-author of *Getting to Yes* (Fisher & Ury, 1981). He is an internationally recognized leader in the field of negotiation and conflict resolution. As a cultural anthropologist, he has shared his wisdom on our need as a species to "change the culture of conflict within our families, our workplaces, our communities, and our world . . . to create a culture where even the most serious disputes are handled on the basis not of force and coercion but of mutual interest and coexistence" (2000, p. ix).

REEL PERFORMER

The King's Speech is a dramatic example of solving a major problem laden with emotional land mines. Prince Albert has struggled with a painful stammer since he was four or five. His older brother is supposed to be king but abdicates as World War II is brewing; Great Britain needs to have confidence in their king at the time that the spoken word is just beginning to be broadcast on the radio. Prince Albert has finally started speech therapy with a very unusual person, Lionel Logue. Although there are many challenges, the two work together successfully and form a tight bond. The prince becomes King George VI and boldly leads the country through the war. The problem is well addressed, and to do so the prince and Lionel had to confront, accept, and resolve many emotional challenges.

Reality Testing

WHAT IS IT?

Our reality testing determines how clearly we discern what is actually happening in the world around us. We have learned to interpret and color our objective experience with all sorts of desires, fears, and distortions. In order to avoid mistaking our overly negative or overly positive perceptions of experience for reality, we must develop reliable processes for confirming the objective correspondence of our feelings, perceptions, and thoughts with the immediate situation.

An important aspect of reality testing is that it must occur in the "now" moment. Stein and Book state that "reality testing involves 'tuning in' to the immediate situation....it is the capacity to see things objectively, the way they are, rather than the way we wish or fear them to be. Testing this degree of correspondence involves the search for objective evidence to confirm, justify, and support feelings, perceptions, and thoughts" (2011, p. 159).

It is also important to remember that in one sense we can never see reality directly; we only see it through our own perceptions. Our perceptions are learned from our experience and our society, and they give us a map of our reality, but no matter how accurate that map may be, it is never the whole territory. Improving our reality testing means verifying how well our perceptions match those of others and adding detail to that map, but in order to be as accurate as possible, it must also always honor the mystery that lies beyond all we can ever perceive.

WHY SHOULD WE CARE ABOUT REALITY TESTING?

If there is an absolute reality out there, it is very likely that no human being knows it with perfect clarity, because we have all learned to see, experience, and construct our world out of a learned perceptual bias. Because we use only three of our five senses to construct the vast majority of our experience of reality, it is always very helpful to verify that what we see, hear, and feel/ sense in the world around us is accurately perceived. Likewise, it is very helpful to periodically check out our reasoning processes to confirm that the conclusions we are drawing actually follow logically from all the information that is available to us.

When we fail to do this, we are not testing reality well enough to achieve consistently the results we desire. We may avoid reality testing either because we are reluctant to engage fully in the world or because we are conditioned to expect results that are consistently better or worse than objective reality shows them to be.

HOW CAN WE BUILD REALITY TESTING?

 Be a little bit skeptical! Ask yourself:

- "What evidence am I relying on when I believe this is as it appears to be?"
- "Who wants me to believe this is reality? What are his or her motives?"

The best way to assess and develop our reality testing skills is by calling our perceptions and desires into question on a regular basis. This can be done effectively in several ways.

First, check in with your body at the sensory level—"How is my body feeling now? Hot? Warm? Cool? Centered? Upset? Out of balance?" What does that information tell you?

Then ask questions like: "What kinds of sounds am I hearing around me? Soothing? Abrasive? Scary? Angry? Seductive? Supportive? Challenging? How accurately am I seeing the situation in which I find myself? Do people really feel the way they appear to? Am I exaggerating the significance of what I perceive—either positively or negatively?"

Another way to check the quality of your reality testing is to figure out all who have a significant stake in the outcome of the situation at hand. Observe them and notice how they are responding. If it is appropriate to do so, tell them your take on the situation and ask whether they concur.

TRANSFORMATIONAL BENEFITS

The benefits of developing good reality testing skills can be expressed very succinctly—these skills are what help us avoid the unexpected loss, disappointment, and bad luck that we can inadvertently cause for ourselves and others when we haven't assessed a situation accurately. Moreover, they help us get on the same page with everyone who is involved and keep our efforts coordinated.

STAR PERFORMER

Good reality testing is tempered by optimism; Secretary of State Hillary Rodham Clinton is a champion at demonstrating the courage to take chances, to go for the gold while also tempering her hopes and dreams with the reality of the situation. She has demonstrated this skill in running for office as U.S. Senator from the state of New York—and winning—and again in her dramatic bid for President of the United States in 2008. She came quite close to winning and forged a new path for women in the United States. She continues bringing her skills in reality testing, optimism, courage, and brilliant dignity to her service as Secretary of State and responding to significant issues throughout the world.

◧ REEL PERFORMER

The Hurt Locker is an intense movie depicting a real-life situation. During the conflict in Iraq, elite U.S. soldiers are engaged in one of the most dangerous jobs imaginable, disarming bombs in the heat of combat. Director Kathryn Bigelow won the Academy Award for this emotional movie where reality testing is required minute by minute due to the bombs as well as a dicey new sergeant.

Impulse Control

WHAT IS IT?

Impulses are urges that compel action. They exist beyond logic and rationality and spring from our subconscious minds with persistence and intensity. They pulsate with primal urgency and are fueled by psychological or physiological factors. Impulses can be helpful or harmful to us. We must look to the results and consequences manifest in our lives to determine how much we need to control our impulses.

Our discussion focuses on controlling impulses that diminish effectiveness. Lack of impulse control is the source of much human misery, including one of the perils of modern society—road rage. Road rage is an uncontrolled display of anger by the operator of a motor vehicle.

Lane (2000, p. 172) describes impulse control as "not taking a particular action aimed at short-term gratification in order to avoid possible negative long-term consequences. To not act on an impulse requires that a mental representation of possible future consequences influence the behavioral expression of the impulse before it occurs. Thus, impulse control involves recognition of an incipient approach behavior and the ability to anticipate the negative consequences of that course of action....Impulse control thus involves suppression of approach behavior."

Bar-On (2002, p. 18) defines impulse control as "the ability to resist or delay an impulse, drive, or temptation to act. It entails a capacity for accepting one's aggressive impulses, being composed, and controlling aggression, hostility, and irresponsible behavior. Problems in impulse control are manifested by low frustration tolerance, impulsiveness, anger control problems, abusiveness, loss of self-control, and explosive and unpredictable behavior."

WHY SHOULD WE CARE ABOUT IMPULSE CONTROL?

The ability to control or resist harmful urges is essential to functioning at a high level of effectiveness. Let's get real—if one cannot put the bottle down, stop stuffing food into his or her mouth, or quit hitting his or her spouse, self-regard and interpersonal relationships become impaired.

Type A personalities—action oriented, constantly in motion, multi-tasking—may take a dim view of controlling their impulses. They may embrace their Type A–ness as the key to their success and see it as their competitive advantage and an essential success trait. They may not assess how much time they or others spend in cleaning up the broken glass that is left in their wake. People who don't manage impulses well *should* care because the type of impatience and free-floating hostility that can characterize their personalities increases their risk of heart disease and can be costly in the workplace.

HOW CAN WE BUILD IMPULSE CONTROL?

Building impulse control requires identifying, analyzing, and changing unproductive behavior. Controlling impulses requires emotional self-awareness and a willingness to trade the immediate satisfaction of a knee-jerk reaction for the strategic benefit of a thoughtful response. Your client must clarify the WIIFM ("What's in it for me?") and create alternative solutions that also answer the question, "What's in it for others?!"

IMPULSIVENESS IMPACTS RESULTS

- Think strategically and avoid impulsiveness by using effective self-talk such as "This time I will look before I leap!"
- Remember that the aftermath of impulsiveness may not be worth the satisfaction of the moment.

Questions

- What satisfaction does your client derive by acting impulsively?
- What feels good about it in the moment?

TRANSFORMATIONAL BENEFITS

Controlling impulses will increase productivity and improve self-regard. It is liberating and empowering to use determination and higher-order reasoning to overcome compelling urges. When you or your clients enhance this skill, improved results in the daily challenges of life are certain to appear. New experiences could include:

- Waiting for an appropriate time to discuss an issue with an employee or co-worker, rather than "spouting off" in the heat of the moment.
- In business meetings, allowing others to complete their sentences instead of "over-talking" them.
- Emerging from the car in a reasonably relaxed state. It can happen when we do not react to every "idiot" driver who got in our way.
- Inhabiting a slimmer, more toned body.

 STAR PERFORMER

Georgia O'Keefe was a highly disciplined, imaginative, and creative artist. O'Keefe was one of the leading artists of the 20th century. Much of her work was done in northern New Mexico, now often known as O'Keefe country.

She mastered her work by being willing to devote her attention fully to developing her skill. Her commitment reflected strong impulse control and resulted in the gift to all of us of her artwork.

▣ REEL PERFORMER

Gregory Peck plays lawyer Atticus Finch in *To Kill a Mockingbird.* It is the early 1930s in Alabama, at the height of the Depression. Racism is the order of the day. By providing legal representation for Tom Robinson (Brock Peters), a black man wrongly accused of raping Mayella Ewell, a white woman, Atticus incites the ire of Bob Ewell, Mayella's father.

What actually happened was that Mayella invited Tom into her house to repair a door. Once Tom was inside the house, Mayella made sexual advances toward him, which he rebuffed. Her father saw the interchange and told his daughter he was going to kill her. Bob was primarily infuriated because his daughter was attracted to a black man, which was a taboo of the highest order. After Tom left, Bob savagely beat his daughter. Later both Mayella and Bob claimed that she was raped and beaten by Tom. The bottom line is that Bob, in his convoluted logic, wanted the completely innocent Tom to hang because Mayella was attracted to him.

Atticus has ample opportunity to demonstrate impulse control. For example, Atticus exhibits impulse control when Tom informs Atticus of his displeasure in the most derogatory terms. Another instance is when Bob spits in his face. Bob has clearly been itching for a fight. Atticus controls his impulses and restrains himself from responding in kind.

Flexibility

WHAT IS IT?

Flexible people are resilient, able to bend when the wind starts blowing in a surprising direction. People with a strong capacity for flexibility might be compared to a willow—they can bend a long way in many directions in storms that tear the branches off harder, stouter trees. The network of deep roots that supports the willow and gives it that remarkable flexibility is similar to the deeply held core values that guide an individual or organization. When we exercise true flexibility, we must still honor our core values, because if we compromise those, we will lose the connection with the roots of our strength, our purpose, and our credibility.

Not everyone appreciates flexibility to the same degree. One worker described a colleague as "quick to adapt to new information, a skill that significantly contributes to her success." Meanwhile, another says, "Her attitudes blow with the wind or the boss's current fancy; she's unreliable, manipulative, and wishy-washy." How and why we are flexible is important; it is also important to notice if and why we judge other people when they exercise their flexibility.

Webster's (1993) defines "flexible" as "willing or ready to yield to the influence of others (tractable; manageable), and characterized by ready capability for modification or change, by plasticity, pliancy, variability, and often by consequent adaptability to new situations." Synonyms listed are elastic, resilient, springy, and supple.

When they define flexibility, Stein and Book emphasize, "This component of emotional intelligence applies to your overall ability to adapt to unfamiliar, unpredictable, and dynamic circumstances. Flexible people are...able to change their minds when evidence suggests that they are mistaken" (2011, p. 187).

Flexible people are often characterized as adaptable, agile, open, and tolerant of differences. Flexible people are not dogmatic, nor always convinced they are right. This is an example of how two of these sixteen skills influence one another. Happiness and flexibility often influence one another. One of our favorite questions to clients comes from *A Course in Miracles* (Foundation for Inner Peace, 1975) and we phrase it as "Would you rather be happy, or would you rather be right?" Flexible people are on the right track to choosing happiness.

Not all terms are positive; sometimes flexible people are defined as manipulative or fickle or unreliable. President Clinton was highly flexible, which brought him great success and great criticism. He would test the waters to understand how far he could take an issue, and then make a strong push in that direction. It was a strategy that valued making some progress rather than maintaining a firm ideological stance and getting nowhere. Some people praised this strategy; others decried it.

Highly flexible people may be thought of as people who will compromise their principles to please an authority. When these labels are accurate, the behavior is not emotionally intelligent. One needs clarity to exercise flexibility properly. Primarily, it must be applied with concrete reality testing, with regard for others, and without compromising our values. Thus, as with all EQ skills, flexibility must be applied in the context of the other skills. No skill is successful in a vacuum.

With true flexibility, this capacity to easily make a shift pays off when something unexpected occurs, such as when new data arrives, when circumstances change, even when we come to a new understanding of "old" information. Perhaps an "a-ha" has occurred and a truly better solution has finally been discovered! However, those who abuse others' flexibility sometimes manufacture phony changes in order to manipulate a situation or the people involved. For example, an employee with a flexible manager who doesn't want to do a task in the way directed may overstate obstacles to try to get out of work.

As with everything, flexibility must be applied in context. Lauren [not her real name] learned this by participating in Emergenetics® seminars. As an HR director for her city, she brought Emergenetics to several parts of her organization and participated in several of the workshops. Lauren was the first person hired to create a discrete HR department for the city, and others in the city had many ideas as to how she and the department should operate. Lauren is quite bright, empathic, and flexible. She could see the value of most of the suggestions she received and recognized that the staff was hungry for a big menu of services.

However, she spread herself too thin, trying to make everyone happy. Lauren was working far too many hours, and her successes seemed limited because she was working on so many things at once that it took a long time for anything to be completed. One day in the middle of one of the Emergenetics workshops, she finally saw her problem. Her super-flexibility had a cost that outweighed some of the benefits. That was a turning point for Lauren's success, her happiness, and the success of her new department. Successful expression of flexibility requires boundaries as well as the willingness to change.

WHY SHOULD WE CARE ABOUT FLEXIBILITY?

Change is one of the greatest constants in our fast-paced world. The ability to adapt to change rapidly is a predominant characteristic of successful people. It allows them to avoid or take advantage promptly of the critical factors affecting any situation in which they are involved, rather than getting caught up in an ego-dominated struggle of how it *should* be. Inflexible people may stick to deadlines instead of the deeper goal, thus alienating co-workers rather than building up the team.

Would you rather live in a world of *should*'s, *supposed to*'s, and *wanna be*'s, or would you like to be free to *get on with the show*? While the answer is obvious, this question reflects a very real struggle that is documented by the thousands of business and self-help books written on how to deal with change. There would not be such a strong need to embrace change and demonstrate flexibility if there was not such an abundance of flux in our increasingly complex world. However, the large number of books on the topic indicates that many people struggle in numerous processes and settings to learn the wide range of appropriate ways to express flexibility.

Futurists are giving us amazingly similar forecasts—everything they are writing depicts a world of ever-increasing change, often experienced as turbulence. So we can count on the skill of flexibility remaining crucially important. This skill is particularly valuable when we feel there is too much change leading to the tendency to be rigid and *batten down the hatches* rather than to open to the new possibilities.

In Tai Chi, flexibility begins with bending the knees slightly, so we can move with the flow of energy. It's not giving up your stance but, paradoxically, strengthening it. Using flexibility in our interactions is similar. Those who will be successful in today's and tomorrow's worlds will be able to bend and flow, while applying reality testing, self-regard, and empathy.

Thus, the results from caring about strengthening your flexibility skills will certainly include:

- Enhancing your ability to work with a world changing at a radically increasing pace,
- Increasing your effectiveness as it lets you shift to use the best data instead of being caught up in saving face, and
- Expanding your happiness, as you can be satisfied with what is, rather than seeking to force a reality not supported by the circumstances.

We are betting that you can add some of your own reasons. What are they?

HOW CAN WE BUILD FLEXIBILITY?

Apply brainstorming strategies when faced with a challenge. Give yourself ten minutes just to think of possibilities before you begin to look for answers.

There is a direct connection between feeling afraid and becoming less flexible. How can we help our clients expand their trust in a way that will enable them to incorporate the skills of reality testing and optimism in assessing an unfamiliar situation? Taking time to do that assessment before jumping into a dramatic response can give them resilience and expand their credibility, and others will appreciate their thoughtful responses.

Notice limiting beliefs, such as "I usually make mistakes on important projects," and ego defensiveness, such as "I have to protect myself from attacks by all superiors." Are there areas your clients can work on in expanding their personal skills and the nature of their responses to help them choose greater flexibility?

TRANSFORMATIONAL BENEFITS

The benefits of increased flexibility can be astonishing—more freedom, less often needing to be right, life balance, lightened workload, less stress and defensiveness. People might even live longer and be happier because positive thoughts increase DHEA, an important hormone that supports youthfulness in the body. You can be a more successful leader and mentor. Increased flexibility translates to not sweating the small stuff, and that means more joy in your life!

STAR PERFORMER

Meryl Streep is a highly acclaimed actress; nominated for the Academy Award an astonishing sixteen times, she has won it twice. She is a perfectionist in her craft as an artist, meticulous and careful. At the same time, she's highly flexible, playing roles with great credibility that call for seeing her in widely different circumstances, from a razor-sharp businesswoman in *The Devil Wears Prada* to a free-spirited singer in *Mama Mia*. She's literally flexible too—see her do the splits in *Mama Mia* when she's jumping on a bed!

REEL PERFORMER

In *Lilies of the Field*, Sidney Poitier's poignant performance is a direct example of the strength and focus of flexibility. He was remarkably amenable to working with the nuns and meeting their needs, so much so that some could have thought him passive and accomplishing little. Yet, he never compromised his overall focus and intent and successfully completed his mission.

Stress Tolerance

WHAT IS IT?

Life is filled with stress. The sources of stress are plentiful and varied—being cut off (or flipped off!) in traffic, preparing a critical business proposal, making a presentation to the management team, preparing for a wedding, dealing with the death of a loved one, caring for a newborn child, moving to a new dream house, or getting that great new promotion. Paradoxically, stress is caused by both happy and sad situations. The stressors in our lives are inescapable.

Dealing with stress is not an *if* question, it's a question of *when* and *how often.* When it happens, EQ can help one analyze the situation and resourcefully deal with his or her feelings. The problem we face is that our primary response to stress is fight or flight. In past eras, much of our stress was due to threats to our physical safety, such as being chased by a wild animal. Our bodies automatically geared up to deal with the situation, and we physically responded to the problem— stood and fought or ran like heck. When the crisis ended, our bodies returned to normal through a process called the "relaxation response."

The stress we experience today does not usually require a physical response. However, our bodies and minds still instinctively respond to perceived threat as if a wild animal were involved. We automatically gear up with the fight or flight response, but must then suppress the impulse. We often experience the never-ending pressure of chronic stress, which includes ongoing pressure at work or home, persistent financial issues, or ongoing relationship problems. Doc Childre (1994, p. 3), founder of the HeartMath Institute, asserts, "Stress stimulates the perpetual release of the hormones adrenaline, noradrenalin, and cortisol, which eventually sear the body like a constant drizzle of acid. If left unchecked, chronic stress—along with attitudes like hostility, anger, and depression—can sicken and eventually kill us."

Given the dramatic impact of unchecked stress, to remain healthy, we must expand our ability to tolerate and manage it—along with all its implications.

Bar-On defines stress tolerance as:

"The ability to withstand adverse events and stressful situations without 'falling apart' by actively and positively coping with stress. . . . This ability is based on (1) a capacity to choose courses of action for coping with stress (i.e., being resourceful and effective, being able to come up with suitable methods, and knowing what to do and how to do it), (2) an optimistic disposition toward new experiences and change in general and toward one's ability to successfully overcome the specific problem at hand (i.e., a belief in one's ability to face and handle these situations), and (3) a feeling that one can control or influence the stressful situation (i.e., keeping calm and maintaining control)." (2002, p. 17)

WHY SHOULD WE CARE ABOUT STRESS TOLERANCE?

Are you kidding! The quality of one's life is profoundly impacted by his or her ability to tolerate stress. If a person cannot tolerate stress, he or she cannot live well. Being constantly stressed out leads to physical and psychological damage and negatively impacts one's effectiveness. Handling stress supports health and boosts effectiveness.

People who do not deal effectively with mounting stress often resort to self-medication—drug or alcohol abuse, tobacco use, abnormal eating patterns, or unhealthy lifestyles.

Stress increases heart attack risk. According to the Mayo Clinic, "Stress and anger may increase your risk of coronary artery disease . . . " (www.MayoClinic.com). Johns Hopkins University School of Medicine and School of Hygiene and Public Health followed a group of more than 1,055 men for thirty-two to forty-eight years to study their incidence of premature heart disease compared with anger responses to stress. Those who had the highest level of anger and reported experiencing irritability and expressed or concealed anger were more than three times as likely to develop premature heart disease and over six times more likely to have a heart attack by age fifty-five (Chang, Ford, Meoni, Wang, & Klag, 2002).

Bar-On and Handley (1999) emphasize the relationship between strengths in stress management and impulse control. When we control our impulses, we reduce potential stress factors. This is one of many links that can be made between effective stress control and enhancing other emotional intelligence factors.

HOW CAN WE BUILD STRESS TOLERANCE?

 STRESS TOOLKIT—BE PREPARED

- Perfect techniques to manage the psychological and physiological impacts of stress, for example, structured breathing, visualization, and affirmations.
- Develop strategies for coping with stress so they are readily available in the heat of the situation, for example, "The next time I get a 'snippy' voicemail from Chris, I will do a brief meditation before responding."
- Get more exercise!

Who does your client know who tolerates stress well? Have your client ask that role model for tips and pointers.

Stress tolerance and optimism present us with a classic "chicken and egg" conundrum—which came first? In reality, they are very symbiotic. Strength in one area contributes to mastery in the other. As Bar-On implies, optimism and stress tolerance are inexorably intertwined. You must maintain a positive outlook and have confidence that you will successfully ride the roller coaster ride of life.

Develop strategies and techniques for preventing and dealing with stress. Research what is available, identify what seems most interesting and doable to you, and then try it out. Available approaches include exercise, meditation, visualization, deep-breathing exercises, muscle relaxation techniques, biofeedback, and massage therapy. Apply these methods as you work with your clients to choose the most appropriate strategies for their situations.

Other methods of managing stress involve reprioritizing activities and involvement. Shift from stress-producing to stress-reducing activities, including exercise, recreational activities, or mini-vacations. Diet is another key ingredient in managing stress. Eating too many unhealthy foods and not enough healthy ones creates a drag on one's body, which is saddled with processing junk and trying to maintain health with insufficient fuel.

One way to build stress tolerance is to enhance communication skills and muster some courage. Many times people avoid chronically stressful issues rather than resolve them with constructive discussion. You might urge your clients to improve their ability to talk about and resolve sensitive issues using openness and appropriate consideration while maintaining respect for themselves and others.

Finally, apply generous doses of humor. Maintain a sense of humor during difficult situations. It helps to regulate hormone levels and produces those much sought after endorphins!

TRANSFORMATIONAL BENEFITS

Success breeds success. As one improves his or her ability to deal with stress and expands his or her portfolio of stress management strategies, confidence builds because the person knows he or she can handle it. As one's confidence builds, so does one's optimistic outlook regarding managing future stressful situations.

STAR PERFORMER

Tom Hanks shows up smiling, calm, gracious, and happy to support others in succeeding. He's a gifted actor, winning the Academy Awards for best actor for *Philadelphia Story* and for *Forrest Gump* and for director and producer. He is quoted on The Internet Movie Database as saying, "My work is more fun than fun but, best of all, it's still very scary. You are always walking some kind of high wire. I guess it's like being a sportsman. When people ask great football stars or cricketers what they will miss most when the time comes to stop, they'll tell you that it's that moment when the ball comes to them. In that moment, there's that wonderful anxiety, that feeling of 'Please don't let me screw this up.' If I didn't have the chance to do what I do, it's that I would miss more than anything. That terror is what makes me feel alive. It's a wonderful feeling, unlike anything else in the world." What a great description of using stress tolerance to move forward but not let it become debilitating.

🎞️ REEL PERFORMER

Precious was originally released as *Push: Based on the Novel by Sapphire* and stars Gabourey "Gabby" Sidibe as Precious Jones, a high-school girl struggling at a level that makes success seem impossible. She is pregnant with her father's child—for the second time. She can't read or write, and her schoolmates tease her for being quite overweight. Her home life is horrific, given the incest from her father and a tyrannical mother (Mo'Nique) who keeps her imprisoned at both a physical and emotional level. Out of this apparently dire situation, Precious rises to the glory of learning to read. After she is thrown out of school for her second pregnancy, Precious is referred to an alternative school, where she finally experiences someone caring for her. Precious is a young woman who—with creativity, humor, and ferocity—finds the strength to turn her life around. She does not let herself become sabotaged by the enormous stress in her life.

Optimism

WHAT IS IT?

Optimists believe that good events are frequent and long-lasting and that bad events are limited and temporary. Even if they have not found the solution to a problem, they're certain it is just around the corner and that they have some control over the problem.

Optimism correlates closely with success. Merely the mention of this fact gets most people to sit up and take notice! "How can growing my optimism make me more successful?" they ask. Success is directly related to how we manage our expectations. However, the kind of success we experience depends on how we define it. People often think of money first and all the things it can buy. But before long they also include the more enduring factors, such as good health, a happy family, and a safe and prosperous community. Optimism can help us achieve all of these. But what is it?

Webster's (1993) defines optimism as "a doctrine or opinion that reality is essentially good or completely good; or as good as it conceivably could be; an inclination to put the most favorable construction upon actions and happenings; to minimize adverse aspects, conditions, and possibilities, or to anticipate the best possible outcome."

Martin Seligman (1990), author of *Learned Optimism*, points out that optimistic people tend to think of defeat as a temporary setback that is not their fault. A difficult situation can be reframed as a challenge . . . an opportunity to do something novel and innovative or as a call to try harder.

Bar-On (2002, p. 18) defines optimism as "the ability to look at the brighter side of life and to maintain a positive attitude even in the face of adversity. Optimism assumes a measure of hope in one's approach to life. It is a positive approach to daily living. Optimism is the opposite of pessimism, which is a common symptom of depression."

We act optimistically when we respond to good events with a positive attitude, believing they are permanent. We give ourselves messages such as "Life is good today because I'm making sure to get enough exercise and making a conscious effort to be friendly" rather than "Life is good today, but I don't know why or what tomorrow will be like." Furthermore, we respond to bad events with a specific explanation, framing the event as temporary. Thus, we would say, "My workload is pretty heavy right now, which means I'm almost to the point of hiring some help" rather than saying, "I am so busy and tired, I will never get out of this cycle of working too much."

WHY SHOULD WE CARE ABOUT OPTIMISM?

As Seligman (2002, p. 128) writes, "Being optimistic brings about less depression, better physical health, and higher achievement, at a cost perhaps of less realism." How many of those would you like to see more of in your life? All of them? Clearly, our lives will work better if we increase our optimism.

Optimists are much more likely to be survivors. Mark Jenkins (2003, p. 53) wrote about survivors, including Aron Ralston, the climber who was trapped in a slot canyon in Southern Utah and cut off his arm to save his life. Jenkins quotes Peter Suedfeld, professor emeritus of psychology at the University of British Columbia, as saying that "people under high stress are more likely to become rigid, which only decreases their chances of survival." He continues by saying that, even in a jam, "survivors are extremely adaptable people. They know how to improvise. . . . They keep an open mind, searching for options, developing strategies." Notice that this brings together several subscales in the EQ-i, all of which influence the effectiveness of optimism, and that optimism, in turn, influences the effectiveness of other skills.

Certainly emotional intelligence is much more successful when our skills are well integrated!

Optimism is also linked to improved physical health, as demonstrated by an American Psychological Association report on a study in 1995 and 1996 by Martin Seligman and Gregory Buchanan. They worked with two groups of university freshmen who were inclined toward depression and volunteered to participate in the research. One group had no training; the other group participated in a workshop on cognitive coping skills. The group with training reported fewer adverse mental health concerns, as well as fewer physical problems, and was more active in getting checkups to maintain their health (American Psychological Association, 1997). The excellent results these types of studies cite are enough to inspire many to do the work it takes to develop and maintain a truly good attitude!

HOW CAN WE BUILD OPTIMISM?

 BE SOLUTION FOCUSED

- Focus on the possibilities and the answer rather than on the problem.
- Be grateful. Go out of your way to be thankful. Make sure you express gratitude at least ten times a day.

Possibly the most critical aspect of developing optimism is learning that you have a choice about your attitude. Many people think they are born optimists or pessimists and that it is something they just have to live with. Not so! Cognitive development strategies such as learning to dispute negative statements make a big difference. If your clients have a tendency to evaluate a bad event as permanent, help them learn to challenge themselves and change the message. As they will find by implementing the exercises in Part Three, they *can* change their lives by learning to give themselves more optimistic messages. Imagine the impact this attitude has on developing self-regard. Naturally, the more positive we feel about our capabilities, the more positive we feel about ourselves as a whole. This is one of the many examples of the multiple connections among the sixteen skills.

Another valuable strategy is to expand gratitude. What are you grateful for right now? Stop, take a breath, and name five things. Right now! We really mean it! Stop right now before you read any further and list five things you are grateful for. We guarantee your state just changed if you did this quick exercise, as it will every time you do it! Now your attitude is more open and positive and ready to move forward with helping your clients to avail themselves of the many opportunities in this book.

TRANSFORMATIONAL BENEFITS

Increasing your optimism may very well change every part of your life—and we do not make such broad, sweeping statements carelessly! You will find data on the positive effects of optimism, for example, in *Learned Optimism* (Seligman, 1990), and much more in *Authentic Happiness* (Seligman, 2002), *Flourish* (Seligman, 2011), *The EQ Edge* (Stein & Book, 2011), the Positive Psychology Center at www.positivepsychology.org, and the Consortium for Research on Emotional Intelligence in Organizations at www.eiconsortium .org. There is so much research supporting this statement that we can confidently assert that the business case for optimism is robust and convincing. The cost-benefit ratio is top-notch. For very little investment, your clients can learn to change their thoughts to more positive ones, which will result in better heath and in better engagement with others. What our clients believe is manifested through the messages they give themselves. Their self-talk has an enormous influence on what their future reality will become.

STAR PERFORMER

Nelson Mandela has been hailed by many as one of the most inspirational leaders in the world. Mandela was willing to be imprisoned for years if that's what it took to achieve the right result. He continually held out the possibility, even the probability, of the high-level transformation he envisioned. His undying optimism led him and his country to an entirely new way of being together with much greater respect for all. His service as president of South Africa rallied his people's optimistic belief that the hurdles could be handled successfully. He gave people the courage to show up and vote and to continue participating in their government.

▣ REEL PERFORMER

The Wizard of Oz is a treasure of characters learning to believe there are answers to the problems they face. Dorothy is the leader. This child's "can do" optimism in the face of her own great challenge inspires the Tin Man, Scarecrow, and Cowardly Lion to face their fears and achieve what they truly desire.

After a tornado in Kansas knocks her unconscious, Dorothy finds herself in the Land of Oz. She is encouraged to be optimistic that she can find her way home by the good Witch of the North, who says she must travel to find the Wizard of Oz. On meeting Scarecrow, she draws on her growing reservoir of optimism and convinces him the Wizard will help him find what he most desires, a brain. She next inspires the Lion to believe that he will find courage and the Tin Man to believe that he will find a heart.

They go through many trials getting to the Wizard just to learn that he is a phony. However, in the midst of this challenge, each one recognizes that acting as if he or she would get what was most wanted actually caused him or her to develop the desired skill. If we are feeling deeply challenged, even scared, we suspect that Dorothy would advise us to remember that we just don't know the answer *yet*. If we will just act as if we are confident that the problem will be resolved, our faithful action will make it so! Finally, she'd advise us to focus our intention and willingness while we click our heels and say, "There's no place like home!"

Happiness/Well-Being

WHAT IS IT?

We all think we know what happiness really is. But do we? The new EQ-i$^{2.0}$ has changed the way happiness is presented; it is now separate from the fifteen subscales and incorporated with a new concept referred to as a Well-Being Indicator. As such, it doesn't contribute to the Total EI score; rather it is presented as a composite picture together with self-regard, optimism, interpersonal relationships, and self-actualization. The report focuses on viewing happiness as a barometer of emotional health and well-being, which ties together well with the research by Bar-On.

Bar-On (2002, p. 18) says happiness is "the ability to feel satisfied with one's life, to enjoy oneself and others, and to have fun." He continues by saying that "happiness combines self-satisfaction, general contentment, and the ability to enjoy life." Most importantly perhaps, Dr. Bar-On found in doing his extensive research that happiness is a "by-product and/or barometric indicator of one's overall degree of emotional intelligence and emotional functioning."

Notice that the definition indicates that our level of happiness is an indicator of all of our emotional intelligence. Certainly one of the most important words in the definition is *satisfaction*. Our level of satisfaction with present circumstances will greatly impact our ability to be happy and the whole range of our emotional intelligence.

Webster's (1993) definition helps us notice the range in levels of happiness that are possible: "a state of well-being characterized by relative permanence, by dominantly agreeable emotion ranging in value from mere contentment to deep and intense joy in living, and by a natural desire for its continuation."

Three types of happiness are discussed by Martin Seligman (2002) in *Authentic Happiness*—"the Pleasant Life, the Good Life, and the Meaningful Life." Simple pleasures, often physical ones, dominate the Pleasant Life, a concept that is also identified with hedonism. This entails a focus on maximizing pleasures such as money, food, and clothes, while minimizing pain. American consumerism is a glaring exemplar of this strategy for happiness.

Getting what we desire is central to Seligman's definition for the Good Life. This could be standard hedonism, like a great dessert, but it often goes further, such as a quest for knowledge and career advancement. Building your career may be so important to you that you are willing to endure substantial discomfort and even pain from working the long hours it takes in order to attain your goal.

Making the world a better place for others is central to the Meaningful Life. With this form of happiness we seek to give to others. It is about coming more alive through generosity.

WHY SHOULD WE CARE ABOUT HAPPINESS?

How often do we say we want to be more productive? Increased productivity means more successfully achieving our goals and fulfilling our desires. For some people these achievements are so closely identified with happiness that they become their only meaningful criteria. For others, happiness requires more abstract conditions, such as a healthy environment and inner peace.

The extensive amount of research on happiness has established the links between happiness and several factors, including health, truly rewarding career development, and being a useful and contributing member of an organization, community, and/or family. Your level of happiness affects the development and exercise of all your skills and relies on all the elements of your emotional intelligence.

HOW CAN WE BUILD HAPPINESS?

 GROW YOUR HAPPINESS

Would you rather be happy or would you rather be right?

Every day for a month notice whenever it seems like you have to be right in order to be happy. Choose to be happy and forego being right. See what happens.

Seligman (2002, p. 80) cites a traditional saying:

"If you want to be happy . . .

. . . for an hour, take a nap.

. . . for a day, go fishing.

. . . for a month, get married.

. . . for a year, get an inheritance.

. . . for a lifetime, help someone."

What kind of happiness do you want? What is your purpose? It is interesting how core philosophical questions become so vital to our choosing the most effective strategies in building happiness. Basic strategies to grow happiness include:

- Getting good exercise and releasing endorphins
- Reflecting—either on your own, such as through journal writing, or with a colleague
- Paying attention to your "wanting." How will you know when you have enough?
- Sharing what you have with others in need

TRANSFORMATIONAL BENEFITS

In his book *The Art of Happiness,* the Dalai Lama (1998, pp. 13–14, 20) asserts that "the purpose of life is to seek happiness. . . . [and] happiness can be achieved by training the mind. . . . [H]appiness is determined more by one's state of mind than by external events."

To experience the transformational benefits of expanding our happiness, we must pay attention to our self-talk. If we are both intentional about our quality of life and hopeful, the transformational benefits of happiness will have an expansive effect on our entire lives.

As we seek happiness, particularly when we center on the Meaningful Life, we slow down and open to our inherent compassion. This brings about a chain reaction; life unfolds with a natural flow, rather than with all the fits and starts so common to our enormously fast-paced lives. This relaxation of our self-importance helps us to connect being and doing.

With increased happiness you can also experience valuable changes in your physical well-being, being more at ease and more cheerful. Happy people live longer and more fully enjoy the time they are alive.

STAR PERFORMER

Dame Julia Elizabeth Andrews is a British film and stage actress, singer, and author. She is the recipient of numerous awards, including the Golden Globe, Emmy, Grammy, Screen Actors Guild, and Academy Awards. She is well known for musicals such as *My Fair Lady* and *Camelot,* and for appearing in musical films such as *Mary Poppins,* for which she won the Academy Award for Best Actress, and *The Sound of Music,* the roles for which she is still best-known. Through her brilliant, smiling performances, she has brought and continues to bring smiles to millions of people around the world, whether she's flying on a broom in *Mary Poppins* or singing that the hills are alive in the *Sound of Music.*

REEL PERFORMER

Happythankyoumoreplease is a warm and interesting movie where young adults dare to express their emotions, honestly connect with each other, and mature. It's based on six New Yorkers juggling love, friendship, and the challenges of merging into adulthood.

Emotional Intelligence Exercises to Build Effective Skills

Part Three contains the experiential learning scenarios we call "exercises." There are four to five exercises for each of the EI skills discussed in Part Two. In using these exercises, it is important that you understand the EI skill you are seeking to grow, are sensitive to the potential vulnerability of your clients when addressing these topics, and understand the process of behavioral change.

BE INFORMED

We recommend you refer to the appropriate content in Part Two before using any exercise. Depending on the circumstances and your knowledge about the skill, you may need to do additional reading and research. The References and Resources sections at the back of this book contain information to assist you in your developmental effort.

FACILITATOR SKILLS

Pay careful attention to the necessary facilitator skills and to the best practices recommended when working with emotional intelligence. We have indicated the level of skill usually needed for each of the exercises. However, what will be easy for some clients could be difficult for others. Thus, you will need to apply your own judgment and knowledge about the specific situation you are working in as you use these exercises.

Working in this field requires that the trainer, facilitator, coach, therapist, or manager be particularly attentive to his or her client's skills, capabilities, and needs. Fortunately, there are two excellent sources of best practices for training and development with emotional intelligence. The Consortium for Research on Emotional Intelligence in Organizations provides Guidelines for Best Practice, which are found at www.eiconsortium.org, and *Promoting Emotional Intelligence in Organizations* by Cherniss and Adler (2000) is entirely focused on this topic.

While all the points in these best practices lists are valuable, a few of the most important aspects to address include the following:

- *Provide a safe environment.* Work at a pace that is comfortable for your clients. Use strategies to empower them to influence their learning process and acknowledge their concerns and their successes.
- *Establish and observe rules governing confidentiality and disclosure.* From the first time your client(s) become aware of the work they will be doing, they should know what, why, and how any information about them will be used. Be certain that you are clear about what you will discuss and with whom after your interventions. The norm is that you will not discuss any information with anyone else. This norm creates an environment of trust that is essential for the deep work of change to be addressed successfully. If you are working with a team or group, the first ground rule is usually "What is said here, stays here."
- *Get the learning in the body.* It takes concrete experience to make change. Cognitive understanding of new concepts complements this work, but behavioral change is based on a repeatedly reinforced experiential process. Practice number 16 in the EI Consortium list correctly states: "Rely on Experiential Methods: Active, concrete, experiential methods tend to work best for learning social and emotional competencies. Development

activities that engage all the senses and that are dramatic and powerful can be especially effective."

- *Pace your clients.* Just like the saying in real estate—that it's all about location, location, location—to successfully guide transformative EI development, you need to pace, pace, pace your client(s). If they are concerned about doing the work and don't have any experience, go slowly. Start with simple challenges and move to more difficult ones as understanding and trust grow. If they already have considerable experience in this area, keep your work at a more challenging level to maintain their interest.

- *Follow through.* Long-lasting behavioral change happens only when there is a neuronal change. Old habits must be extinguished and new ones developed. This is possible, but it doesn't happen overnight. It takes repeated practice and reinforcement.

- *Evaluate your work.* Some of the first questions to ask when you begin working with your client(s) are, "How will you know your objectives have been accomplished?" and "What specifically will be different?" Be alert to the situations in which research on the results might be possible. The more data we can gather on the benefits of this work, the more reliable and relied on the field of developing emotional and social intelligence will become.

CHANGE

Perhaps the most critical ingredient in the work to build emotional intelligence skills is the ability to facilitate change. As discussed above, follow-through is essential to support effective change. Other key practices listed by the EI Consortium include the following:

- Build in support, such as support groups.
- Use examples of people well known in society or in the organization who exemplify the skill.
- Encourage using these skills and the language of EI on the job.
- Develop an organizational culture that supports learning. To the best extent you can, seek to have your work supported by the organization where you are working and to be role modeled by the top leadership. After all, the phenomenon of "monkey see, monkey do" is still the fundamental learning strategy for us homo sapiens.

If you are working with an assessment tool, you may be able to measure your results using that tool. For example, you could use the EQ-i$^{2.0}$ or one of the other measures for a pre-test and post-test.

USING THE EXERCISES

The exercises can be used with intact teams, groups, or individuals. The instructions are written for teams/groups, but most activities are easily adapted for use with individuals. Where necessary, we provide additional instructions to help with the adaptation. You may also have special dynamics for your group or a team that must be anticipated and addressed carefully. For example, if you are running a session across teams, you'll need to be aware of all the issues discussed above and work with any situations where you find differing levels of capability or buy-in. Go slowly and pay attention. This can be tricky. Further, addressing issues of confidentiality can be even more important. If you are working with a group of individuals who do not work together, you will need to address the near certainty that they will be at different levels of readiness for your work, and, again, it will take careful work to establish a safe environment so that they will open up with one another.

The first three sections of each exercise—Purpose, Thumbnail, and Outcomes—explain the following:

- Purpose answers WHY you would have the people do this exercise;
- Thumbnail tells you HOW participants will engage with the instructional material to generate the learning experience;
- Outcome explains WHAT your target is—the desired results they can achieve.

The exercises contain reproducible handouts (also available at www .pfeiffer.com/go/Hughes/EIAction2) that you may copy for your participants. When reproducing handouts, please be sure to retain the copyright footer. Although the instructions precede the handout, it will always prove helpful to familiarize yourself with the handout before expecting to understand the instructions at the level of fine detail in which they were written!

Self-Regard

Lighten Up with Self-Compassion

Purpose

To recognize the power of being compassionate with oneself.

Thumbnail

60 minutes

Participants discuss what it means to be self-compassionate rather than being personally judgmental and harsh. They reflect on their own behaviors by working through the handout and then talk with others to support personal understanding and taking action for positive change.

Outcomes

- Participants recognize the power of being kind to themselves
- Participants increase the frequency with which they express personal kindness

Audience

- Intact team
- Unaffiliated group
- Individual working with a coach

Facilitator Competencies

Moderate

Materials

- Lighten Up with Self-Compassion Handout

Time Matrix

Activity	Estimated Time
Discuss benefits and challenges of self-compassion	10 minutes
Distribute handout and ask them to fill it in	15 minutes
Get in pairs and discuss their reflections	20 minutes
Discuss as a whole group, including action steps	15 minutes
Total Time	**60 minutes**

Instructions

1. Discuss key aspects of self-compassion, including the following:
   Ask: Do you treat yourself as well as you treat others you care about? Treating ourselves with kindness can bring big benefits, including the much sought after goal of losing weight, as well as possibly less depression and anxiety. Surely a positive interaction with oneself supports the EI skills of happiness and optimism, and this includes the way we talk to ourselves internally. What kind of self-talk do you engage in when you are feeling discouraged? Angry? What messages do you give yourself when you are successful and life is a breeze? Sometimes a significant challenge to our self-regard can be that we don't remember to speak positively to ourselves and about ourselves when life is going well, but critical internal voices are almost automatic!

   A study titled "An Examination of Self-Compassion in Relation to Positive Psychological Functioning and Personality Traits" by Neff, Rude, and Kirkpatrick (2007) examines the relation of self-compassion to positive psychological health and the five-factor model of personality. Self-compassion entails being kind toward oneself in instances of pain or failure; perceiving one's experiences as part of the larger human experience; and holding painful thoughts and feelings in balanced awareness. The study found that self-compassion had a significant positive association with self-reported measures of happiness, optimism, positive affect, wisdom, personal initiative, curiosity and exploration, agreeableness, extroversion, and conscientiousness. It also found a significant negative association with negative affect and neuroticism. Self-compassion predicted significant variance in positive psychological health beyond that attributable to personality.

Ask: What are the obstacles to self- compassion? Give your participants time to discuss. One component is fear. Many believe if they are kind to themselves they will become self-indulgent and lose their motivation. Yet the opposite seems to be the truth. What do you think about this? Have you ever been afraid to be kind to yourself? Is it a deeply ingrained habit to be self-critical? What if you changed your self-talk and emphasized compassion instead?

2. Give each person the Lighten Up Handout and ask them to take fifteen minutes to reflect on how much compassion they give themselves.

3. Then ask them to form pairs and discuss their reflections and desired changes.

4. Bring the full group together to discuss. Emphasize the importance of making sustainable change by committing to specific actions and a time frame. Remind your clients that it helps to agree to tell someone else periodically about your successes and challenges. Often it's what is scheduled that gets done. Thus, scheduling a talk about your progress in being more self-compassionate can help you actually take those positive steps.

LIGHTEN UP WITH SELF-COMPASSION HANDOUT

Think of a time you were recently kind to yourself. Write about what happened and what kind of self-talk you engaged in. Why were you kind? How would the outcome and your self-concept be different if you had been unkind?

Think of a time you were recently unkind to yourself. Write about what happened and what messages you gave yourself. Why were you unkind? How would the outcome and your self-concept be different if you had been kind?

Emotional Intelligence in Action

Self-Regard

Of Thine Own Self Be Aware

Purpose

To expand recognition of the process for building self-regard.

Thumbnail

45 minutes to 2 hours

The facilitator will create a reflective process by having participants respond to a list of questions while they are given time in a quiet environment for self-reflection, followed by discussion on what is learned. There must be a high level of trust before this exercise can be shared productively among team members.

Outcome

Begin drafting a powerful map for initiating a self-exploration process that over time will build healthier positive self-regard.

Audience

- Intact team
- Individual working with a coach

Facilitator Competencies

Moderate to Advanced

Materials

- Of Thine Own Self Be Aware Handout
- Paper and pens

Time Matrix

Activity	Estimated Time
Brief background on self-regard	5–10 minutes
Self-reflection and responding to questions	30–60 minutes
Group debriefing	10 minutes per member
Total	**45 minutes to 2 hours**

Instructions

1. Briefly explain self-regard and discuss the intent of the exercise, which is to build awareness of self-regard and develop it by adding something of real value to participants' lives.

2. Read aloud (or to one's self if this is applied as an individual exercise): "In a quiet space of self-reflection, get in touch with something you want in your life. It should be something significant, meaningful, and important, not necessarily an object, although it can be. Humans tend to use objects as symbols or placeholders for values that are actually more abstract. Someone might say, for instance, 'I want a new boat for water skiing,' when actually he wants the feelings of importance, success, and power he associates with people who have new ski boats. Merely getting the boat may or may not bring the feelings sought.

   "In this exercise you will set a goal to feel more congruent and worthy in some aspect of your life (work, family, personal, etc.) by achieving the goal you have just identified. The process of fully accomplishing it will naturally take a more extended period of time beyond this exercise, during which you will practice new behaviors, attitudes, and expectations. The scope of this exercise is to focus on clearly defining what those new conditions will need to be, how you will be able to recognize them, and how you will motivate yourself to persist in your efforts to incorporate them."

3. Distribute the handout, pens, and extra paper and instruct participants to take thirty minutes for self-reflection and consideration of the questions on the worksheet, then write down the answers. Emphasize that this is a personal exercise and the answers are only for themselves. Encourage the participants to be honest with themselves.

4. Conduct a group debriefing and encourage the participants to make a commitment to continue the learning from this exercise. *Note:* Participants should not be asked to share personal matters in a team setting unless the team is well integrated and a proven foundation of trust exists. You can still ask questions like: Was this an enjoyable exercise? Why or why not? What is the value of this kind of exercise? What sorts of questions or insights did it generate for you?

OF THINE OWN SELF BE AWARE HANDOUT

Answer the following questions in detail. Use as much extra paper as you need. This is confidential—for you alone.

1. What is something I want to accomplish in my life that, when achieved, will lead me to feel really good about myself?

2. How will I have to think about myself and my life differently to accomplish this goal?

3. What feelings about my life and myself will have to change for me to accomplish this goal?

4. How will I have to act differently?

5. What has kept me from thinking and feeling and acting in these ways up to this point?

Emotional Intelligence in Action

Self-Regard

Reconciliation

Purpose

To give participants an experience of increased self-regard through a reconciliation process.

Thumbnail

35 minutes or more, depending on number of participants, plus individual working time between sessions

The participants revisit two situations—one in which they feel like they caused hurt or harm to someone else, and one in which they felt that they were harmed—and undertake to reach better resolutions. This also can be used as a self-directed practice.

Outcome

To experience the elevated sense of self-regard that comes from initiating a reconciliation process.

Audience

- Intact team
- Unaffiliated group
- Individual working with a coach

Facilitator Competencies

Advanced

Materials

- Reconciliation Handout
- Writing paper and pens

Time Matrix

Activity	Estimated Time
Facilitator explains the process of reconciliation	20 minutes
Individuals conduct steps one and two	On their own
Each individual discusses the experience	15 minutes per person
Total	**35 minutes or more + individual time**

Instructions

1. Provide writing paper and pens.
2. Distribute the handout. Tell the participants that this is an exercise on forgiveness and reconciliation, that it's not necessarily an easy process for anyone, but making apologies and repairing relationships is actually a normal and common part of human behavior. Since they are choosing the incidents to deal with, and because at least this step of it is only hypothetical, they should generally be able to handle the tension okay. Be optimistic and suggest to them that new behavior is easy once a new understanding of the situation becomes available.
3. Ask them to list three relationships in their lives where they hurt or offended someone and would like to repair things. Have them rank the incidents in order from the apparently least difficult to the apparently most difficult to repair.
4. Ask them to read Step One from the handout and then, starting with the apparently least difficult incident, ask them to write down the actual things that they would say to the person whose forgiveness they seek.

Have them write the responses they realistically anticipate they would receive in response to each of their comments.

5. Explain that this exercise provides them with an off-line opportunity to thoroughly think through the exchange of feelings and reasons they will be having with this other person—someone who may still feel like the damage cannot be undone. It's true that the facts cannot be changed, but what they mean most assuredly can be. (Ask the participants to do this with the other two incidents as well, now if they have time, or later on their own.)

6. Encourage them to follow through and actually have these conversations and remind them that much of who we think we are gets built up around our experiences of being treated unfairly, so there are likely to be some strong emotional responses from the other person as the emotional energy patterns are released.

7. Now ask them to read Step Two, list three incidents in which they felt harmed, and proceed in a similar manner.

8. Ask them to write for five or ten minutes about what they learned from this exercise and again encourage them to follow through and actually have these conversations.

9. If you have time, and wish to do so, invite participants to share some of their reflections using the kinds of questions below:
   - Was it more difficult to work with the incidents in which you are asking for forgiveness or those in which you were offering it?
   - How important was it to get into the other person's point of view to be able to complete the exercise?

RECONCILIATION HANDOUT

People benefit from conducting a reconciliation process because two kinds of emotional anchors drag on our productivity and impede our enjoyment of life—guilt and rejection. If you look carefully, you will notice they are the flip sides of the same coin: When we choose not to forgive others, we are putting a barrier between them and us that they cannot remove, and regardless of how justified our rejection may seem, at least at the subconscious level, we feel guilty for excluding them, just as they feel guilty for having injured us. Self-regard can't help but grow when those sorts of burdens are relieved.

Step One

First, you are going to seek reconciliation with someone you have hurt or offended or who thinks you have. Obviously, sincere humility and apology are crucial ingredients, but it does not mean you should grovel. It is important that you bring your healthiest level of appropriate self-regard with you so the other person can recognize he or she is not dealing with a needy beggar but an intact individual who sincerely wants to repair a valuable relationship. When you approach someone who feels that you have harmed him or her, expressing your vulnerability (instead of concealing it as we usually do) is generally the best defense.

Tell the person that you have been thinking about the incident a lot lately and feel that it is time to make a new effort to resolve it. Tell the person that you'd like to start off by offering a sincere apology and ask forgiveness for whatever it was you did (or he or she says you did). Sometimes people may still feel very hurt and harbor a level of hostility and resentment that causes them to try to extort a confession from you for something that you never did. It's okay. This is no longer a contest about who's right and wrong. Sincerely say the following sentence (exactly!), "I have never felt as if I did that, but if you do, then I need your forgiveness more than ever."

If the person is ready, it will unfold pretty easily and naturally from there. If he or she is not, say that you understand and that you just wanted to do whatever you could to get things started. Eight out of ten times the person will be ready. In the other two you'll have done your best and know you can feel good about it. But in that instance be careful not to start judging and blaming the person for not accepting your invitation. He or she also did his or her best. Otherwise, the good results you started may be further delayed for both of you.

Remember that much of our identity and who we think we are gets built up around our experiences of being treated unfairly, so there are likely to be some strong emotional responses from both of you as the patterns that had been holding this energy in place begin to dissolve and are released.

Step Two

The second step in this exercise is to extend reconciliation to someone who has hurt or harmed you in some way that is still unresolved. This is a little tricky because if you just walk up to someone you haven't been speaking to and say, "I forgive you for the terrible thing you did to me!" it's a bit more like a fresh accusation than a genuine attempt at reconciliation.

In fact, things will probably proceed best if you begin pretty much like you did when you were asking for reconciliation from another. Say that you've been thinking about the way things ended up and you want to do whatever you can to get your relationship into better balance. It's true that the facts cannot be changed, but what they mean to your relationship most assuredly can be.

Whether the other person shows it or not, one of his or her biggest concerns is that you are condemning him or her for what happened. However, if you maintain an open, non-judgmental attitude and posture, it will help remove this stumbling block. Whether you are standing or sitting, fold your hands loosely in front of you in a relaxed manner. Make gentle, brief but repeated eye contact in a manner that says, "Just curious . . . just wondering." Let your body seem a little tired, as if you are tired from carrying the weight of this matter.

These kinds of nonverbal cues for openness will make it easier for the person to connect at a deeper level and begin to express how he or she feels about the situation. Just to start talking about things again will help lead toward the person's ability or desire to ask for your forgiveness.

To encourage an atmosphere of communication, you can give the person two messages that will help. Whether you say it directly or not, convey, "I don't like to have these awkward feelings between us" and "We are both losing out on something valuable as long as they persist."

If the person shows a willingness to go further, after having had a chance to say something about what it's like from the other side, you can respond matter-of-factly, "Look, it hurt, but I've been healing, and I'm not stuck on this the way I used to be." Then you will be conveying your forgiveness honestly and sincerely, whether he or she feels worthy of receiving it yet or not.

After you complete the writing assignment in preparation for each of these conversations, take some time to reflect about what you learned and how you feel about yourself, your strengths, and your shortcomings. Then follow through, have conversations, and see how much better everyone feels!

Self-Regard

Toot Your Horn and Scratch Your Back

Purpose

To encourage people to give themselves a break. To shift the focus away from all the things they need to accomplish in the future and the things they regret not accomplishing in the past. To zero in on the successes they have had—small and large. To identify what they are not giving themselves enough credit for and to celebrate their accomplishments.

Thumbnail

25 to 45 minutes

Facilitator or coach provides a list of the different roles people may play throughout their lives and asks participants to identify the areas that apply to them. They articulate the good things they have done in those areas and celebrate their accomplishments. The facilitator may need to help participants surface their successes and view them as accomplishments.

Outcomes

- Greater self-appreciation
- Enhanced self-regard

Audience

- Intact team
- Unaffiliated group

Facilitator Competencies ◯

Easy

Materials

- Aspect and Roles Handout
- Back scratchers, whistles, toy horns, or noisemakers and bags to keep them in
- Tissue paper to cover contents of bags

Time Matrix

Activity	Estimated Time
Discuss self-regard	5–10 minutes
Select areas and list accomplishments	5–10 minutes
Discussion in pairs	10–15 minutes
Debrief and celebrate	5–10 minutes
Total	**25 to 45 minutes**

Instructions

1. Have people sitting in table groups with an even number of people at each table.
2. In the center of each table have two bags:
   - Bag containing back scratchers
   - Bag containing whistles, horns, or noisemakers

   Make it evident that something is being hidden to create curiosity.

3. Distribute the Aspects and Roles Handout.
4. Discuss self-regard. Ask participants whether they ever find themselves focusing so much on what they want to accomplish that they forget to stop and appreciate the small everyday successes they have had.
5. Ask participants to check off those categories on the Aspects and Roles Handout that pertain to them. Ask them these questions:
   - Which of these types of groups do you participate in?
   - Are you ever in any of these roles?
6. Have them select three areas and list things they have accomplished in each area. Give them examples such as the following:
   - Work—individual, project, or team success; help another employee, help your boss, help develop or coach an employee; assume a new responsibility
   - Home—clean the house, cook, do repairs, pay bills, decorate, make it safe
   - Health—exercise, watch diet, do special things to mitigate a particular disease or condition, sleep, meditate
7. Ask them to divide into pairs (or threes if necessary) and take turns sharing their accomplishments. When listening to the other person's accomplishments, each should provide positive feedback such as "great job" and "that was a lot to get done." Tell them they don't need to share anything they feel is too personal.
8. Reconvene the group and debrief by asking:
   - Did anything surprising happen? Any *a-ha*'s?
   - Did you realize you have been overlooking things you achieved?
9. Have them take a few moments to appreciate themselves:
   - Retrieve the back scratchers and have them scratch their own backs. An alternative would be to have them pat themselves on the back (their own backs).
   - Retrieve the whistles, horns, or noisemakers from the bag and have them toot their own horns!
10. Ask them to take their back scratchers and noisemakers with them and use them as reminders to stop and appreciate themselves.

ASPECT AND ROLES HANDOUT

_____ Team   _____ Friend
_____ Work   _____ Spouse
_____ Home   _____ Child
_____ Health   _____ Employee
_____ Church   _____ Boss
_____ Community   _____ Citizen
_____ Parent

List your accomplishments in three of the preceding roles or areas.

1. _____ (selected area)

2. _____ (selected area)

3. _____ (selected area)

Self-Actualization

Leverage Your Time with a 2% Solution

Purpose

To develop a personally focused project that will cause participants to stop and pay attention to themselves in a way that will be richly rewarding.

Thumbnail

70 to 90 minutes

Participants focus on how self-actualized they feel now and how self-actualized they would like to feel. They focus on what they need to give themselves to feel more fulfilled and develop a way to make that investment by exploring their 2% Solution.

Outcomes

- Focus on the aspect of self-actualization that is based on taking care of oneself.
- Develop a plan to implement a project that responds to something they would really like to happen, that their hearts crave, and craft plans to spend 30 minutes a day on the project.
- Include reflective self-awareness as a part of the project.

139

Audience

- Intact teams
- Unaffiliated group
- Individual working with a coach

Facilitator Competencies

Moderate

Materials

- Leverage Your Time with a 2% Solution Handout
- Your 2% Solution Handout

Time Matrix

Activity	Estimated Time
Answer Questions 1 through 3 on handout and explore Question 3 in pairs or with coach	15 minutes
Discuss 2% Solution and individual writing	35 minutes
Report and commit	20 to 40 minutes (depends on size of the group)
Total Time	**70 to 90 minutes**

Instructions

1. Distribute the handouts and ask everyone to write answers to items 1 through 3 on the Leverage Your Time handout.
2. Explore Question 3 in pairs or with the coach.
3. Discuss the description provided in the Your 2% Solution Handout and then ask each person to take reflective time to explore creating his or her own 2% Solution. Give participants a full 30 minutes, as this should not be rushed.
4. Ask each person to make a few comments about what he or she is considering as a 2% project (or discuss with you if this is an individual

Emotional Intelligence in Action

coaching session). Invite each person to make a commitment to implement his or her project and to state some specifics about how and when he or she will carry out his or her intentions.

Stretch Goal (Optional)

Revisit in a few weeks and ask everyone to report on his or her progress and challenges with the project.

LEVERAGE YOUR TIME WITH A 2% SOLUTION HANDOUT

1. On a scale of 1 to 10 (10 is highest), how meaningful do I seek to make my life? Write your numerical answer and then write about why you gave yourself that number.

2. Imagine it's six months from now and you're working with this handout again. What number do you want to give yourself then?

3. Explore how you are defining a meaningful life for yourself. How much of your definition has to do with taking care of others? How much is nurturing yourself? How much is meeting external goals that satisfy others? How much is because it feels wonderful to you because it is truly soul nurturing? Write a few notes and then talk with someone in your group or with your coach.

YOUR 2% SOLUTION HANDOUT

Your 2% Solution is a strategy for building your personal success by giving yourself focused time to do what your heart or soul is deeply calling for you to do. It's called 2% because it only takes 2 percent of your time, thirty minutes a day; it's powerful because your time is well spent—on you—and because it includes time to notice how you feel and why while you're engaged with your 2% Solution. The book, *Life's 2% Solution* (Hughes, 2006) provides detailed guidance on the process. The structure is straightforward; the application is where the transformative potential lies. Research shows that taking this small but focused time for oneself contributes strongly to being successful throughout one's life. Without doubt, if you pay attention to your life and refill your own well, you will have more capacity to give to others. This is a major contributor to experiencing your life as being actualized.

To implement your own 2% Solution, follow these steps:

1. Take time to truly reflect and consider your life now. Ask what you would really love to do but you're waiting until you have more time so you can do it really well. It could be pottery, writing poetry, meditation, playing an instrument, or any number of other things. The point is that it needs to be something you really want to do for you. That means no matter how much you'd like more time to read to your children, that is not your 2% Solution. This is for you.
2. During this exercise you will begin your exploration process. You may find you need more time, so list possibilities for now and consider one as a potential while being willing to further consider your choice later.
3. Answer the following:
   - My potential 2% project might be _____.

   List the choices and write a few ideas about what the project means to you. For example: I'll engage in a quiet meditative walk every day for 20 minutes and spend 10 minutes journaling my thoughts and reflections that come up as I become more in touch with myself. Unless you are really certain about the right project for you, consider two or three possibilities.

- Choose one of your possibilities and write a few notes about how and when you will conduct your process. You may need to adjust the schedule but having a structured intention of when you'll take this time for yourself helps you give yourself this time.
- Write about your hopes and worries about giving yourself this time.

REFERENCE

Hughes, M. (2006). *Life's 2% solution*. Boston: Nicholas Brealey.

Self-Actualization

The Scavenger Hunt

Purpose

To assist participants in playing a game that requires striving to actualize some of their potential capabilities. They will need to exhibit drive and set goals to be competitive. The game will require using their underlying skills for self-actualization, including optimism, problem solving, and assertiveness.

Thumbnail

80 minutes to 2 hours and 40 minutes

The facilitator will guide the group in conducting a scavenger hunt—a game that requires team action and a motivation to compete to win. The items are a challenge to find and require team problem solving and coordination. Each team, and then the group as a whole, will debrief and understand the motivational strategies they used, how they set goals, cooperated, and solved problems as a team. The group will compare their recognitions to the normal working environment and identify the specific learnings and strategies for incorporating improved motivation and engagement.

Outcomes

- Increased awareness of how the team applies its drive and sets goals
- Better understanding of how the underlying eight emotional intelligence skills impact our abilities and our accomplishments
- Take-away learning on improved ways to motivate one another, problem solve, and integrate EI skills back to the work environment

Audience

- Intact team
- Unaffiliated group

Facilitator Competencies

Moderate to Advanced

Materials

- The Scavenger Hunt Handout—one copy for each participant
- List of team assignments
- List of scavenger items and ground rules, prepared in advance (see Step 2)
- Prizes
- Flip charts, pens, and paper

Time Matrix

Activity	Estimated Time
Organize group into scavenger hunt teams	10–15 minutes
Scavenger hunt. Give prizes once all return	30–60 minutes
Team discussion with handout	10–20 minutes
Full group discussion—apply to workplace	20–45 minutes
Identify next steps for back at the workplace	10–20 minutes
Total Time	**80 minutes to 2 hours, 40 minutes**

Instructions

1. If you are working with an intact team and are able to do pre-work with the leaders for the team, develop learning goals for how you assign your teams. The teams should be pre-assigned to accomplish those goals. If you have assessment information from an EQ measure or other profiles, such as Emergenetics, MBTI, FIRO-B, or others, use this information to build teams with different strengths so they experience the diversity—or teams that are very similar so they experience the dynamics of similar strengths and preferences. This allows the opportunity for participants to witness the differences within and between their teams and to build intentions for how they will work together most effectively in their normal workdays. This question will be revisited in Step 6.

2. Set up the game—build expectations for great prizes and the impression that those who do better will get better prizes. Send the teams out with ground rules on when to return, how far they can go, anything else relevant to your particular group and environment, and a list of items to obtain. You will need to create the list and ground rules based on the environment you're working in and the type of teams. Here are some examples to draw from:

Scavenger Hunt Sample Items
- Snow ball
- Six-pack (they can be creative, it can be flowers, pop, etc.)
- A woman's shoe (not from anyone in the whole group)
- Something fifty years old or more
- A collage representing every color in the rainbow
- A man's tie clip
- A box of mints
- A plant
- An object from another nation
- Something that symbolically represents your team (and be prepared to tell us why)
- Other (Compile your list to represent the type of team you're working with and what might be found within the time frame for the hunt in their location.)

Scavenger Hunt Sample Ground Rules

- You must stay together as a team.
- You must be back by X (tell them the specific time).
- You cannot buy any item.
- No item can come from any member of your team.
- You may go anywhere you want.
- Other (Again, create your rules to fit the dynamics of the team you are working with. Generally, only a few ground rules are needed.)

3. After all have returned, have a lively celebration and give out prizes.
4. Give each person a copy of the handout and a pen. Direct each team to meet to talk over and write answers to Questions 1 through 10. Tell them to write on the back of the handout if they need more room, or give them more paper.
5. Next have all the teams meet as a whole group to listen to one another and to discuss similarities and differences in their answers. Use the same set of questions from the handout as the small groups used, but this time record key points on flip-chart pages.
6. Instruct each person to take five to ten minutes to individually answer Question 11 on the handout.
7. Close by gaining commitment from participants to implement the action steps they proposed in Item 10 on the handout.

THE SCAVENGER HUNT HANDOUT

Answer Questions 1 through 10 within your scavenger hunt team first and then discuss them with the whole group.

1. Mark on the scale below to indicate your team's motivation to succeed:

   1   2   3   4   5

low   high

2. Mark on the scale below to rank each individual member's motivation to succeed (give each team member a number):

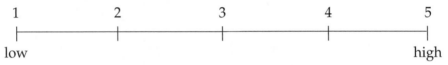

   1   2   3   4   5

low   high

3. Discuss and write a few points about why you gave the scores for Items 1 and 2 above.

4. Take a few minutes for individual reflection. How did each of you individually define success? Is this similar to your response in the workplace? How?

5. Now work as a whole to discuss how your team defined success. Write the definition here. Is this similar to your response in the workplace? How?

6. Discuss how playing this game reflects your ability and drive to set and achieve goals.

7. Were you involved and committed to the pursuit?

8. Self-actualization is built on many other emotional skills. Reflect on how the following factors came into play in this exercise, and then on how they are relevant to your work.
   - Happiness

   - Optimism

   - Self-regard

   - Independence

   - Problem solving

- Social responsibility

- Assertiveness

- Emotional self-awareness

9. Discuss how your team worked together. Did you have different approaches or similar ones to problem solving? How well did you maximize your team's differences and similarities?

10. If your full group is an intact team, develop at least two action steps that you want to take back to your work environment based on your learnings from this exercise.

11. Complete the following item individually when instructed to do so by your facilitator:

    Take five to ten minutes, as your facilitator directs, and each person record some awareness you've gained in this exercise. Do you believe you are meeting your own goals for success in life? Most people say they are meeting some, but not all of their goals. How is it for you? Based on your experience in the scavenger hunt, what two items do you want to pay attention to so you meet your own criteria for success? This is a rich topic; you may want to continue exploring your thoughts during your personal time later to enhance your own self-actualization.

Self-Actualization

Becoming All That You Can Be

Purpose

To explore what self-actualization means to each individual and to develop an action plan to enhance this skill.

Thumbnail

60 to 65 minutes

Individuals and groups work to understand what self-actualization means to them and how important it is personally and professionally. They develop action plans.

Outcomes

- Understand the value of self-actualization in each individual's life
- Learn how others see this value through discussion (for groups only)
- Develop action plans for increasing their self-actualization

Audience

- Intact team
- Unaffiliated group
- Individual working with a coach

Facilitator Competencies

Moderate to Advanced

Materials

- Becoming All That You Can Be Handout
- Writing paper and pens

Time Matrix

Activity	Estimated Time
Each person responds to prepared questions	10–15 minutes
Group discussion	15 minutes
Rate importance of self-actualization	10 minutes
Develop individual action plans	15 minutes
Group reflections	10 minutes
Total Time	**60 to 65 minutes**

Instructions

1. Distribute the Becoming All That You Can Be Handout and additional paper and pens as needed. Instruct each person to take ten to fifteen minutes to answer the questions on the handout. This guides them to begin exploring the underlying questions that lead to self-actualization.
2. Lead a group discussion (or talk with the individual you are coaching) about the questions. Bring in facts related to the importance of self-actualization. For example, Stein and Book (2011, p. 62) report in *The EQ Edge* that they found that this is the number one factor supporting workplace success.
3. Ask the group to rate, as individuals and as a group (individually only for coaching), the importance of self-actualization to them on a scale of 1 to 10. Each person should write the number down for him- or herself. Then work with the group to come up with a group answer; it may be a range. Discuss the results.

4. Now ask them to rate on the same 1 to 10 scale how self-actualized they feel their lives are now. Lead a discussion on their answers. In the discussion, the participants may give the numbers they wrote down and an explanation of why. Or they may give a more general statement, such as, "I gave myself a low score because I need to change jobs and I'm just not working on it." Ask whether the score reflects that they are living within their values of meaningful success for themselves. If so, what should they keep on doing? If not, what should change? Explore whether they feel their scores reflect good alignment with their values or whether change is indicated.

5. Instruct each person to take fifteen minutes to outline his or her personal action plan to achieve ongoing self-actualization. Encourage anyone who is interested to take more time to fully develop his or her plan on his or her own at a later time.

6. Wrap up with group reflections on where they would like to take this awareness. Ask them to explore ways in which they might be of support to one another.

7. (*Optional*) Have an intact team develop a group plan to enhance team self-actualization. Tell group members to take time to make the features of their collective identity explicit by exploring what values, strategies, and personal behaviors make their team unique.

BECOMING ALL THAT YOU CAN BE HANDOUT

Respond to each question below. Use as much paper as you would like.

1. Name five of your core values—in order of priority if possible—and describe why they are important to you.

2. How do you bring your values into your professional and personal lives? How good a job do you feel you are doing at living your values?

3. What really interests you? How do you (or could you) actualize your interests even more, whether at work, in a community setting, or as a hobby?

4. How much time do you set aside each week to do what truly interests you, and how significant is the reward you receive?

5. What are the key skills you bring to life?

6. How fully are you able to express them at home? In the workplace? In your community?

7. Describe how well you are able to accept yourself and others unconditionally.

8. Name some circumstances where you have found yourself expressing awe and/or gratitude.

9. Briefly discuss the level of trust and depth you experience in your personal relationships.

Emotional Intelligence in Action

10. When and where in your life do you feel creative or inventive?

11. Do you feel that your life path is leading you to live up to your potential?

12. What else seems important to you as part of this reflection?

Self-Actualization

Applying Inspiration

Purpose

To help participants understand self-actualization as a process to use to answer the question *What/How/Who do I want to be?* in contrast with the process of problem solving, which tends to answer the question *What do I want to have/get/achieve?*

Thumbnail

70 minutes

Participants will develop a process for building in themselves qualities, states, and behaviors that they have identified as contributing to the success of others. By following the instructions for reflective journaling in response to the selected questions, participants will be able to re-access behavioral and attitudinal resources that were originally inspired in them by others.

Outcomes

Re-connect with some of the feelings of greatness that others have inspired in you and with feelings and/or goals that you would still like to actualize.

Audience

- Intact team
- Unaffiliated group
- Individual working with a coach

Facilitator Competencies

Moderate to Advanced

Materials

- Applying Inspiration Handout
- Writing paper and pens

Time Matrix

Activity	Estimated Time
List thoughts and feelings about goals, models, and success	20 minutes
Write what you will see, hear, feel when goals are actualized	30 minutes
Write down what has kept you from actualizing them in the past	10 minutes
Notice why it might have been appropriate to have avoided them earlier in life	10 minutes
Total	**70 minutes**

Instructions

1. Distribute paper, pens, and the Applying Inspiration Handout.
2. Ask participants to list their feelings and thoughts about Item 1 on the handout.
3. To respond to Item 2, have them explore the various aspects of what they will *see, hear, and feel* when they have accomplished their goals.
4. As directed in Item 3, ask them to discuss what has blocked their past efforts.

5. For Item 4, discuss how to develop a six-week plan using what they have discovered in this exercise and the principles of graduated goals, positive self-talk, accountability to an ally, and appropriate celebration at the end of their quest and all along the way!

APPLYING INSPIRATION HANDOUT

1. Think back to the stories you know of people who faced serious challenges and whose efforts to overcome them resulted in an inspiring success that impressed you deeply. Notice what the general similarities are between the challenges they faced and your own situation. What is it you must overcome to achieve the goals you want to accomplish? Consider what it was about those people that impressed you and why. What were some of the important qualities and abilities that you admire in them? Revisit how it felt to read or hear or watch their stories being told. List your feelings and thoughts about this in the space provided below.

2. Inspiration is the ability to behave in such a way that other people feel and believe that they too can succeed as you have and can overcome the challenges in their lives. Step 1 was designed to help you reconnect with some of the sources of "Can Do!" enthusiasm you have incorporated from your own past learning. Now imagine how it will feel when you are empowered with more of the qualities and abilities that you admire in these individuals. Write down what you will see, hear, and feel that will be different when you have actualized more of your own capacities in these areas. For instance, "When I am more assertive/expressive I will *see* looks of surprise on the faces of people who know me as shy. I will *hear* comments about how I've changed, and I will hear more people challenging me, since I will be taking a stand more often. I will *feel* scared at first but also more congruent and self-respecting, and that will be a relief.

3. Now notice what has prevented you from expressing these qualities and skills in the past, and write down your thoughts in the space provided. Are there any useful ways in which these limits of expression have served you constructively in the past? For instance: "Expressing my opinion as a child often meant hostility and rejection." Is it still appropriate to observe those limits today? Why? Or why not?

4. Using the thoughts and feelings that you have reactivated in your awareness during this exercise, develop a six-week plan for bringing to life more of what it is you truly want to be. If you have a coach, mentor, or partner in your workgroup with whom you are doing this exercise, review it with him or her, incorporate suggestions, and meet with him or her at least once a week to report and reinforce your progress.

Emotional Self-Awareness

Expanding Your Uncommon Awareness

Purpose

To help increase your awareness of your external and internal emotional environments and be able to adjust your level of sensitivity to emotional signals.

Thumbnail

40 minutes

By changing the focus of participants' attention to include more of the sensory data in their environment, they are able to filter out some of the pressing cognitive information that tends to dominate their awareness and get more in touch with their emotional states.

Outcomes

- Increase your awareness and sensitivity to your current emotional energy states
- Learn about how to use your emotional self-awareness to help manage stress and improve your stress tolerance

Audience

- Intact teams
- Unaffiliated group
- Individual working with a coach

Facilitator Competencies

Moderate

Materials

- Expanding Your Uncommon Awareness Handout
- Paper and pens

Time Matrix

Activity	Estimated Time
Introduce exercise	5 minutes
In pairs, follow handout instructions	25 minutes
Discuss as a full group	10 minutes
Total Time	**40 minutes**

Instructions

1. Distribute the Expanding Your Uncommon Awareness Handout and instruct the participants to find partners to work with, preferably someone that they do not know. Tell them they are going to take turns reading the instructions to each other and taking notes on their experience. Each person will have about ten minutes. Hand out paper and pens for note taking.
2. Before they start, ask them to practice the instructions in the second paragraph of the handout. Tell them to support their chins on their palms while using their index fingers to cover the center of their visual fields. Once that feels comfortable for both members of each pair, whoever wants to read first can begin.
3. Bring the full group together to debrief the experience.

EXPANDING YOUR UNCOMMON AWARENESS HANDOUT

First, get your paper and pencil ready so that you can take a few notes at the end of these instructions.

Next, practice blocking the center of your visual field (called your foveal vision) by placing your elbows on the desk or table in front of you, or even on your knees will do. Place the heels of your hands together, creating a V shape. Next rest your chin on the space between your palms and fingers, keeping your ring fingers up and gently adjusting them so they cover your pupils. Close one eye and look directly at the center of your fingerprint, then close the other and do the same so that your fingertips are covering the center of your visual field approximately half an inch away from your eyes.

Now that you have practiced this technique, it's time for one of you to read the rest of the instructions to the other. Please do so in a pleasant, relaxing, and reassuring manner, perhaps using the tonality you might if were reading a happy bedtime story to a child.

Instructions to Read Aloud

We are going to begin this exercise by shifting your awareness to your peripheral vision. We spend most of our waking time focused on the words and faces and cars and images of our highly visual world, but very little time defocused, sensitive to the amazing amount of information that comes to us through our peripheral field. We tend to focus on the named objects of our world, glancing from thing to thing, connecting them with the threat of consciousness. Knowing what they are and what they're called and how they are likely to behave is the foundation of our safety, and keeping this world in focus is a highly conscious process. Allowing the awareness of the peripheral world to "seep in"—since we can never look at it directly—gives us more awareness of the whole world, that is more forest, fewer trees. This attention is one of the sources of our intuition, the things we know without necessarily knowing how we know them.

Now use the technique you practiced earlier and place your chin between your hands while you gently position your ring fingertips to block your foveal vision. Without moving your eyes, let your awareness drift up toward your eyebrows . . . then down toward your nose . . . now gently over to the right. . . . And slowly back to the left. . . . Then finally return to the

Exercise 3.1. Emotional Self-Awareness

center again and just see everywhere. You may be tempted to notice something specific, but if you're doing it correctly you really won't want to. You don't need to. Take longer and deeper breaths and just hang out like this for a while. Just be aware without trying to "capture" anything.

If it feels more comfortable to sit normally now, you can return your hands to your lap, but allow your visual awareness to remain defocused while you shift your attention to your ears . . . and notice what you're hearing. Notice what is the loudest sound in the environment. . . . And the next loudest. . . . Then the next loudest after that, until you become aware of the very quietest sound that you can just detect with some awareness.

Just enjoy listening for a few more moments, then shift your attention to your sense of touch. What is touching your skin with the most pressure? The force of gravity is always pushing us against the planet. If we're sitting in a chair, we will feel it pressing against our back and legs. If we're standing, we'll feel it in our feet. What else can you feel touching your skin? Do you notice a breeze from the wind or the air conditioning? What about the air temperature? Is it cooler or warmer than your skin?

Now, if you haven't done so already, close your eyes, and pay attention to your heartbeat. It is virtually certain to be slower than it was when you first started this exercise. Now notice your breathing. It is probably slower and possibly somewhat deeper too. Take a deeper than normal breath and just let the air rush out of your lungs and keep exhaling. Repeat that once more, then with your eyes still closed continue breathing in a generally relaxed fashion.

Now take a few moments to reflect on earlier in the day. How have you been feeling? What events led up to those kinds of feelings? Looking back over yesterday and the last week, how have you been feeling in general? Were there any significant events that you notice that led up to a change in the way that you've been feeling?

After a while, gently open your eyes when you're ready, and jot down a few notes about how and what you have been feeling and what kinds of events you associate with those feelings. Summarize the experience for yourself silently by filling in the blanks for yourself: "Hmmm, I guess I've been feeling_____, because_____."

Now it will be your time to read the instructions to your partner.

When both of you have completed the written exercise, take about five minutes to discuss your observations.

Emotional Self-Awareness

Are You in Touch?

Purpose

To demonstrate how quickly emotions can change and how seemingly insignificant things can impact emotions. The exercise also provides a technique to calm emotions and regain emotional footing.

Thumbnail

25 to 40 minutes

The facilitator or coach will introduce an irritating influence to cause people to feel unsettled. The influence will cease and people will be asked to focus on how their emotions were changing during the "irritating interval." The facilitator will then lead the group through a calming visualization. Finally, the group will be asked to reflect on the entire experience and relate it to how they can manage the emotions in their lives. The facilitator needs to have a comfort level with leading a physical exercise to increase self-awareness.

Outcomes

- Increased awareness of the capricious nature of emotions
- Better understanding of how ancillary events can impact emotions
- Greater sensitivity to how changing emotions can affect human interactions
- Gain a new technique to regain emotional centeredness

Audience

- Intact team
- Unaffiliated group
- Individual working with a coach

Facilitator Competencies

Moderate to Advanced

Materials

- Are You in Touch? Handout
- Flip chart and markers
- Cacophonous music that is jarring and unsettling
  - Suggestion: James Tenney *Selected Works 1961–1969,* New World Records. www.newworldrecords.org
  - Please adhere to copyright laws when using recorded music.

Time Matrix

Activity	Estimated Time
Talk to group on a subject of interest	5–10 minutes
Debrief using the handout	5–10 minutes
Conduct Hook-Ups exercise	5 minutes
Participants record experience on handout	5–10 minutes
Review extended exercise on handout	5 minutes
Total	**25 to 40 minutes**

Instructions

1. Talk to the group or individual client about emotional intelligence (or another subject of your choosing).
2. After speaking for a couple of minutes, turn on the cacophonous music. Have the music loud enough for everyone to hear but not so loud they cannot hear you. You (the facilitator) respond as if the music is not playing. You do not react in any way to the music—no wincing, twitching, eye rolling, or body stiffening.
   - If someone asks you to stop the music, calmly tell him or her you will stop it in a little while.
   - If someone asks you to turn the music down, pretend to do so, but do not change the volume.
3. At the conclusion of your brief discussion of emotional intelligence, ask the group the ten questions on the Are You in Touch? Handout. Do not distribute the handout at this time.
4. Have the group do the following physical exercise called Hook-Ups, which is designed to increase self-awareness and reduce tension. The exercise helps re-establish emotional centeredness and can be used when feeling angry, confused, or sad.

   *Hook–Ups**

   Hook-Ups connect the electrical circuits in the body, containing and thus focusing both attention and disorganized energy. As the mind and body relax, energy circulates through areas blocked by tension.

   Part One: Sitting, the student crosses left ankle over right. Student extends arms, crossing left wrist over right. Student then interlaces fingers and draws hands up toward chest. Student may now close eyes, breathe deeply, and relax for about a minute. *Optional:* Student presses tongue flat against the roof of mouth on inhalation and relaxes the tongue on exhalation.

   Part Two: When ready, student uncrosses legs. Student touches fingertips of both hands together, continuing to breathe deeply for about another minute.

---

*Taken from *Brain Gym*, Teacher's Edition, Revised, by P.E. Dennison and G.E. Dennison, 2010, Edu-Kinesthetics, Inc., Ventura, CA. Used with permission of the authors.

5. Distribute the handout and review with the group the Extended Exercise, which is at the end of the handout. Obtain commitment from the participants to take and record their emotional pulse in this regimented way until it becomes second nature and they find themselves automatically checking in with their emotions.

ARE YOU IN TOUCH? HANDOUT

1. How did you feel when we first started?
2. What are you feeling right now?
3. Why do you feel differently?
4. How did you emotionally react to the music? Did it impact your attitude?
5. Did it happen immediately or take a few minutes to build?
6. Did the music lead you to feel more or less open to positive interactions with others?
7. How did you feel about the facilitator or coach while the music was playing?
8. List all the ways in which you were aware of the music's effect on your emotions and attitude.
9. What did you feel when the music was turned off?
10. When the music was turned off, did any of the negative emotions caused during the time it was playing disappear automatically?
11. Think of a situation in your life in which you were feeling pretty good (or pretty bad) and some event or new information suddenly caused your feelings to change dramatically. What happened? What impact did it have on you and on the quality of your interactions with others?

Extended Exercise

Do this in the course of your normal day.

At selected times, stop and check your "emotional pulse," and write down what is happening.

- Determine the specific times during the day and evening that you will stop and check.
- Regularly record your responses to the following questions in a notebook, personal digital assistant, or appointment book:
  - What are you feeling now?
  - When did you start feeling this way?
  - Why are you feeling this way? What is the cause?

Emotional Self-Awareness

It Just Bubbles Up

Purpose

To connect with the emotions that drive unproductive behavior.

Thumbnail

35 to 50 minutes

Team members (or individuals) identify situations in which they regret the way they acted. They pinpoint the unproductive behaviors and recall what was going on physiologically at that point in the process.

Outcomes

- Be more in touch with changing emotions
- Build understanding of how emotions drive behaviors
- Recognize cues that emotions have changed

Audience

- Intact team
- Unaffiliated group
- Individual working with a coach

Facilitator Competencies ◯ ◑

Easy to Moderate

Materials

- It Just Bubbles Up Handout
- Flip charts and markers
- Pens

Time Matrix

Activity	Estimated Time
Identify situations, feelings, and responses	15 minutes
Discuss physical reactions	15 minutes
Debrief	5–20 minutes
Total	**35 to 50 minutes**

Instructions

1. Distribute handouts and pens to the participants.
2. Ask the team members (or individuals) to recall a significant situation (as recent as possible) in which they regret acting the way they did. Then ask them to write a brief description of what they regret specifically.
3. Ask them to write down in Steps 2 and 3 of the handout how they felt in the above situation, such as fearful, anxious, defensive, happy, embarrassed, and why they felt that way—for example, because they felt publicly insulted. Handout Steps 2 and 3 complete this model:
   "I felt _____ because _____."
   For example, "I felt foolish because no one volunteered when I asked."
4. In Steps 4 and 5 of the handout, have them write how they responded to those feelings.
5. Ask them to write about how they would have felt if it had gone perfectly, in accordance with Step 6 of the handout.

6. Have your participants look back and do their best to assess how others around them were feeling at the time. Did others know how they were feeling? What evidence did participants rely on to come to their conclusions? Upon reflection, do they feel they assessed the situation correctly? Did they do sufficient reality testing? Record their answers on a flip chart.

7. Ask them to evaluate their decision making from as objective a point of view as possible and record their thoughts on a flip chart. Did they feel as if they were under pressure? Could they have supplemented their emotional self-awareness with better impulse control in this situation? How?

8. Debrief the participants. Have them discuss what they are most often paying attention to instead of the sensory cues from their bodies. Write their answers on a flip chart. Most of the time at work we are preoccupied with intellectual, symbolic, verbal issues. Increasing our sensitivity to our body's internal states requires that we "shift brains," slow down, and pay conscious attention to the sensory input we generally tend to process subconsciously. Ask whether anyone wants to share his or her insights with the group, but don't push anyone to share.

IT JUST BUBBLES UP HANDOUT

1. Have you recently been in a situation in which you wished you had not acted or responded in a particular way? Describe the situation.

2. What were you feeling in the above situation?
   ____ Fearful
   ____ Defensive
   ____ Anxious
   ____ Happy
   ____ Embarrassed in a positive way—for instance, someone paid you a compliment and you were glad he or she did and felt it was appropriately done
   ____ Embarrassed in a negative way—for example, you were publicly insulted
   ____ Other
3. Why did you feel that way?

4. How did you respond to those feelings listed in Step 2?

_____ Withdrew completely from the situation

_____ Stayed in the situation but tried to steer the interaction in a different direction

_____ Stayed in the situation and pretended you were in agreement

_____ Became verbally or physically abusive

_____ Disparaged the other person or people

_____ Tried to out-talk the other person or people

_____ Other

5. How was your body responding while you were feeling in the way you indicated

_____ Folded arms

_____ Clenched jaw

_____ Sweat—lip, brow, under arms, scalp, palms

_____ Twitching

_____ Tapping foot

_____ Drumming fingers

_____ Stomach clenched

_____ Other

6. Identify how you will act differently in the future when you notice the reactions from Step 4 or your physical cues from Step 5.

Emotional Intelligence in Action, Second Edition. Copyright ©2012 by Marcia Hughes and James Bradford Terrell. Reproduced by permission of Pfeiffer, an Imprint of Wiley. www.pfeiffer.com

Emotional Self-Awareness

Moving Toward and Moving Away

Purpose

To help participants understand how the body's basic biological response of "moving toward" and "moving away from" influences all of their emotional activity.

Thumbnail

70 minutes

Participants will observe and explore a list of emotional scenarios that they regularly encounter, notice the distinctions among them, and describe the differences they discover.

Outcome

By exploring the suggested situations and feelings, participants will become more aware of how they respond emotionally to those issues they want to approach and those they want to avoid in their lives.

Audience

- Intact team
- Unaffiliated group
- Individual working with a coach

Facilitator Competencies

Moderate

Materials

- Moving Toward and Moving Away Handout
- Paper and pens

Time Matrix

Activity	Estimated Time
Have participants think about which things they naturally approach and avoid	10 minutes
List specific instances for each feeling	15 minutes
Write distinctions between states	15 minutes
Ask them to notice how these emotions and states affect their choices	10 minutes
Have them explore in pairs how they actually communicate the listed feelings	20 minutes
Total	**70 minutes**

Instructions

1. Provide paper and pens, and distribute the handout.
2. Ask participants to think about how fundamental the act of moving toward and moving away from is for all life—even plants.
3. Ask them to build a list in each category under Number 1 on the handout of the kinds of things and situations that they naturally move toward and those they naturally move away from.

4. Have participants describe a specific instance for each of the feelings under Number 2 on the handout.

5. When they have responded to each of the seven different feelings, have them go back and add descriptions of how their bodies felt physically while they were experiencing those emotions.

6. Now ask the participants to recall specific instances for the different states listed in Number 3, and have them write down the physical and emotional distinctions they experience.

7. In Number 4 have them fill in the blanks.

8. Finally, ask them to work in pairs for Number 5. Here they will express the described emotional attitudes to their partners as realistically as possible, and their partners will observe and take notes of all the nonverbal components of the message. Remind them to notice tonality, volume, posture, skin tone, eye contact, and so forth. Have participants discuss what they learned.

MOVING TOWARD AND MOVING AWAY HANDOUT

Developing this competency in emotional self-awareness increases your ability to know *what* you are feeling, *when* you are feeling it, and what *causes* those feelings in you, as well as their degree of intensity. In beginning this exercise, take a moment to reflect on the fact that human beings, along with all living organisms, share the same two fundamental responses to the events in their environment: approach or move toward, and avoid or move away from.

1. Now think about what sorts of things you naturally tend to approach and avoid, and list three or four in each category below.

   Things, situations, and kinds of people I approach:

   Things, situations, and kinds of people I avoid:

2. Now, think of a *specific instance* in which you felt each of the following feelings. Address all, but you can start with whichever one seems most appealing. Describe what sort of situations and conditions and what sorts of behavior by other people has prompted you to feel . . .

Stressed

Excited and Hopeful

Frustrated

Playful

Worried

Relieved

Furious

Now go back to each category and add a few descriptions of the ways your body feels when you are experiencing each emotion. Where is there tension? Heat? Coolness? Pain? Pleasure? Weakness? What other body feedback do you notice?

3. Write down a few of the distinctions (physical and emotional) that you experience in the following states: jealousy, a job interview, expressing condolences for a death, and successfully completing a big project. Please take enough time to access real memories of specific emotional situations. It will help you be able to differentiate how strongly you feel when you experience different kinds of emotions.

4. Considering what you have learned about how you feel and the situations in which you feel that way, now make a two-column listing of what causes you to move toward some things and away from others. Use the model below:

   I move toward _____ because _____.

   I move away from _____ because _____.

Move Toward	Move Away

5. The way in which we communicate to others that we want them to move toward us or to move away from us is clearly a critical skill; they are two of the most important messages we ever give! So, using specific situations from memory as your reference, work in pairs to discover and describe what you do to communicate to other people that you are experiencing the following emotions:

- Enthusiasm, excitement—that you are eager to begin a new project and hope they will want to work on it with you.
- Frustrated, thwarted—that you need some new suggestions, but they'd better be good!

Emotional Expression

Expressing Resistance

Purpose

To help individuals develop effective ways of resisting requests that do not seem as well founded as they need to be.

Thumbnail

25 minutes

This exercise will help leaders and team members answer the questions, "How do you know when to push back, and how much?" and "In what way to do so?"

Outcomes

- Improving understanding of how to express emotions in challenging situations
- To have several ways of politely but effectively resisting requests that are emotionally and/or rationally unintelligent

Audience

- Intact teams
- Unaffiliated group
- Individual working with a coach

Facilitator Competencies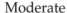

Moderate

Materials

- Expressing Resistance Handout

Time Matrix

Activity	Estimated Time
Describe the strategies	10 minutes
In pairs, apply one each	10 minutes
Debrief	5 minutes
Total Time	**25 minutes**

Instructions

1. Distribute the Expressing Resistance Handout and discuss the following with your participants. There will be times in everyone's career when he or she is requested to take actions that may seem rational from one point of view but equally irrational from another. When it really is a rational request, there is probably an information gap involved in the situation; however, often a lack of emotional reality testing also contributes to the mixed feelings. This could be, for example, because a person doesn't want to disappoint/confront his or her boss's unrealistic expectations. Review each of the ways to push back respectfully and effectively provided on the handout.

2. Ask participants to form pairs and experiment with the strategies by applying one to a situation in each of their lives. The person who goes first will briefly explain the situation and then practice using the strategy he or she chooses as if the situation is current. Then the pair should discuss the likely success of that strategy. Then the second person follows the process, and again the pair should discuss what is likely to happen.

3. Bring the full group together to debrief their experience and insights.

EXPRESSING RESISTANCE HANDOUT

The following are some ways to push back respectfully and effectively. Choose one that might work in a situation you are in now or have experienced in the past and discuss with your partner how the method could work for you. Then trade and the other person picks a method to discuss.

- *Offer an Exclamation!* Often a great way to challenge someone's enthusiasm for the impossible right out of the box is simply to start with an exclamation such as, "Wow, that's optimistic!" Or you might say "Gee that sounds pretty ambitious!" This part of the communication can sound a little incredulous, but follow it up with a respectfully curious tonality and ask, "Can you tell me about the details?" This lets the person know you're not completely on board at the very beginning.

- *Reflective Listening.* This could be the next step or an independent step in the intervention. It is a simple and powerful one. Use good reflective listening skills to make sure you heard the person correctly. For instance, "Okay, so if I hear you correctly, you don't think draining the swamp with the alligators still in it will pose any serious problems for the team, even though we are only being given shovels to get the job done." In addition to serving to clarify accurate understanding, this can be an invitation to do better reality testing and is accomplished through changes in your tonality depending on what words you emphasize. Try it using several different kinds of tonal emphasis.

- *Challenging the Assumptions.* If you hear something like, "No, that shouldn't be a problem" or "Well, there's hardly any gators out there anymore," you can reply enthusiastically, "So you don't think we'll run into any problems?" And when the person reassuringly says "No," you can counter with (hesitantly, of course): "But what if there are?" Pause for a moment here, and if there is no reply you can shift the table a little bit by asking, "What I guess I'm asking is, if there were any problems, what do *you* think we might run into?" This objectifies the problem and appeals to the person's managerial expertise, so for the moment it's not an emotional confrontation. It puts you on the same side because you're asking, "What do you think WE might run into?" At this point, if he or she is honest, he or she will begin to explore some concrete issues. If the person is only partially honest, he or she will probably invite you to suggest problems that you might anticipate. But *don't* take this bait or you can be seen as a whiner, a pessimist, a naysayer, or insubordinate. Simply say, "I really have no idea, but you would probably understand that better than I do."

- *Covering Your Bases.* If the person is still unwilling to be honest or realistic, you can simply say, "I guess we just disagree on the way we're seeing this. It seems unrealistic to me, and I'm just afraid if we don't think it through more carefully we're going to run into some serious problems." Your tonality here will be critical. It's often best to deliver this with as light an emotional charge as possible. You want this to come off as a *rational* cautionary remark, *not* an emotional warning that challenges the other person's authority. In any case he or she has been warned, you have done the best you can, and if there are problems you can say, "Wow, I was worried we might run into something like this" (not "I told you so!").

Emotional Expression

Say It Nonverbally!

Purpose

To practice learning how to use nonverbal communication more effectively.

Thumbnail

20 minutes

This exercise helps people notice their own nonverbal communication in a variety of emotional situations and shows them how to consciously use those behavioral cues to be more effective when communicating intentionally with others.

Outcome

- Increase awareness of one's own nonverbal communications

Audience

- Members of intact teams
- Members of an unaffiliated group
- Individual working with a coach

Facilitator Competencies ◯

Easy

Materials

- Say It Nonverbally! Handout

Time Matrix

Activity	Estimated Time
Discuss nonverbal communication	10 minutes
Practice exercise and debrief	10 minutes
Total Time	**20 minutes**

Instructions

1. Discuss the value of nonverbal communication, such as the power of a shrug when you ask whether someone really likes the plan, or the person chuckling when it sounds as though he or she is making him- or herself too important.
2. Distribute the handout and ask each person to practice the exercise in the handout, and then discuss the experience with the entire group.

SAY IT NONVERBALLY! HANDOUT

In this exercise, you will imagine yourself in the various situations suggested in the following instructions. Notice how your body communicates—how it feels, what is it saying, and how it is saying what it is saying, and without speaking! Jot down a few notes to remind yourself. This will work much better if you cover your list with a separate piece of paper and expose the next example after making your notes from the prior experience.

- 1 minute ago your favorite football team just won the Super Bowl.

- 1 minute ago your favorite football team just lost the Super Bowl.

- Your daughter has just announced that she's going to marry a man she has known for three months whom you have met twice and distrust and dislike.

- Your daughter has finally announced that she and her fiancé of ten months have set the date to be married next year. You think he is perfect for her.

- You are surprised to hear the VP of your work group announce he's excited to be implementing a cost-saving measure that you developed, but he gives all the credit to a co-worker, who accepts it proudly.

Exercise 4.2. Emotional Expression

- You need some product information from a vendor who does a lot of business with you. You have been calling and e-mailing all your contacts there for several days, but no one appears to be making any effort to get back to you.

- Your six-year-old has been working diligently all weekend on an art project to surprise your spouse when he returns from a business trip. Thinking she has already presented it, you accidentally spoil the surprise and she runs out of the room in tears.

- You and your team have been working on a project for three weeks, ten and twelve hours a day, including some weekends. Finally, you turn it in by the deadline Thursday morning. Everyone feels exhausted but proud and relieved. At 2 p.m. Friday, your boss calls you into his office and tells you the customer is not happy and wants you to make some changes. It will take you most of the next three days.

- Your boss has a new haircut and it's a lot shorter. It looks good, but the change is pretty dramatic. Everyone is saying she's trying to look younger. You walk into the break room just as the conversation dies down and joke that maybe she's actually trying to lose weight. She is walking in right behind you and clearly hears your comment.

Emotional Intelligence in Action

Emotional Expression

Tell a Story

Purpose

To practice recognizing and talking about emotions and listening to those of others.

Thumbnail

25 minutes (plus 3 more minutes for each person in the team or group)

Each person tells a story about the selected topic including commenting about how he or she felt during the event being described. The group or team discusses the value and challenges with expressing emotions and the value of storytelling.

Outcomes

- Increase comfort in expressing emotions
- Invite willingness and commitment to express emotions
- Become aware of the value of telling stories and how that can reconnect the team or group with their passion

Audience

- Intact teams
- Unaffiliated group
- Individual working with a coach

Facilitator Competencies ◯

Easy

Materials

- None needed

Time Matrix

Activity	Estimated Time
Select topic in advance	5 minutes
Each person tells a story	5 minutes per person
Discuss	15 minutes
Total Time	**25 minutes (plus 3 more minutes for each person in the team or group)**

Instructions

1. In advance, select the type of subject for the story you will ask your team, group, or coachee to tell. The subject could be a current project at work; a key event or relationship at work, such as working with a mentor; a meaningful personal event; or any other appropriate possibility.

2. Ask each person to take a few minutes and think about a story he or she will tell regarding the topic you have selected. They will have three minutes to tell their stories to the team or group or to you as the coach. Ask them to start telling their stories. The ground rules are

   - Each person speaks without interruption; this is not a time for questions or corrections. It is the speaker's story.
   - The person must include at least two descriptions of how he or she felt and why regarding events in the story.

3. If you have a large team or group and are time-constrained, have them tell their stories in groups of three or four.
4. Invite discussion on what they are noticing and feeling having heard one another's stories. Guide them to discuss:
   - Becoming aware of their own feelings as they tell their stories and as they listen to those of others.
   - Their level of comfort in expressing their emotions and their comfort in hearing others discuss their emotions.
   - What they could do to invite increased emotional expression and why they would want to do so.
   - Their feelings now that they have told their stories and heard the stories of others. Do they feel more connected to one another (and to their work or project if that was a subject of the stories)?
   - Ask what else they would like to comment on or ask others about.

Emotional Expression

Expressing Emotions in Social Media

Purpose

To allow participants to explore the effectiveness of their emotional communications when using social media.

Thumbnail

30 minutes

Participants explore how they use emotions in the social media formats they use, discuss the benefits of and lost opportunities from their approaches, and then make a commitment to improve their emotional communication.

Outcomes

- Build awareness of how people communicate emotions in social media interactions
- Recognize where change would be valuable

Audience

- Intact teams
- Unaffiliated group
- Individual working with a coach

Facilitator Competencies ◯

Easy

Materials

- Expressing Emotions in Social Media Handout
- Pens

Time Matrix

Activity	Estimated Time
Participants fill in handout	10 minutes
Discuss what they wrote in handout	10 minutes
Commit to enhanced strategies	10 minutes
Total Time	**30 minutes**

Instructions

1. Give everyone the handout and a pen. Ask all participants to fill in the handout so that they:
   - Make a list of the social media formats they use
   - Write how they express emotions in each of the formats
   - Candidly notice when the use of emotions works well and when it doesn't work well by leaving important information out or actually getting them in trouble.

   For example, you could tell your participants:

   > "Imagine you have an important dinner date; it's with someone you want to impress about an important topic (or it's a romantic date). You are so frustrated because your boss kept you late, you are racing out of the building, your date is probably already at the restaurant, and . . ."

In one scenario, you text your date saying "Running late c u soon, maybe 45 minutes."

In the other scenario, you call your date and give him or her emotional context and say, "Susie, I'm so sorry I'm running late. My boss needed a project from me and I just couldn't get out. I'm frustrated because I'm so eager to see you. I can get there in about 45 minutes; will that still work for you? Have a drink on me while you wait."

Now which scenario is likely to produce the best results?

2. Ask participants to reflect on how their engagement does or doesn't work and what changes they want to make. Get the participants together and ask for comments. Depending on the size of the group, you can ask each person to comment or just gather representative feedback. Invite exploration of what works and what does not work and what changes can be useful. Discuss that nonverbal communication is a big part of human communication and this is always left out of social media interaction. Ask when it would be better to call or go see the person with whom one is communicating rather than using social media.

3. Ask each person to turn to someone next to him or her and make a commitment about ways in which he or she will improve the emotional content of his or her communications.

EXPRESSING EMOTIONS IN SOCIAL MEDIA HANDOUT

Social Media Formats I Use

I express emotions thus:

This works well when:

This does not work when:

Comments

Assertiveness

Developing Appropriate Assertiveness Within Your Team

Purpose

To help teams and individuals use the appropriate level of assertiveness.

Thumbnail

30 minutes

Participants will discuss the interrelationships in the way that several emotional effectiveness skills can contribute to the successful use of assertiveness. They will then have an opportunity to explore ways to improve their assertiveness skills by increasing or decreasing their assertiveness as needed.

Outcomes

- To understand that several emotional effectiveness skills co-influence assertiveness.
- To help team members and individuals who tend to overdo their assertiveness to restrain it and those who tend to underplay their assertiveness to build it up.

Audience

- Intact teams
- Unaffiliated group
- Individual working with a coach

Facilitator Competencies

Advanced

Materials

- Developing Appropriate Assertiveness Within Your Team Handout

Time Matrix

Activity	Estimated Time
Discuss the concepts and practices in handout	10 minutes
In pairs, discuss applying one of the practices	10 minutes
Debrief as a full team/group	10 minutes
Total Time	**30 minutes**

Instructions

1. Explain that assertiveness is one of those skills that people are either good at or not so good at. Within the team environment this can have a high impact on team performance. Assertiveness is not a stand-alone emotional effectiveness skill, although none of the EQ-i or TESI skills really are. Assertiveness requires flexibility, impulse control, independence, empathy, interpersonal relationships, and self-regard to be functioning optimally for assertiveness to reach its full potential. Let your group or team know that they will begin by discussing the interrelationships between several emotional effectiveness skills, then have an opportunity to explore ways to improve their assertiveness skills.

2. Distribute the handout and go over the concepts described. Review the practices for improving assertiveness when it's too high and too low and ask for examples of how participants have seen both forms of

assertiveness demonstrated. Ask them to discuss using the practices—who has used the ideas and how they have worked for them?

3. Have participants form pairs and ask them to identify a specific part of their lives where they could use one of the practices and create a plan to do so.

4. Bring the full team or group together to debrief. You might:

- Ask for some examples of what practices they thought of using.
- Ask whether anyone wants help in brainstorming how to develop his or her plan to make changes.
- Ask for any "a-ha's" as they considered their own assertiveness. Would they be better off increasing or decreasing their assertiveness, or does it depend on the context?
- Ask how much they need to gauge their assertiveness based on the culture they are working with.

DEVELOPING APPROPRIATE ASSERTIVENESS WITHIN YOUR TEAM HANDOUT

Assertiveness and Its Relationships to Other EI Skills

When you want to adjust your assertiveness, it is helpful to first consider the relationship between the skill of assertiveness and other EI skills, especially the following:

- Self-Regard gives one a belief in one's worth and the worth of what he or she has to say. It also gives people the confidence to say it.
- Independence gives one the courage to act independently with or without the support of others' opinions.
- Assertiveness motivates one to be sure that others know what one likes and wants more of and what one dislikes and wants less of or none at all.
- Interpersonal Relationships gauge the amount of our energy that we like to spend developing and maintaining social friendships. It has somewhat of a biological set point. To the extent that it correlates with extroversion and introversion in the MBTI, we will tend to see less extroverted members of the team reflecting more and commenting less often. As a result, they will tend to have more carefully prepared remarks to contribute. While these people, with practice, can learn to be more assertive, it is also the shared responsibility of the leader and other team members to invite the comments and observations of the quieter team members when their contributions are noticeably absent.
- Impulse Control gives one the restraint to be able to suppress or delay one's reactions and diminish their intensity, even when one is under emotional pressure.
- Flexibility enables one to recognize and engage the full range of one's effective choices so that one does not feel constrained to choose the most obvious course of action.
- Empathy allows one to feel how one's actions affect others emotionally and to communicate more effectively with others. Are we intimidating, or interrupting, or supporting others?
- Social Responsibility empowers the generosity one needs to be able to recognize and support the needs and best efforts of others.

Practices to Improve One's Use of Assertiveness

When Assertiveness Is High

When a team member's scores in assertiveness (and perhaps independence as well) are high, but his or her scores in empathy and impulse control are significantly lower, practicing to improve the lower skills will help balance this person's expression of assertiveness. Improving in social responsibility and flexibility can also help offset the tendency to dominate in discussions. Slowing everything down will be one of the first steps to take in building effectiveness, remembering that good impulse control is the ability to increase the amount of time between stimulus and response.

To build social responsibility and flexibility while being assertive, ask yourself to answer the following two questions before speaking:

- "How will I look to others if I make this statement?"
- "How will others feel if I reply in this way?"

To grow flexibility while being assertive, use this challenge:

- "Instead of this obvious reply, what is another way to make my point?"

Using social responsibility while being assertive might require considering:

- "Is this course of action going to provide the best result for the greatest number of people?"

When Assertiveness Is Low

When a person's assertiveness is lower than scores in flexibility and impulse control, he or she may need to offset those strengths by strengthening behaviors in independence and assertiveness to increase his or her influence in the team's decision-making process.

Increase assertiveness and decrease impulse control by:

- Speeding things up by being less deliberative
- Trusting your intuition and speaking up much earlier in the conversation
  Increase assertiveness and decrease flexibility by:

- Forgetting the other options for a moment and stating your thoughts about the one under consideration

Other Assertiveness Tips

- A great way to start practicing assertiveness is to start telling everybody what you like about inconsequential matters. For instance, "I really like it when it rains late in the afternoon" or "I really like lots of oregano in my spaghetti sauce" or "I just love it when the bad guys in the movie get caught in the act!" So what?! No one is going to take issue with these preferences any more than they're going to get upset when you say, "I hate it when the ice cream in my cone is all soft and runny!" or when you declare, "I can't stand a bouquet that's mostly lilies." Again, who cares? But for someone who has never spoken up before and told other people what he or she likes and dislikes, practicing making these kinds of strong pronouncements can be great exercise!
- This kind of practice lays a strong foundation for then being able to say, "I really prefer that you call me instead of reply with an e-mail when I leave you a voice message" or "I really don't like it when I have to remind you that your weekly report is due by 3:00 on Thursday." An empathy challenge might simply phrase it a different way: "How do you think I feel when I have to hunt you down to get a report that's due every week at the same time?"

Assertiveness and the TESI

The Team Emotional and Social Intelligence Survey (TESI) uses concepts like, "Our team is more important than its members" and "We are honest with one another" to help teams move past the self-importance and turf protection mentality that undermine effective team performance and that are frequently expressed with inappropriate assertiveness. It takes every member's courage, honesty, and commitment to belong to a highly effective team. . . . But boy does it feel good to go to work when you do!

Assertiveness

Ramp It Up

Purpose

To help build assertiveness in those who are reticent. It will push them beyond their normal comfort zones and make them stretch their capabilities.

Thumbnail

40 to 110 minutes

Individuals in coaching identify areas in which they need to be more assertive and then select one specific situation from the list. To practice the skill, they then role play until they feel more comfortable. Their follow-on assignment is to be more assertive in two real-life situations. Team members identify lack of assertiveness issues that impact the group's effectiveness. They select the top two to three issues and role play to be more assertive. Their follow-on assignment is to take the learning back to the organization. The facilitator will need to be able to help more aggressive team members calm down so they use the skill of assertiveness with respect and so they model assertiveness effectively and respectfully to those who are not as assertive.

Outcomes

- Increased awareness of areas in which participants can be more assertive
- Overcoming barriers to being assertive
- Integrate the learning into their daily lives

Audience

- Intact team
- Individual working with a coach

Facilitator Competencies

Moderate to Advanced

Materials

Team

- Role-play handout to be created prior to group exercise from template provided
- Flip charts, markers, masking tape

Individual

- Ramp It Up Handout

Time Matrix

Activity	Estimated Time (Individual)	Estimated Time (Group)
Discuss assertiveness	10–15 minutes	10–15 minutes
Select areas and list barriers and possible remedies	5–15 minutes	20–35 minutes
Role play	15–20 minutes	20–30 minutes
Debriefing	10–15 minutes	15–30 minutes
Total	**40 to 65 minutes**	**65 to 110 minutes**

Instructions

Individual

1. As a coach, you should guide the participant through this exercise, helping identify areas for correction, discussing why some behaviors are ineffective, and implementing corrective strategies during the role play.
2. Discuss the concept of assertiveness and why a lack of assertiveness can be an issue in the workplace.
3. Give a copy of the Ramp It Up Handout to the participant. Work through each step with the participant.
4. Based on issues raised, offer to role play some scenarios with your client.
5. Review the assignment at the end of the handout.
6. Set up a time to meet again with the participant and review how the assignment went. Ask questions such as:
   - Which real-life situations did you select?
   - Were you able to be more assertive?
   - What was your comfort level while doing this?
   - What results did you get?
   - Will you do it again in the future?

Group

1. Prior to the exercise, identify those in the team who are considered to be assertive. You want the assertive people, not the aggressive ones. Ask them to help you with the exercise by sharing with the group their perspectives, techniques, and strategies.
2. With the group, discuss the concept of assertiveness and why a lack of assertiveness can be an issue in the workplace.
3. Ask participants to identify issues that impact the team's effectiveness and write what they say on a flip-chart page.
4. Ask them which of those issues listed in Step 3 may be impacted by a lack of assertiveness. Record the responses on another flip-chart page. Stimulate thought with the following examples of problems caused by lack of assertiveness:
   - A surgeon operated on the wrong body part because no one mentioned discrepancies between the documentation and the procedure that they noticed prior to the surgery.

- A company faced financial ruin partially because the people who noticed accounting irregularities did not speak up.

5. Have them discuss the benefits that could be achieved if team members were more assertive. Could problems be avoided or corrected sooner? Would morale improve because people would feel they had more of an impact on the organization?

6. List the barriers to being assertive on a flip-chart page. What stops people from being more assertive? Why do they hold back? Could they lack the skills to effectively express what they are thinking or feeling? Could they be afraid of repercussions?

7. Identify some ways to overcome the barriers. Do people need to enhance their communication skills, build confidence, or practice being assertive in a safe environment?

8. Tell the participants they will take turns role playing more assertive behavior. Ask them to form pairs and distribute the role-play handout.

9. Discuss with the entire group how everyone felt during the role plays.

10. Give the following assignment: Over the next two weeks, be more assertive in two actual work situations.

11. (*Optional*) Find a time after you have completed the assignment to review how it went with a partner or coach.

ROLE-PLAY TEMPLATE

Instructions for Facilitator

Based on the feedback from the team, select an issue similar to one from Step 3 of the team instructions and create a role play. If you are already familiar with the team's issues, you can select an issue yourself. Otherwise, you'll need to do some pre-session research to find an appropriate issue from which to create a scenario. The scenario should include elements similar to the following:

- Person A identifies a problem and brings it to the attention of someone at a higher level of authority—Person B.
- Person B is initially not happy to hear about the problem.
- Person A perseveres by asserting the benefits of addressing the issue sooner rather than later.

The following is the template to be re-created as a handout with the specifics added in for the participants.

Person A = Hunter
Person B = Jordan

There is a problem with _____*(problem area)*_____. Hunter notices it and is determined to make Jordan, the __*(title of person in authority)*__ aware of it.

Hunter:	Jordan, I'd like a few minutes of your time to talk to you about something.
Jordan (a little abruptly):	Yes, what is it? I really don't have much time.
Hunter:	This won't take very long.
Jordan:	Okay, let's hear it
Hunter:	I've noticed that __*(description of problem)*__

Jordan responds less than enthusiastically and doesn't seem to be very interested in hearing about this.

Hunter must convey to Jordan the benefits of addressing the problem now rather than waiting until later, when it will be harder to fix. He should let Jordan know that his concern is to help the organization be as effective as possible.

RAMP IT UP HANDOUT

1. Name a few specific situations in your personal or professional life when you have lacked assertiveness. It might be helpful to think of times when you regretted not speaking up.

2. Why did you lack assertiveness? What stopped you? Why did you hold back?

3. What are the barriers to being assertive? Do you lack the skills to effectively express what you were thinking or feeling? Are you afraid of repercussions? Were you conditioned as a child to be unassertive?

4. How can these barriers be overcome? Do you need to enhance your communication skills, build your confidence, or practice being assertive in a safe environment?

5. In which situations are you willing to be more assertive in your life?

Assignment

Over the next two weeks, in two real-life situations, act more assertively than you would have in the past.

Assertiveness

Dial It Back

Purpose

Help aggressive people move from aggressive behavior to assertiveness. This requires them to reduce the size of their normal comfort zone by restraining aggressive behaviors.

Thumbnail

50 to 80 minutes and follow-up assignment

A coach works with a client to identify areas in which the individual needs to be assertive rather than aggressive. They select one specific situation in which to practice dialing back the aggressiveness. To practice the skill, they then role play until the client feels more comfortable. The follow-on assignment is for the client to practice being assertive rather than aggressive in two real-life situations and then to discuss them with the coach.

Outcomes

- Increased awareness of the value of being assertive rather than aggressive
- Learning to be more aware of the intensity of aggressive behavior and dial it back so it can be expressed through appropriate assertive behavior

Audience

Individual working with a coach

Facilitator Competencies

Advanced

Materials

- Dial It Back Handout
- Paper and pen

Time Matrix

Activity	Estimated Time—Individual
Discuss assertiveness	10–15 minutes
Select areas and list barriers and possible remedies	15–30 minutes
Role play	15–20 minutes
Debriefing	10–15 minutes
Total	**50 to 80 minutes**

Instructions

1. Discuss the concept of assertiveness. Zero in on situations in which the client is behaving aggressively and wants to dial it back to an appropriate level of assertiveness.
2. Give a copy of the Dial It Back Handout to your client and go through all of the steps.
3. With your help, ask the client to reenact one of the situations listed in Step 1 and role play being assertive instead of aggressive.
4. Calibrate the tipping point between being assertive and being aggressive and help your client move back and forth between assertiveness and aggressiveness until the client sees he or she can choose to behave assertively whenever he or she wants. The calibration is set by helping your client become aware of factors such as the different

responses he or she receives when assertive rather than aggressive behavior is used.

5. Discuss how the client felt during the role play and which specific behaviors he or she had to change in order to accomplish the shift.

6. Give the client the following assignment: Over the next two weeks the client should commit to being more assertive rather than aggressive and practicing his or her new skills in two real-life situations.

7. Set a time for a follow-up meeting during which you and your client can discuss the results of the assignment.

DIAL IT BACK HANDOUT

1. In which specific situations in your personal or professional life have you been too aggressive? It might be helpful to think of times you regretted being overly forceful or times when people were obviously intimidated by you.

2. What do you do when you are being too aggressive? Do you raise your voice, use a condescending tone, or look angry and hostile?

3. How would you explain your aggressive behavior? Have you been angry? Do you want to win at all costs?

4. Explain what the barriers are to being assertive rather than aggressive. Do you lack the skills to effectively express what you were thinking or feeling? Are you afraid of appearing to be weak?

5. Describe how these barriers can be overcome. Do you need to enhance your communication skills, calm down, or practice being more assertive and less aggressive in a safe environment?

Assertiveness

Getting Your Point Across

Purpose

To practice different ways of communicating disagreement so that others will understand what you want, what you do not want, and why.

Thumbnail

35 to 40 minutes

In pairs, practice different styles for communicating disagreement. Then take time to understand which strategies are effective and why. In one-on-one coaching, the coach is the other person in the pair.

Outcomes

- Learn effective ways to be assertive
- Be able to disagree and still respect the other person's opinion

Audience

- Intact team
- Unaffiliated group
- Individual working with a coach

Facilitator Competencies ◯

Easy

Materials

- Getting Your Point Across Handout
- Pens

Time Matrix

Activity	Estimated Time
In pairs, practice different ways of disagreeing, taking time to reflect on the differences	15 minutes
As a group, discuss the learnings and apply to real-life situations	10–15 minutes
Individually write about a couple of challenges that require assertiveness and apply what was learned	10 minutes
Total Time	**35 to 40 minutes**

Instructions

1. Distribute the Getting Your Point Across Handout and review the "In Pairs" instructions.
2. Ask the group to form pairs and to complete the "In Pairs" section of the handout. Tell the pairs they will have approximately fifteen minutes to complete the role plays and pair discussions. Emphasize the need to follow the language patterns given in the models carefully.
3. After fifteen minutes, reconvene the entire group and discuss the questions in the Group Debriefing section of the handout.
4. After ten to fifteen minutes, conclude the group discussion and ask the participants to individually complete the Individual Activity section of the handout.

GETTING YOUR POINT ACROSS HANDOUT

In Pairs

Exercise 1

Working in pairs, make direct eye contact with the other person. While Person A speaks, Person B will listen, then reverse roles. In each of these scenarios, the one speaking should talk about a matter on which he or she has an opinion and state that opinion in no uncertain terms. For example: "When it comes to cutting back eligibility for overtime, the union is going to go ballistic!" Be conscious of how you are using your posture (body language) to convey this message. If you are congruent, your muscles will be more tense, your posture more angular and stiff, and your gestures will be more emphatic.

After Person A has spoken, Person B will reply by folding his or her arms across his or her chest, using a similarly confrontational tonality, and saying, "No, I disagree with you; that is not how I see this." Person B's body language will tend to mirror Person A's.

Notice how you feel, both when saying and receiving these messages. Record your observations; then switch roles and repeat. When you have each been in both roles, discuss the experience with your partner.

Exercise 2

Repeat Exercise 1, only this time Person B will stand in a comfortably relaxed posture, hands at sides, and briefly restate to the best of his or her ability what the other person has said. Then when you express your disagreement, begin with the word "and." For example, "I know you think the cut in overtime is unfair to the people who make the least money, AND I really disagree *about that* [instead of "with you"]; I'm sure there is another way for *us* to look *at* this."

Notice how you feel, both saying and receiving these messages. Record your observations; switch roles, and when you have both been in each position, discuss the experience with your partners.

Group Debriefing

Discuss how it felt to confront the other person.

- How did it feel when you were being confronted?
- Did changing the tonality and body language have much of an effect on your experience when you were receiving the communication? When you were delivering it?
- Do you feel more comfortable having rehearsed some basic assertive confrontational scenarios? Could you do this more effectively now in real life?

Individual Activity

Write about the experience and list two situations in which you will practice your new skills. Who are the specific individuals you will be disagreeing with? Describe how you anticipate they will respond, and then describe how you will respond to their response.

Independence

Virtual Decision Making

Purpose

To practice making decisions more rapidly and to understand one's own decision-making process and how it compares to those of others.

Thumbnail

25 minutes

Review the process for making good decisions quickly and consider its valuable as a business skill! Practice making quick decisions as initial questions arise. Acting with independence means that we can decide confidently when we have enough authority and enough information to do so.

Outcomes

- Practice rapid decision making in virtual, no-risk simulations
- Improve intuition

Audience

- Intact teams
- Unaffiliated group
- Individual working with a coach

Facilitator Competencies ◯

Easy

Materials

- Virtual Decision Making Handout
- Virtual Decision Notebook for each participant

Time Matrix

Activity	Estimated Time
Discuss independent and quick decision making	5 minutes
Individually work through handout and then discuss in pairs	15 minutes
Full group debriefing	5 minutes
Total Time	**25 minutes**

Instructions

1. Discuss the process of decision making, using intuition, and being able to act intuitively. When we talk about our intuition, we're referring to understandings we have that come from instinct, feelings, or some other internal awareness that creates a sense of "this is how it is," even though external evidence isn't gathered to support the awareness. People often refer to a "gut" sense. If they make a decision based on that gut sense or on a hunch, they are making an intuitive decision.

2. Distribute the handout and the notebook. Explain to the participants that as part of the ongoing exercise described in the handout that they will need to record information in their virtual decision notebooks.

3. Ask participants to fully work through all points in the handout and then form pairs to discuss results and considerations.
4. Bring the full group together to debrief. You might explore:
   - What was your most interesting observation?
   - What did you learn about your intuitive awareness in problem solving?
   - What event at work could you apply this process to first?

VIRTUAL DECISION MAKING HANDOUT

You are probably relatively clear about how much authority you have. Theoretically this is determined by your job description, but in fact it is determined by your ongoing relationship with your leader and other top decision makers. Independence is a critical skill in supporting your decision-making power because there will be plenty of times when you want or need to influence the people who are leading you. This certainly takes a blend of all the EQ-i skills, but self-regard and assertiveness stand out as first lines of support you may need to draw on to strengthen your independence.

In this exercise, you are encouraged to simulate making a variety of kinds of decisions early and often and to record brief notes on your thoughts about what you've decided to do and why. For example, you hear your boss talking about needing to fund some new tech support positions. Right away begin to guess at the optimal number, what skill and pay grade would be good, how soon you can bring them on board, and any other kinds of relevant decisions that will need to be made (whether you will be making them or not). Jot down your ideas, any thoughts or reasoning about why your initial thoughts seem to be the best decision at this point and stash it away.

Congratulations! You have made your first virtual decision. It's mostly intuition and guesswork at this point, but your job is to keep updating your observations every time you receive new information or have a new insight. Reality testing is also an important part of this exercise because you're going to follow your virtual decision through to the end, observing how it matures and develops to the final outcome. This is like a game you're playing, and one of the rules is that you have to update the simulation every time you obtain more information. You have to record your changes in your virtual decision notebook or you will not be able to learn nearly as much as you need to from your efforts. The value of this is that you will be able to compare similar kinds of decisions over the course of a year or more at some point, noticing when you had it right early on, when others had better decisions than yours and how they came about, as well as noticing how accurately your intuition was operating on your behalf.

If the decision does become your real responsibility, you will be far better prepared. If your boss keeps the responsibility, you may be able to offer useful suggestions to him or her. If a colleague has the responsibility and it's not appropriate to collaborate with him or her, it may be harder to obtain information for updates, but you can compare your process with the final result and whatever you can learn about how it matured to that end.

Be careful about kibitzing on other people's responsibilities, as this will not be appreciated, especially if the person feels that you are constantly second-guessing him or her! This is a private practice in independent decision making for your professional development.

Exercise 6.1. Independence

Independence

Cut the Apron Strings

Purpose

To move beyond uncertainty and into independent action. To surface the reason you have not been as independent as you want to be.

Thumbnail

25 to 45 minutes

Participants identify the characteristics of independence. They discuss when it is easy and when it is hard to be independent. Next, they explore their current environment. They determine how they can act more independently in the current environment and practice the new behaviors.

Outcomes

- Deeper understanding of the impacts of lack of independence
- Greater comfort level with acting more independently
- Commitment to select coaches to help them rehearse their practice of independence

Audience

- Intact team
- Unaffiliated group
- Individual working with a coach

Facilitator Competencies

Moderate to Advanced

Materials

- Cut the Apron Strings Handout
- Flip charts and markers

Time Matrix

Activity	Estimated Time
Discussion of independence	10–15 minutes
Examine current environment, including personal examples	5–15 minutes
Handout Steps 1–4	7–10 minutes
Debriefing	3–5 minutes
Total	**25 to 45 minutes**

Instructions

1. Lead a discussion about independence. Ask participants for the characteristics of independence and write their responses on a flip chart.
2. Ask when it is easy to be independent and record participants' ideas.
3. Ask when it is hard to be independent and record participants' ideas. Use the following examples to generate discussion if responses are few. Ask what could make it hard for them to think independently in the following situations:
   - Benefits accrue to you because you are favored by these people or groups (you're in the "in" crowd):

High school—the most popular person or clique

Work—the opinion leader, the best producer, the smartest one, the boss's favorite

Community—the one with the most influence and political clout

4. Clarify the current issues in the workplace. Ask, "What are some examples in which you do not believe people are acting independently?" Explain that they should not confuse contrariness with independence. Independence and rebellion are not necessarily synonymous. Ask, "What is the impact on the workplace?"

5. Ask them to think of specific behaviors that would make them more independent in the current environment. How could they exercise more initiative, be more self-directed or self-controlled? Ask them to share one of their examples if they feel safe and comfortable doing it. If no one volunteers, do not press it.

6. Distribute copies of the Cut the Apron Strings Handout, and ask participants to complete Steps 1 through 4.

7. Have them pair up with someone in the group and have each partner rehearse one of the scenarios they listed in Step 2 of the handout using the new behaviors they listed in Step 3.

8. Debrief:
   - Discuss how the rehearsal went and what they are willing to do to improve.
   - Ask them to identify someone they can ask on an ongoing basis to help them rehearse. Have them write that person's name in Step 5 of the handout.

CUT THE APRON STRINGS HANDOUT

1. Describe the environment (work, home, community, specific situation) you selected for this exercise.

2. List examples from your life in which it would benefit you to be more independent—have more initiative, be more self-directed or self-controlled, or less emotionally dependent.

3. Select one or two of the examples you listed above and identify at least one or two specific new behaviors you would like to be able to do that would express an increased level of independence.

4. If you did the things you listed, how would it affect your confidence? Your efficiency? Your relationships with the other people in your life?

5. Find someone who is willing to work with you as a coach on an ongoing basis and set up several weekly or bi-monthly meetings in which you commit to rehearse the new behaviors. Ask the person to help you develop and practice powerful, appropriate responses to those who would challenge your independence.

Emotional Intelligence in Action

Independence

Solitary Effort

Purpose

To have participants experiment with increasing their independence by doing some activities alone that they usually do with others.

Thumbnail

20 minutes

To create the feeling of being independent, participants select an activity to do alone from a list of activities they usually do, and prefer to do, with others. In the session, they fully visualize and act out mentally what it would be like to do the activity alone. To achieve the desired level of independence, they commit to put into practice in their lives what they visualized in the simulation.

Outcomes

- Develop a method to support you in acting more independently in the world
- Increase your confidence in your ability to interact effectively when you are alone

Audience

- Intact team
- Unaffiliated group
- Individual working with a coach

Facilitator Competencies ○

Easy

Materials

- Solitary Effort Handout
- Pens

Time Matrix

Activity	Estimated Time
List activities and select one	5 minutes
Visualization	10 minutes
Debriefing	5 minutes
Total Time	**20 minutes**

Instructions

1. Distribute copies of the Solitary Effort Handout and pens and review the handout with the group (or individual).
2. Ask everyone to complete Steps 1 and 2.
3. Have them visualize what it is like to do their selected activities alone. Ask them to close their eyes and take four deep, slow breaths. While their eyes are closed, read them the instructions in Step 3 of the handout. Play soft music in the background, such as the *Largo* CD from the Relax with the Classics® series (Various Artists, 1987). Follow copyright laws for playing recorded music.

4. Debrief the individual or team with the following questions:
   - Were you able to picture yourself performing the activity?
   - Did you feel some of the anxiety you might feel if you were really doing it?
   - Did you increase your comfort with the idea of doing it alone?
5. Ask them to choose a time in the next two weeks when they will actually do this activity alone. Advise them to take a little notebook or some 3-by-5 cards and jot down notes about their experiences.
6. If you are able to meet again, schedule a time to meet in two weeks to discuss how participants felt doing the chosen activity alone.

SOLITARY EFFORT HANDOUT

1. List activities you usually do, and prefer to do, with others. These are activities that take place away from home.

2. Select from the list above one activity you will do alone in the next two weeks.

3. Visualize yourself doing this activity alone. Imagine each of the steps from when you begin to get ready until after you return home. Begin by picturing yourself:
   - At home just before the activity.
     What are you wearing?
     What are you feeling?
     If you are feeling anxious about doing this alone, imagine taking someone with you who makes you feel more comfortable and secure.
   - Approaching this activity. For example, maybe you see yourself driving to the location and/or walking up to where the activity takes place. Notice the soundscape throughout your imagined adventure. Is there music playing in the car? Do you hear people's voices? How loud or close are they? What are they saying?
   - Starting the activity. If you feel stressed, take a few deep breaths and picture yourself smiling and confident.
   - Completing the activity.
   - Leaving the activity and returning home—still smiling and confident.
   - Returning home safely.

Independence

Going Along with the Group—Or Not

Purpose

To recognize the value of acting independently

Thumbnail

30 to 45 minutes

Review the applications of independence and discern best practices.

Outcomes

- Gain perspective on the value and application of acting independently
- Identify the factors that need to be balanced to achieve real independence

Audience

- Intact team
- Unaffiliated group
- Individual working with a coach

Facilitator Competencies ○

Easy

Materials

- Going Along with the Group—Or Not—Handout
- Flip chart and markers
- Pens

Time Matrix

Activity	Estimated Time
Discuss attached vignettes	10–15 minutes
Review examples of how they've applied independence in their own lives	10–15 minutes
Draft a 21-day development plan	10–15 minutes
Total Time	**30 to 45 minutes**

Instructions

1. Give the coaching client or the group the vignettes on the handout.
   - Ask them to explore how they see the exercise of independence, or lack thereof, in the examples.
   - Ask where they see healthy applications of independence and where the strategies are unhelpful.
   - Follow along this track in discussing group observations. Note that different individuals may see different applications of independence in the same vignette.
2. Ask them to discuss their own experiences with the application of independence.
   - Look for examples of both useful and unhelpful applications of the skill.
   - Work with the group or your coaching client to develop a list of criteria to consider in determining the best use of independence as a skill.

- In your discussion of the pros and cons of behaving independently, brainstorm ways to do so successfully and tactfully.

3. Invite each individual to work with a partner (if that fits the group dynamics; if not, do so alone) to draft a twenty-one-day development plan for increasing his or her own independence. This plan includes the specific new behavior each of them commits to undertake for the next twenty-one days. Examples of elements of the plan follow:
   - To decide on your own two days a week when and where you want to go to lunch instead of waiting for others in your office every day
   - To speak up to authority figures in your life to present your differing view when you disagree on an important point

4. Remind them to look at the nuances of the application of independence so their behavior is respectful and furthers organizational needs as well as their own.

5. Ask each person to make a commitment to change and report back to the group or a designated person in the group in twenty-one days.

GOING ALONG WITH THE GROUP—OR NOT—HANDOUT

Read these scenarios and talk about whether each way of expressing independence was helpful to the individual and to the organization.

Scenario One

A senior management official reports to a board that has been quite pleased with his timely and competent work. He seems to always exhibit a can-do attitude with them and reliably gets things done. It seems whatever they want, he can do, and he never complains. Needless to say, the board members were shocked when they received the results of a 360-degree assessment with statements from his staff showing they were about to mutiny. It turned out that the senior official took whatever the board wanted back to his staff and told them to do it, no matter what. It often meant unnecessary emergencies, late nights, and confusing assignments because they hadn't been thought through well enough. Now the board is wondering whether they can keep this employee.

Scenario Two

A few members of a seven-person team are disgruntled with their boss. The unhappiest person brought the group together to develop a list of concerns that they then decided to take to their boss's boss first, without talking to their immediate boss. One member of the team refused to go along with the strategy, even though his co-workers became very angry with him. He had only been directly assigned to the team for three years, but he'd been working in the field for fifteen years and just didn't agree that this was the right way to go about it. The other team members are going ahead, and the senior boss has agreed to meet with them.

Interpersonal Relationships

Investment in Friends

Purpose

To take personally reflective time to evaluate the value of friendships in life and set priorities for the future.

Thumbnail

45 minutes

Participants are guided to write about the roles of friends and friendship in their lives and then to discuss the value of friendships, the priorities they choose for how they are living their lives, and their related goals for the next year.

Outcomes

- Become aware of the role and value of friendships in their lives
- Set a realistic goal for the role friendships will have for them over the next year

Audience

- Intact teams
- Unaffiliated group
- Individual working with a coach

Facilitator Competencies ○

Easy

Materials

- Paper and pens

Time Matrix

Activity	Estimated Time
Explain exercise	5 minutes
Give writing instructions and time to write	15 minutes
Discuss	15 minutes
Goal-writing	10 minutes
Total Time	**45 minutes**

Instructions

1. Give participants paper and pens and tell them you will ask them to write about a few different items that will help them explore the role friends and friendship play in their lives. Emphasize that this exercise is intended to aid personal reflection and awareness; it is not to be used for judging oneself. It can help them make more personally satisfying decisions in their lives. Give them a few minutes for each of the topics. Watch, and when they stop writing and reflecting, move to the next question. Do not give them a handout with all the questions written out, as this can cause them to answer early questions in order to match the answers they think they should give for later questions.

2. Ask them to do the following:
   - First, ask them to write the heading "My Friends" and then list the names of friends who come to mind. Don't give them any further direction, this is for them to define and clarify. Give them a few minutes to write.
   - Second, ask them to write "Define Friend" and then write their own definitions. Their definitions can be as concise or detailed and differentiating as they wish. Give them a few minutes to write.

- Third, ask them to write the sentence stems below and to complete each of the statements:

  "Friends are important at work because…"

  "Friends are important in my personal life because…"

  "Friends are important in my whole life because…"

  "My best friends are 'best' because…"

  Give them a few minutes to write.

- Fourth, ask them to write "How I Prioritize My Life" on their paper and then write about how they feel about the time they allocate to friends, to work, to family, and to any other key parts of their lives. Encourage them to be realistic while also noticing whether their task lists with all the objective "to do's" ends up running more of their lives than they would prefer in the future. You can ask whether they get caught up in checking items off the list instead of playing or engaging with friends. Give them more time to answer this question than the others. You want to encourage reflective awareness.

3. Bring the group together for a discussion, working with the topics from their writing. Questions you might ask include:

- How did you define friends?

- Is the definition different for extroverts and introverts? Do Facebook or other social media friends count?

- Why are friends important at work, in your personal life, or overall?

- How do you feel about how you prioritize the time you give to friendship? Do you want to make changes?

- How much is enough? People often tend to think any good part of their lives should be bigger. Yet we all have twenty-four hours a day; it's a question of how we allocate our time.

4. You might also want to note that Interpersonal Relations, of which our friends are a major component, is a part of the Well-Being Indicator on the EQ-i$^{2.0}$, which is a recognition that there is a direct link between our friendships and our personal happiness. Ask for their thoughts on this connection.

5. Ask them to write about one more topic, "My Priority for Friendship for the Next Year," and to reflect on their goals for the next year. Remind them to be realistic. You don't want them to set themselves up to fail.

   Note: This exercise can be used well with Exercise 2.1 under Self-Actualization, where individuals create their 2% project and with Exercise 16.1 under Happiness/Well-Being.

Interpersonal Relationships

You've Got Good News

Purpose

To help participants increase their awareness of the power of affirming one another and recognize that interpersonal relationships deepen with positive interaction.

Thumbnail

50 minutes for Phase One; 80 to 110 minutes for Phase Two

This exercise consists of two phases that could be coupled for a half-day team-building experience if management will really commit to participate. In Phase One, team members work in small groups on exercises that focus on affirming one another. In Phase Two they work with management to identify and affirm the group's strengths and goals. The exercise can be limited to Phase One only.

Outcomes

- Feel the experience of group reinforcement and understand the ongoing power of reflection that occurs in our day-to-day interpersonal relationships

- Experience the power of focusing on strengths as a group and recognize how that strengthens effective interactions

Audience

- Intact team
- Unaffiliated group
- Individual working with a coach

Facilitator Competencies

Moderate to Advanced

Materials

- You've Got Good News Handout
- Paper and pens
- Flip chart and markers

Time Matrix

Activity	Estimated Time (Phase One)	Estimated Time (Phase Two)
Discuss the dynamics of group affirmation	15 minutes	
Prepare personal statements on strengths and goals	15 minutes	
Practice affirming goals	10 minutes	
Practice affirming goals	10 minutes	
Coach team members		20 minutes
Coach senior managers and supervisors; work up list of kudos		30 minutes
Managers and supervisors affirm the team together and discuss team goals in terms of future organizational direction		30–60 minutes
Total	**50 minutes**	**80 to 110 minutes**

Instructions

1. Discuss the dynamics of group affirmation, including the valuable effect that comes from receiving positive reflections from other humans in general; how the impact changes when you receive affirmation from people in your family, colleagues at work, and those with authority or prestige; and how powerfully it is magnified when it comes from *everyone* on your team.

2. Emphasize that the following exercises are designed to help the responders build the quality of generosity and enthusiasm in their responses. What they will be supplying and practicing is affirmation, not an evaluation of the person's chosen strengths or goals. Coach everyone to notice how team identification, along with understanding and respect for one another, grow as the exercise proceeds.

Phase One

1. Distribute paper, pens, and the You've Got Good News Handout.

2. Assemble the participants in groups of three; additional groups of four will work if there are one or two left over. Explain that the purpose of this exercise is to experience having a group of peers affirm what you believe (or want to believe) about yourself.

3. Review the handout, and get the groups started with Phase One by instructing each person to take up to fifteen minutes to write down three of his or her strongest, most valuable features and three of the goals that he or she would like to achieve over the next year (these can be personal or professional, but ones that he or she feels comfortable sharing in the group).

4. Instruct them to continue with Steps 2 and 3 of the handout.

5. Guide participants so they take up to ten minutes for affirming strengths and ten for affirming goals. Each person should participate in the small groups.

Phase Two

1. This exercise works best if you start with two separate meetings—one includes all members of the team and the second includes as many levels of the team's supervision as you can interest in the process. If you can persuade senior management to participate and listen to the team's

direct supervisors, it will build self-regard for the supervisors and provide better engagement, insight, and understanding for the senior staff.

2. First, have the coach/facilitator bring the team together and ask the members to discuss their strengths, their strongest contributions, and the key goals they want to achieve in the next year. The coach/facilitator will record this list on a flip chart.

3. Next, the coach/facilitator will meet with all the supervisors who will be participating in the team exercise and instruct them on the nature of the exercise. Be certain to emphasize that this experience is designed to be empowering rather than critical. Have the supervisors compile a list of the team's greatest strengths and accomplishments.

4. After these tasks have been completed, bring the two groups together and ask the supervisors to present the list they created. Next, have the team members share their lists and then guide the group in discussing their observations about each other's lists. The goal is to find everything positive and to discuss only that. Remember, *What you reinforce will be repeated!*

5. Finally, have the team present the goals they want to achieve in the next quarter/year or other selected timeframe, and ask the supervisors to be supportive with comments such as, "Yes, we can see you achieving those goals!" Have the supervisors list some of the reasons why they believe the goals are viable to the best extent possible. If a goal seems to be unrealistic, compliment the effort and work with a positive attitude to reframe it until it is viable.

6. Debrief by acknowledging the value of positive interactions and how they can enhance the interpersonal relationships within the group and, therefore, their effectiveness as a team.

YOU'VE GOT GOOD NEWS HANDOUT

1. Write down three of your strongest, most valuable features and three of the goals that you would like to achieve over the next year (these can be personal or professional, but ones you feel comfortable sharing in the group). Your list of three or more affirmative statements about your strengths might be something like: "I'm a good listener"; "I pay attention to detail"; or "I'm improving my handicap in golf."

2. The learner (Person A) will read the first affirmative statement to the other two people (Persons B and C) and both of them will smile encouragingly and say, "That's what we like about you!" enthusiastically. The purpose is to provide a person with a refreshingly congruent affirmation of him- or herself, so give the person a chance to absorb this feedback before going on to his or her next excellent quality. Now switch roles so that B and C can each have this experience.

3. Next, Person A reads his or her goals one at a time and, after each one, B and C respond with, "Of course you can accomplish that—I can see it now." (Give the person a chance to absorb this feedback before going on to the next goal.) Each of you will read your list of three goals and receive the affirmation from your two partners.

Interpersonal Relationships

Making New Friends

Purpose

To help people who are generally less outgoing feel comfortable beginning new friendships.

Thumbnail

25 to 30 minutes

Participants in this exercise will reflect on their own lives in order to compile a set of historical events that they will feel happy sharing with anyone.

Outcome

Increased comfort in making small talk and the beginning conversations that are the foundation of basic interpersonal relationships

Audience

- Individual working with a coach

Facilitator Competencies ○ ◑

Easy to Moderate

Materials

- Making New Friends Handout
- Pen

Time Matrix

Activity	Estimated Time
Fill out worksheet	15–20 minutes
Discuss	10 minutes
Total Time	**25 to 30 minutes**

Instructions

1. Provide the client with a pen and the Making New Friends Handout.
2. Share with the client that making new friends is in part a function of our conversation skills and that this exercise will help him or her develop enough skills to begin and sustain a conversation with just about any-one who is the least bit inclined. Tell your client he or she will be gathering information from four areas of life and will learn how to share it and that the ways in which he or she listens can encourage other people to share similar stories about their lives.
3. Review the handout and ask the client to complete it.
4. After the client finishes, discuss his or her answers and reactions.

MAKING NEW FRIENDS HANDOUT

Reflect on your life and on the significant events that generally made you who you are. Some of the events will have been happy and successful; some of them will have been less so. Some of them you will enjoy sharing with everyone; some of them you may not want to discuss until you know someone can respect and appreciate that part of your life. Just remember that you have the power to choose whatever you share in the adventure of making new friends!   Write a brief note to remind yourself of at least four of these stories and record them below under the heading of Life Changes.

Life Changes

Now reflect on some background aspects of your life: where you were born and grew up, what your parents did for work, your favorite subject, sport, or hobby in school, how many siblings you have, whether you were the oldest, youngest, and other pertinent information. List the four or five of these facts that are the most fun for you to talk about under the heading of Background Events.

Background Events

Emotional Intelligence in Action, Second Edition. Copyright ©2012 by Marcia Hughes and James Bradford Terrell. Reproduced by permission of Pfeiffer, an Imprint of Wiley. www.pfeiffer.com

Exercise 7.3. Interpersonal Relationships

In the Goals category, list two or three things you would like to achieve: finding a branch in your family tree, improving your golf or bowling or bridge score, getting your baby to sleep through the night, and so on.

Goals

In the next section, list a few details about each of your two most favorite vacations.

Vacations

Now you have a great foundation of supporting material to use when engaged in conversation with someone. If it ever feels like the conversation is dragging, you'll be ready to move it forward.

In addition to having these conversational tools, you will recognize that the act of talking with and listening to someone well has its own power. New friendships start most frequently when people feel that they are being listened to, not talked at! They start when you begin discovering what's interesting about another person by listening and paying attention to him or her in a way that demonstrates your respect. We all get talked at plenty. Finding someone who is patient enough and caring enough to be interested in the details of our lives is rare. We naturally want people such as these to be friends. Yet to have a balance in your friendship, you must reciprocate and tell others about yourself as well.

Starting conversations involves what is sometimes referred to as "small talk." This means very general topics of interest that affect everyone and generally benefit or offend us all equally. That's why the weather is always a great place to start. But from there it could lead to something that happened on one of the person's favorite vacation or to an event in your childhood.

Humans have a natural inclination to swap stories. It's a way of relating our lives together, so if you tell a story about how the weather affected your vacation, be quiet for a little while, and pretty soon someone else will probably tell you about how the weather affected something in his or her life. If silence doesn't encourage someone to talk, then perhaps gently ask a general question. Then whatever sort of an answer he or she gives you, repeat it back by paraphrasing, and he or she is almost guaranteed to give you more details. For example:

"That happened to me one time when I was down in Georgia. Worst thunderstorm I've ever seen in my life. We were about an hour out of Atlanta and the rain was up over the wheel covers."

"You're kidding, 'the rain was clear up over the wheel covers'?"

"Yep, and we had to drive about two miles an hour for a mile or better until the water finally went down."

Well, you get the idea.

Interpersonal Relationships

Fun and Meaningful Relationships

Purpose

To develop a keen awareness of the significant value that respectful relationships contribute to the workplace.

Thumbnail

70 minutes to 1 hour and 25 minutes

Plumb the depths of the meaning of healthy interpersonal relationships and the gifts they can bring.

Outcomes

- Expand awareness of interpersonal relationships
- Develop recognition of healthy goals and boundaries for intact teams, whether in the workplace, community, or nonprofits
- Lay a foundation for expanding the skills of developing and maintaining robust interpersonal relationships

Audience

- Intact teams

Facilitator Competencies

Moderate

Materials

- Flip chart and markers
- Paper and pens

Time Matrix

Activity	Estimated Time
Discuss the value of developing interpersonal relationships that emphasize respect and regard	10–20 minutes
The team defines interpersonal relationships, lists pros and cons, and lists considerations	15–20 minutes
Discuss strategies for maintaining relationships	10 minutes
Create an action plan	15 minutes
Go around the room for reflections	20 minutes
Total	**70 to 85 minutes**

Instructions

1. Lead the group in a discussion about the value of developing compassion and regard for one another, and then note how this can extend to others within the organization or community.
2. Discuss the meaning of interpersonal relationships.
   Healthy interpersonal relationships in the workplace mean taking time to listen to one another, to care that John's daughter is in ballet, that Bill's son just enlisted, that Sarah's mom went into a nursing home. It's covering for Tom so he can go to his friend's graduation from rehab, and it's helping Mary brainstorm the contents of her first presentation to the board and helping her get past her nervousness. The more in touch the members of an organization are, the less likely the chances of workplace violence, as well as many other possible challenges.

Sexual harassment is a big concern in our workplaces and is always inappropriate. Some are concerned that if we develop our interpersonal relationships, it can lead to sexual harassment. If that is a concern with your group or organization, work with them to understand the difference between respectful regard and sexual harassment.

3. Have the group:
   - Develop its own definition of healthy interpersonal relationships. As they brainstorm, write the components on a flip chart.
   - List the pros and cons of strengthening their interpersonal relationships. Help them be honest. For example some personalities and/or values don't mix well. That's Okay.
   - Discuss considerations such as respecting boundaries, timing, and cultural differences.

4. Discuss what it takes to maintain valuable interpersonal relationships outside the workplace. Ask questions such as "What challenges do you experience in some of your valuable relationships because of work demands?" "What do you do to maintain the relationships?"

5. Have the team create an action plan that applies to the team as a whole and has defined check-in times to ascertain their commitment and progress toward enhancing interpersonal relationships.

6. Ask each person to reflect on the work of the team in this exercise and what it means to them individually. Go around the room and ask each person to share his or her thoughts.

Empathy

Recipe for Influence: Curiosity and Compassion

Purpose

Clients learn a focused and easy strategy for building influence by expressing empathy.

Thumbnail

50 minutes

Experience building understanding about the power of influence and the awareness of a strategy for expressing empathy that will expand influence. Demonstrate and practice in pairs.

Outcomes

- Build skills in expressing empathy
- Recognize elegant ways to engage emotions to more effectively influence others

Audience

- Intact teams
- Unaffiliated group
- Individual working with a coach

Facilitator Competencies

Moderate

Materials

- None needed

Time Matrix

Activity	Estimated Time
Discuss the importance of and ways to exercise influence	10 minutes
Present and demonstrate the formula	10 minutes
Practice the formula in pairs	15 minutes
Debrief with full group/team and ask for a commitment to apply	15 minutes
Total Time	**50 minutes**

Instructions

1. Discuss with your group/team or coachee the many ways in which they
   need to be effective at influencing people. Influencing is needed for
   employee management and motivation, for moving people from no to
   yes, and to gain buy-in or be persuasive in many other forms of engagements. To build this awareness:
   - Ask when was the last time they tried to "make" someone do some-
     thing. Ask them to describe what happened and how successful it was
     in the long run. You're likely to hear them say that, even if people are
     direct reports, leaders exercise their success through influencing.

- Note that whenever one is negotiating or seeking to resolve a conflict, the goal is to influence others to move from no to yes.
- Persuasion requires people feeling that you are credible and have useful information for them.

  People are much more likely to follow the advice of someone when they believe that person has his or her best interests in mind. We reflect that positive interest by letting people know that we understand and care about who they are. To do this requires demonstrating empathy. Explain that this exercise will help them build influence by expanding their skills in extending empathy.

2. Explain that empathy is exhibited by paying attention to someone and then reflecting back that you have noticed what is important to him or her and that you care. The formula is: Curiosity + Compassion = Empathy. You can practice this with a client by asking with curiosity about something you recognize he or she cares about; when you do this, you are role modeling to your client a process you'll next ask him or her to do. For example, "You are involved in a big project with your team; how is it going?" Wait for the response and listen attentively. Then reflect back, "You are excited about the potential of this project making a big difference for the whole team, but worried about whether there are enough staff to get the job done in time. I can tell you really are invested in success!" Now suggest a way that your participant can apply influence, such as by saying something like, "I know it adds some time up-front, but how about taking time with each team member to ask how he or she is doing and what you can do to support his or her effectiveness? I've found that when people feel that you care and are paying attention, they are motivated to work more quickly. Also, you might discover ways to easily provide assistance."

3. Now ask your participants to form pairs and trade off applying this strategy for expressing empathy and building influence to something really going on in their lives, whether it's at work or at home. What's important is that it's being applied to a real situation. Experiencing empathy authentically through this formula will help build the desire to use it later. Instruct the pairs to focus first on one person for five minutes and then to trade roles. Explain that you'll debrief when you bring everyone back together again.

4. Bring your participants back together and ask about their reflections. Deliberately discuss some of the applications of empathy they discussed and emphasize the power of this strategy by talking about the potential long-term benefits they can achieve. Ask for commitment to using this strategy by asking each person to turn to a neighbor and name two times in the next week when he or she will use this strategy for building influence through effectively expressing empathy.

Empathy

Connect Feeling with Meaning

Purpose

To build empathy skills by recognizing the importance of listening and responding to what is actually being said.

Thumbnail

35 to 40 minutes

The participants will work in pairs to practice and gain understanding of applying empathic skills through a scripted reflective exercise. Individuals work with their coaches.

Outcome

Gain understanding of a specific reflective strategy that can build their connection with others and reduce conflict

Audience

- Intact team
- Unaffiliated group
- Individual working with a coach

Facilitator Competencies

Easy to Moderate

Materials

Prepared flip chart (see instructions, Step 3)

Time Matrix

Activity	Estimated Time
Summarize empathy and describe exercise	5–10 minutes
In pairs, one person at a time talks about an uncomfortable situation—the other person reflects using the model phrases, then reverse roles	10 minutes
Group debriefing	10 minutes
Second step optional: Repeat with pleasant situation	10 minutes
Total	**35 to 40 minutes**

Instructions

1. Describe the skill of empathy. Emphasize the importance of paying close attention to the other person. Many people think they are good at this, but are not. Such participants are likely to be lax in their efforts.

2. Ask group members to form pairs; the coach pairs up as the other partner when the exercise is used with an individual. In each pair, one person will tell the other about an uncomfortable situation at work in which he or she was involved. The person listening will help him or her explore and validate the experience by reflecting both the emotions the person is feeling and the reasons he or she is feeling them.

3. Instruct the respondent to use the basic "You feel ＿＿＿＿＿＿＿ because ＿＿＿＿＿＿＿" model (which you should display on a flip chart). Respondents can also adapt the model to provide variety and increased accuracy with remarks such as, "Wow, that must have felt ＿＿＿＿＿＿＿. It's so ＿＿＿＿＿＿＿ when people behave that way."

4. Explain that the goal of the respondent is to facilitate the speaker's exploration of the situation by reflecting the feelings he or she experienced and what gave rise to them. *The respondent should not attempt to solve the problem for the speaker!* All the respondent is doing is providing the speaker with a mirror in which to see his or her behavior so he or she can gauge how to change it if a different result is desired.
5. Tell the pairs to begin.
6. After five minutes tell them to reverse roles.
7. Debrief the exercise with the group using questions such as:
   - Which was harder to identify, how the person was feeling or why?
   - How did your partner respond when your reflection was highly accurate for both the feeling and the meaning?
8. (*Optional*) Now repeat the same exercise, using a positive and happy situation (again preferably from the workplace).

Empathy

Mixed Emotions

Purpose

To give participants the opportunity to recognize that many emotions arise when someone is having a strong response to a situation and expand their skills to be empathic when this occurs.

Thumbnail

60 minutes

The participants consider two situations and undertake to become aware of the complex emotions someone else is feeling. They grow their understanding of how different points of view affect someone's emotional responses.

Outcomes

- To gain an understanding of how, when a person has particularly strong feelings, he or she is often experiencing a composite of several emotions
- To recognize how much different points of view affect a situation

- To expand participants' ability to be empathic when talking with friends or colleagues while going through complex situations

Audience

- Intact team
- Unaffiliated group
- Individual working with a coach

Facilitator Competencies

Easy to Moderate

Materials

- Mixed Emotions Handout
- Paper and pens

Time Matrix

Activity	Estimated Time
Read the first scenario and discuss	25 minutes
Read second scenario and record possible feelings	15 minutes
Discuss insights and feelings as a group	20 minutes
Total	**60 minutes**

Instructions

1. Distribute pens, paper, and the Mixed Emotions Handout.
2. Ask participants to work in pairs on the first scenario. If there is an odd number of participants, the last group can contain three. Have them read the handout and proceed with the exercises as indicated.
3. After twenty minutes give them a five-minute warning, and five minutes later ask them to all begin working on the second scenario, which they will do independently.

Emotional Intelligence in Action

4. After ten minutes give them a five-minute warning, and five minutes later ask the participants to discuss their experiences as a group. The following questions may be helpful:

- In Scenario One, who had the most responsibility for improving communications?
- In Scenario Two, how might Linda's relationship with Randall have influenced the way he understood the changes in his life and how he felt about them?

MIXED EMOTIONS HANDOUT

In real life, emotions are often bundled together, sometimes with confusing contradictions, and they certainly are interpreted according to our view of a situation. Learning to recognize the implications that someone's perspective has on his or her responses, as well as the complexity of feeling multiple emotions, will greatly increase your ability to be empathic.

When you are in a conversation with someone, you can often best demonstrate your empathy by reflecting back the two critical parts of the message he or she is trying to communicate, namely the meaning and the feeling. As the situations in our lives become more and more complex, we often find ourselves adrift in a puzzling array of emotions. These feelings are chemical and electrical responses occurring in several different locations within our bodies, so they don't always announce themselves in precise words that tell us what they mean. Accurate reflection promotes clarity.

Scenario One: Ships in the Night

The Story

Imagine that your college-aged daughter leaves a message on your home answering machine saying that she has Friday off and she'll be driving home for the weekend. You expect her about noon. She arrives at dinnertime with a girlfriend, and they stay only long enough to change clothes, as they are going to the grand opening of a new dance club. They get in about three o'clock in the morning and then sleep until eleven the next day.

They go out shopping and catch lunch at the mall, getting home in time for dinner, when at last you get to talk. It's a very interesting discussion, but you have expensive tickets for a play you've been waiting to see for months, and by the time you return home they are out again. They get up when you are at church and have already left for the long drive back by the time you get home. She leaves a note saying, "Thanks, it was great to see you—I had a wonderful time." How do you feel?

Instructions

Working in pairs, take five to ten minutes to discuss how the parent could have reached out to the daughter to let her know what was going on with him or her better at the critical points during the weekend. Put yourselves in the role of being close friends of the parent. The value of talking with close friends is that they can help us contextualize what we're going through by reflecting what they hear us saying and how they sense we feel. A good listener can serve as a multidimensional mirror for us, showing us parts of ourselves that are out of view or out of focus. One of you role play being the parent; the other be the friend talking with the parent about this scenario. Write an abbreviated list of the feelings the parent had and why in the first column below.

Now do the same thing for the daughter. Reverse the role play so that whoever was the parent last time is now the friend; the friend in the last role play is now the daughter. Discuss how you could have responded more empathically to your parents and still had the good time you were looking forward to with your best friend. List the feelings the daughter had and why in the other column.

Parent's Feelings and Why	Daughter's Feelings and Why

Here is one possible set of feelings for the parent:

After hearing her message on the answering machine you feel warm and happy and have a strong feeling of anticipation. When she's not home by three o'clock Friday afternoon, or by four o'clock or five o'clock, you feel increasingly anxious, stressed, and nauseated. When she arrives, you feel tremendously grateful and relieved, but when you realize she has a friend with her, you feel hurt and a little disappointed. This grows worse

Emotional Intelligence in Action, Second Edition. Copyright ©2012 by Marcia Hughes and James Bradford Terrell. Reproduced by permission of Pfeiffer, an Imprint of Wiley. www.pfeiffer.com

when she leaves immediately. By the time she gets home at 3 a.m. the next morning, you feel downright angry and used because you know she'll sleep in . . . which she does. When you finally get to see her at dinner, you feel eager and grateful to hear what she has to say, but part of you is still fuming.

Although you've been looking forward to seeing the play ever since you bought the tickets, now you wish you didn't have to go so you could spend more time with your daughter. You have a hard time paying attention because you worry that you're losing contact with her. When you leave for church in the morning you feel crestfallen, knowing that she'll probably be gone when you return. On reading the note, you feel proud of how grown-up she is and how thoughtful it was to write a nice note, but then you feel angry about how she seemed to avoid you, and then you become anxious thinking about her on the long drive back to school.

Discuss your observations in comparison with this possible rendition. Notice how your empathy for the different points of view grows. Now tell the daughter's story from her point of view from when she leaves the phone message.

Scenario Two: Complex Feelings

Instructions

Filling in the blanks as this scenario unfolds will help you recognize the complex emotions Randall and Joe felt. Working independently this time, list some of the ways that Randall might have felt and why. There are many possibilities, so provide at least two in each of the response patterns below. Use extra paper or the back of the handout if necessary.

Randall was a junior in high school in September of 2001 and was deeply upset by the World Trade Center bombings, as were all his classmates and their families.

He felt _____, because _____.
He also felt _____, because _____.

[*Example:* He felt *furious* because *Americans shouldn't ever be attacked on their own soil!* He also felt *scared* because *he never thought that this could happen.*]

In order to deal with some of the anger and helplessness they felt, he and his friend Joe put together a plan to graduate first semester in their senior year and join the Marines. They worked out at the gym a lot together,

Emotional Intelligence in Action

hung out with the local recruiter, and carefully studied the materials they were given about life in the Corps. Now Randall felt _____ because _____. Joe, who had always been recognized as a natural leader, felt _____ because _____.

Randall's birthday wasn't until August, so he would not be old enough to join the Marines without his parents' permission at the semester break, and they weren't about to let him go. When it came to this, he felt _____, because _____.

Joe was old enough, and his mother was unable to influence him to stay in school and go to college, so he left according to their plan and had everyone's attention, receiving much admiration from his classmates during the last several weeks before it was time to go. This left Randall feeling pretty _____ because _____. Joe, on the other hand, was feeling quite _____ because _____ _____. He left for basic training the day after New Year's.

Joe's younger sister Linda started calling Randall frequently after Joe left, and they often talked for hours. It wasn't long before they started dating. About a month before Randall's birthday they learned that Joe had gone into combat; in his first firefight he had killed someone who was later identified to be a civilian.

Using a descriptive pattern similar to the model that follows, describe Randall's developing understanding of the world and how it must have felt as he moved through these stages of his life.

At first he felt _____ because _____ _____. Then he felt _____, _____, and _____, because _____ _____. Now he feels _____ because _____ _____.

Similarly, describe Joe's developing understanding of the world and how it must have felt as he moved through these stages of his life.

Even though this seems like a formula (which it is), you can still tell a pretty good story if you fill in the blanks creatively from an empathetic point of view.

Emotional Intelligence in Action, Second Edition. Copyright ©2012 by Marcia Hughes and James Bradford Terrell. Reproduced by permission of Pfeiffer, an Imprint of Wiley. www.pfeiffer.com

Exercise 8.3. Empathy

Share your reflections on this process with the group.

Emotional Intelligence in Action

Empathy

Do as the Empathic Do

Purpose

To promote more meaningful connections with key people in your life.

Thumbnail

60 minutes

Working with a coach, each individual discusses the value of focused listening and how to understand another person's reality. The client will choose a specific relationship in which he or she wants to strengthen his or her connection using empathy, create a reminder card, and practice the new behaviors.

Outcomes

- Increased ability to hear what others are saying and understand what they really mean
- Enhanced capacity to respond effectively

Audience

- Individual working with a coach

Facilitator Competencies ◑

Moderate

Materials

- Do as the Empathic Do Handout
- 3 x 5 cards
- Pens

Time Matrix

Activity	Estimated Time
Value of listening discussion	20 minutes
Practice paraphrasing the meaning	15 minutes
Practice reflecting the feeling	20 minutes
Create practice card	5 minutes
Total	**60 minutes**

Instructions

1. Give the client the Do as the Empathic Do Handout, which contains a case study.
2. Ask the client to read the case study; then ask these questions:
   - Have you every experienced or observed a similar situation?
   - Does the case study solution seem actionable? Does it seem as if it could be implemented?
   - Do you think something that simple could make a difference? If so, how? If not, why not?
3. Now have the client focus on his or her situation. Ask the client to select one or more of the relationships in his or her life in which he or she wants a more meaningful connection.
4. Discuss what is lacking in that relationship currently and ask the client how the other person(s) might perceive it.

5. Ask the client to review his or her current schedule and behavior patterns and decide when in the day it will be most efficient to engage with this person(s) and give him or her the time and attention that focused listening requires.

6. To help your client learn the powerful value that paraphrasing gives to communications, compose some model statements to practice paraphrasing until he or she feels comfortable. Suggest that your client use the following types of introductions as a way to help get the hang of it: "So you're telling me. . . . " "What I hear is that you want (need). . . . " "Okay, it sounds like. . . . "

7. Have your client practice suggesting how others feel about what's happening, using patterns like, "And that leaves you feeling pretty. . . . "Wow, you must feel . . . about that." "And so naturally you feel kind of. . . . " Reassure the client that if someone doesn't feel the specific way suggested, the person will usually correct the suggestion by describing his or her actual feeling more accurately.

8. Tell the client that if he or she needs help remembering, make a card on which the new behaviors are described clearly and briefly, including who specifically the client will be practicing with and the times he or she has committed to use the new behaviors.

DO AS THE EMPATHIC DO HANDOUT

Case Study Points

- Executive manager has great leadership skills and believes she really cares about her employees.
- Employees think she is a talented manager, but they are troubled by her seeming lack of interest in them. It's beginning to affect morale.
- She is a very task-focused person and she spends her commute to work thinking about the things that need to be done that day. Since the only thing on her mind when she gets to work is getting those things done, when she arrives at work she makes a beeline to her office. She doesn't take the time to check in or touch base with her staff. She often forgets to even say hello.
- The manager becomes aware of the impact of her behavior on her employees when she receives the results of a 360-degree assessment. Subsequent discussions with her staff help her understand how they feel and how they would prefer to be treated.
- She and her coach devise a simple strategy for her to connect with her people to let them know she values them. They created a pocket card with the following reminders:
  - Stop to greet people, make eye contact, and call them by name.
  - Ask what they're working on and how its going. Stop and listen to the response!
  - Ask if there are any problems I can help with.
  - Paraphrase what I've heard and "guess" about how they're feeling— "Sounds like you're feeling skeptical about this." (Having a long list of feeling words will be helpful. Merely saying "You feel sad, mad, or glad" every day will quickly wear extremely thin.)
- She reads the card two or three times a day and rehearses the behaviors mentally at these times:
  - In her office parking lot before getting out of the car
  - Right after she gets back from lunch
  - Toward the end of the day when she will occasionally make a brief round for "Good-byes"
- Taking the time to be other-directed helped her connect with her employees and positively impacted morale.

Emotional Intelligence in Action

Social Responsibility

*Focus on Something Bigger
Than Yourself*

Purpose

To emotionally connect with a big topic that matters to all humans and connect that awareness to the value of appreciating who we are as people and to being successful at work.

Thumbnail

15 minutes in advance; 25 to 45 minutes in session

Show an inspirational YouTube video clip or movie clip on a topic bigger than what the individuals work on daily. Each person writes emotions he or she felt when watching the video, then all participants discuss what it means to focus on bigger topics and how that can help them be better employees and people.

Outcomes

- Expand awareness of the value of caring about something bigger than oneself
- Connect the value of that awareness to being more effective employees and more of the persons they want to be

Audience

- Intact teams
- Unaffiliated group
- Individual working with a coach

Facilitator Competencies

Moderate

Materials

- Paper and pens
- Capability to play YouTube or movie clip and the link to the clip or the video

Time Matrix

Activity	Estimated Time
Prior to Exercise: Select YouTube or movie clip	15 minutes (could take longer)
Show the clip; participants write emotions	10–15 minutes
Discuss	15–30 minutes
Total Time	**15 minutes in advance; 25 to 45 minutes in session**

Instructions

1. Prior to using the exercise, select a YouTube or movie clip about a big project designed to help accomplish significant social change that everyone can relate to. Be sure to select something that will engage your coachee, team, or group emotionally. You can search YouTube and find videos on topics relevant for your clients, such as Thank You from Habitat for Humanity, which is focused on everyone having a simple and warm home; the Golden Rule, with a demonstration of the value of treating one another well; or Lemonade Day, which emphasizes financial literacy and entrepreneurial awareness for children. Be sure you

Emotional Intelligence in Action

have the equipment and audio capacity to show the video. If you are using a movie clip, be sure to comply with relevant laws. The clip should be about three minutes long.

2. Show the video clip prior to having any discussion. Then give everyone paper and pens and ask them to write three to five emotions they felt while watching the video clip. If people get stuck, show it again; that will deepen their experience and their awareness of their own emotions.

3. Guide a discussion on what it means to focus on something bigger than yourself because it's a social topic or project that benefits members of society who are in some way disadvantaged. Whether the area of concern, such as adequate housing, is something people work on at work or simply care about as human beings, noticing what they care about and why helps give their lives purpose. Invite discussion on:

   - The value of caring about something bigger than oneself
   - How taking time to experience and express a bigger focus at work is relevant to being productive team members and employees
   - How it feels to be altruistic and to express caring about others
   - Other topics the group wants to discuss

   Ask whether they would like to make a commitment to paying attention to big topics regularly and make plans to continue the process if that is a goal.

4. (*Optional*) Stretch goal: Facilitate a process in which the group takes on a project, such as painting houses for the elderly, for a day. Follow the activity up with a discussion on how doing this work supports their engagement as employees and as members of their own community. Be sure to include emotional awareness by discussing how participants feel and why.

Social Responsibility

Reflect the Best

Purpose

To shift the participants' primary focus and frame of reference away from themselves and onto the people around them.

Thumbnail

50 to 65 minutes

Participants take the time to shift their attention from the problems and deficiencies of the workplace to the resources that are currently present and available to support the people and their enterprise. This exercise draws from the theory and practice of appreciative inquiry. The facilitator must be able to model sincere appreciation and assist participants in dealing with any discomfort that this unfamiliar orientation might arouse.

Outcome

Participants will have a direct experience of the ways in which they can influence their own emotional states in the direction that will facilitate building stronger and more integrated socially responsible relationships.

Audience

- Intact team
- Unaffiliated group
- Individual working with a coach

Facilitator Competencies

Moderate

Materials

- Reflect the Best Handout
- Flip chart and markers
- Pens and paper

Time Matrix

Activity	Estimated Time
Give background on social responsibility	5 minutes
Step 1 and discussion	10–15 minutes
Step 2 and discussion	10–15 minutes
Step 3 and discussion	10–15 minutes
Group discussion of beliefs and values	15 minutes
Total Time	**50 to 65 minutes**

Instructions

1. Provide pens and paper.
2. Give participants a brief explanation of social responsibility and what makes it such an important quality in the workplace.
3. Distribute the Reflect the Best Handout.
4. Have the participants work through the first three steps of the exercise in pairs. Take ten to fifteen minutes for each step, including a short period for discussion.
5. For Step 4 have the entire team work together. Additional discussion time will not be necessary.

REFLECT THE BEST HANDOUT

With your partner, do your best to notice and comment on only the positive aspects of the workplace and your relationships with the others who make up your organization.

Step 1

First discuss how unusual an assignment this is and share your thoughts and feelings about undertaking this rather curious kind of communication in the workplace.

Then each person acknowledges at least three different positive things about the physical structure of your work environment that you appreciate. For example, the office is comfortable and attractive. These need to be sincere appreciations, not cleverly disguised ways of avoiding the unfamiliar and possibly uncomfortable positive orientation required by the exercise. In other words, saying, "Well, at least it doesn't smell like sewage" would not be an acceptable appreciation—unless of course it did last week and they just recently fixed the problem.

Step 2

The next step is to acknowledge to each other at least two things you appreciate about upper management.

Step 3

Now acknowledge at least one thing you sincerely appreciate about each of the other members of your team or work group.

Then begin to acknowledge the things you genuinely appreciate about your partner in this exercise. When someone offers you an appreciation, your *only* response will be to say, "Thank you."

Step 4

When we are able to consciously manage our beliefs, it is easier to improve our attitudes. When we pay attention to those attitudes and notice how we are approaching the *present* activity in our day, it is easier to manage our emotional states. When we are feeling safe, optimistic, respectful, and so on, then managing our behavior is a much simpler task and it is easier to be intentionally supportive and appreciative of the others around us, *and* our efforts begin to generate virtuous (rather than vicious) cycles in the workplace environment.

Now the whole team together discusses the following four beliefs to see whether they would be generally acceptable to the team. Be sure to explore the possible costs, downsides, and changes that would be required to adopt these beliefs and list the upsides in one column and downsides in another.

1. Simply by being alive, all people possess intrinsic value and a unique way through which they share their value.
2. There is a real bottom-line payoff in taking a little extra time to care for others.
3. Today I'm going to do my best to leave people feeling more resourceful than I find them.
4. It is good for me to give sincere praise generously. (This means looking long enough to find what is genuinely praiseworthy.)

Now fill in the list for each of the four beliefs above, noticing the pluses and minuses for the team adopting these beliefs.

Upsides	*Downsides*
1.	
2.	

Upsides	*Downsides*
3.	
4.	

Now agree to spend the rest of the day doing your best to reflect the best in everyone and see how your team blossoms!

Bonus

Some tips for managing *your* emotional state include making eye contact with the people you encounter and smiling before greeting them with a welcoming comment in a friendly tone. This is about changing your behavior, which you *can* consciously control, in order to positively affect your own emotional state (and that of others).

Social Responsibility

Who Do I Work for?

Purpose

To give participants the opportunity to explore the many expectations/demands that they experience as social beings.

Thumbnail

60 minutes

Participants explore the kinds and numbers of social expectations that they experience and how to determine what the appropriate balance is.

Outcome

Experience significant insight into the different kinds of pressures and the different kinds of rewards that we experience as social beings.

Audience

- Intact team
- Unaffiliated group
- Individual working with a coach

Facilitator Competencies

Moderate

Materials

- Who Do I Work for? Handout
- Paper and pens

Time Matrix

Activity	Estimated Time
Give background on social responsibility and hand out materials	5 minutes
Ask participants to read and answer questions	40 minutes
Debriefing	15 minutes
Total	**60 minutes**

Instructions

1. Distribute pens, paper, and the Who Do I Work for? Handout.
2. Ask participants to read the introduction and questions and write their responses in the space provided.
3. After approximately thirty-five minutes, inform the group that they will begin to debrief in five minutes.
4. Debrief the exercise for the remaining fifteen minutes using questions such as:
   - What did you discover as you began to list all of these expectations?
   - Were the expectations of some aspects of society more concrete than others? For instance, how do you know what your community expects of you?
   - When discussing your own expectations of yourself, did you include things such as income, health, status, self-actualization, and so forth?

WHO DO I WORK FOR? HANDOUT

To some extent we all serve some constellation of different social groups, and each group has its own expectations about what behavior constitutes an appropriate balance between acting out of self-interest and fulfilling our social responsibility. With all of these competing demands, how do you determine the right balance?

Social responsibility relates to how big a part of the world we undertake to serve. On whose behalf do you choose to employ your creativity, skills, and efforts? Are you attempting to climb the corporate ladder and be a superstar at the top? Do you discipline your behavior and tailor your communications to achieve the best that you can with your team? Respond to the following questions to explore your beliefs and feelings about social responsibility.

1. How many different kinds of expectations do I attempt to meet on behalf of the organization (or customer base) that provides my income? (Be sure to consider such things as time, skills, relationships, and so forth.)

2. In what ways are they expecting me to be productive in the workplace?

3. What is the full range of compensation and rewards I receive for my efforts in the workplace?

4. How many different kinds of expectations do I attempt to meet on behalf of my family? Consider such areas as emotions, leadership, education, discipline, morality, and so forth, along with the more obvious areas of finances, recreation, and nutrition. Discuss these expectations both in terms of the people who live under the same roof as well as those of your extended family.

5. What is the full range of rewards I receive for my efforts in the family?

6. How many different kinds of expectations do I attempt to meet on behalf of my community? Consider constituents and interests such as churches or spiritual development, schools, arts, health care, law enforcement, service groups, political parties, recreation and so forth.

7. What is the full range of rewards I receive for my efforts in my community?

8. How many different kinds of expectations do I attempt to meet on behalf of myself? (If we have no identification with some component of the social fabric—for instance Little League baseball—we won't feel or attempt to meet any expectations from that arena, so to some degree self-interest plays a role in all areas covered thus far. Instead of considering any more expectations placed on us from the outside, here is where you can explore how much you personally feel called to contribute to each of the aspects of your society.)

Exercise 9.3. Social Responsibility

Social Responsibility

The Value of Volunteering

Purpose

To gain perspective on the value of volunteering and how it benefits many parts of one's life.

Thumbnail

65 to 80 minutes and follow-up

Learn about social responsibility and its relationship to emotional intelligence. Participants reflect on their experiences of volunteering in the past and for a short time commit to a new volunteer activity. Use this exercise to help the participants understand the connection between volunteering and organizational performance as well as personal well-being. Requires follow-up.

Outcomes

- Expand awareness about the value of social responsibility
- Learn at a personal level, through conducting a volunteer activity, how this connects many different areas of one's life

Audience

- Intact team
- Unaffiliated group
- Individual working with a coach

Facilitator Competencies ◯

Easy

Materials

- None needed

Time Matrix

Activity	Estimated Time
Discuss social responsibility and why it's important personally and to the organization. Note the connection with volunteering	10–15 minutes
Discuss ways each individual is volunteering	10 minutes
Commit to one new volunteer activity for 21 days	15 minutes
Reflect	10 minutes
Follow up 21 days later	20–30 minutes
Total Time	**65 to 80 minutes**

Instructions

1. Discuss social responsibility and why it's important to the organization and to each of us personally. Note the connection with volunteering. Refer to the description of this skill in Part Two of this book.
2. Discuss the ways individuals are currently volunteering if they are. This can be done one-on-one with your coaching client, with the whole group, or in pairs, depending on the size of your group. If you do it in pairs, bring them all together afterward to discuss key points as a group.

3. Ask each person to commit to one new volunteer activity he or she will initiate and continue over the course of twenty-one days.
4. Bring the group together again after twenty-one days to discuss their experiences from the activity and how these affected their engagement with their organization. Also discuss what the activity meant to them personally.

Problem Solving

When Problems Become Conflicts

Purpose

To understand the use of emotions at the individual and team levels to positively influence problem solving when the situation escalates to conflict.

Thumbnail

65 minutes

Participants first evaluate problems they have been involved with that escalated into conflict. They identify the positive and negative emotions that were involved in the situation at the individual and team levels. In small groups they consider the individual skills of the EQ-i$^{2.0}$ and TESI to identify the skills most useful for responding effectively to conflicts. Additional time for taking the assessments in advance of approximately thirty minutes for facilitator and thirty per participant. (Different skills from other assessments can be substituted.)

Outcomes

- Become aware of positive use of emotions at the individual level for resolving complex problems and conflicts
- Become aware of positive use of emotions at the team level for resolving complex problems and conflicts

Audience

- Intact teams
- Unaffiliated group
- Individual working with a coach

Facilitator Competencies

Advanced

Materials

- When Problems Become Conflicts Handout
- Flip-chart paper, easel, and markers
- Pens
- Masking tape

Time Matrix

Activity	Estimated Time
Discuss instances of problem solving escalating to conflict	15 minutes
Distribute handout with list of EQ-i$^{2.0}$ and TESI skills and work in small groups of 3 or 4 to address points on handout	30 minutes
Come together and discuss as a whole	20 minutes (could be more depending on number of groups)

| *Optional:* Ask participants to take EQ-i and TESI in advance | *30 minutes your time;* 30 minutes per participant; potentially 60 minutes more per person if a private debriefing on the EQ-i results will be provided for each person |

Note: Certification is required to use either of these assessments. You should also consider adding in a one-hour debriefing in advance on the EQ-i results for each person individually. Be sure that each person knows he or she will receive the EQ-i results confidentially.

Total Time   65 minutes

Instructions

1. Lead a discussion about problem-solving situations that turned into conflicts because something was avoided or not handled effectively. Using practical examples from your team, group, or coachee, guide your participants to evaluate their examples, seeking to understand interactions at the individual and the team level:

   - What interactions or events caused the problem to escalate to a conflict?
   - How did the people involved engage emotionally with one another throughout the problem-solving process? How did they use emotions negatively? How were emotions used positively?

   Note: Don't let them talk only about difficult or negative emotions and behaviors. Look for signs of emotional awareness, empathy, reality testing, optimism, and other useful engagement of emotions to solve problems. This is an excellent opportunity to build recognition of the power of managing emotions and engaging to accomplish results that couldn't happen absent the skillful use of emotional engagement. Your participants may find they use their emotions better than they thought, which is likely to give them energy and confidence to expand on their skills.

2. With this awareness of emotions, problem solving, and conflict resolution in mind, show them a list of the individual skills addressed as a part of the EQ-i$^{2.0}$ and the team skills addressed by the TESI. Ask them

to consider which skills are called upon to accomplish effective problem solving, especially when the situation has escalated to conflict. Give them the When Problems Become Conflicts Handout and ask them to work in small groups to identify the key emotional intelligence skills that support problem solving and conflict resolution and ask them to identify one or two reasons why they selected each skill. Also ask them to write one or two ways to apply each skill. Give each group a flip-chart page and markers and ask them to write their answers on the page to present to the full group when they come back together. (If you are using this in an individual coaching session, have your coachee write the answers on the handout and then explain his or her answers to you.)

Note: You can substitute a handout with the skills of any other assessment you are using.

3. Bring everyone together and ask each small group to present their thoughts and then discuss the issue as a whole group. Ask what they have learned that they will use the next time they are engaged in difficult problem solving or conflict.

Note: The article "Building Your Team's Conflict-Resolution Skills with Emotional and Social Intelligence," by Marcia Hughes (Hughes, Thompson, and Terrell, 2009) includes many concepts and tips that you can use to support this discussion in working with conflict with teams.

While a case could be made for all of the skills being relevant, likely skills to be named in the individual component of the presentations are:

- Problem Solving
- Self-Regard
- Emotional Self Awareness
- Assertiveness
- Impulse Control
- Empathy
- Social Responsibility
- Optimism
- Flexibility

Optional: Give the EQ-i and TESI assessments to all participants and arrange an individual debriefing for each person on his or her EQ-i results. This should be done prior to the exercise if possible, although it can be a follow-up.

WHEN PROBLEMS BECOME
CONFLICTS HANDOUT

1. Consider the skills of the EQ-i$^{2.0}$ and the TESI listed below. Identify the skills that are called upon to accomplish effective problem solving, especially when the situation escalates to conflict. Notice how individual and team skills influence each other.

   • Choose a minimum of two individual and two team skills. For each skill you choose, identify one or two reasons as to what makes that skill appropriate and effective. Then write one or two ways to apply the skill.

2. Post your flip-chart page and be prepared to present your responses to the full group.

Skills of the EQ-i$^{2.0®}$
Self-Perception Composite

Self-Regard: To accurately perceive, understand, and accept oneself

Self-Actualization: To strive to achieve personal goals and realize one's potential

Emotional Self-Awareness: To be aware of and understand one's emotions and to express them to others

Self-Expression Composite

Emotional Expression: To openly express one's feelings both verbally and nonverbally.

Assertiveness: To effectively and constructively express one's emotions and oneself

Independence: To be self-reliant and free of emotional dependency on others

Interpersonal Composite

Interpersonal Relationships: To establish meaningful and close relationships

Empathy: To be aware of and understand how others feel

Social Responsibility: To identify with and be a responsible and cooperative member of one's social group

Decision Making Composite

Problem Solving: To effectively use your emotions while solving problems of a personal and interpersonal nature

Reality Testing: To objectively test one's feelings and thinking against external reality

Impulse Control: To effectively and constructively control impulses and strong emotions, including anger

Stress Management Composite

Flexibility: To adapt and adjust one's feelings and thinking to new situations

Stress Tolerance: To effectively and constructively manage stress and strong emotions

Optimism: To be positive and to look at the brighter side of life

Happiness/Well Being Composite

Happiness: To feel content with oneself, others and life in general. To have the ability to feel satisfied. This is a general indicator of all emotional intelligence.

Skills of the TESI®

Team identity: Measures the level of pride each member feels for the team as a whole, and how much connection members feel to the team

Motivation: A competency that measures the team's internal resources for generating and sustaining the energy necessary to get the job done well and on time

Emotional awareness: Measures how well team members accept and value one another

Communication: Provides information on how well team members listen, encourage participation, share information, and discuss sensitive matters

Stress tolerance: Measures how well the team understands the types of stress factors and the intensity impacting its members and the team as a whole

Conflict resolution: Measures how willing the team is to engage in conflict openly and constructively without needing to get even

Positive mood: Measures the positive attitude of the team in general as well as when it is under pressure

Problem Solving

Emotions Affect Decision Making

Purpose

To understand that emotions affect decision making and to use a strategy to gain positive results.

Thumbnail

45 minutes

Participants discuss the impact that emotions have on decision making including research by leading neurologist Antonio Damasio. They role play a situation calling on them to ask specific questions to address the role of emotions as decisions are made.

Outcomes

- Understand that emotions affect decisions
- Practice using guided questions to manage the emotional processing and gain effective decisions

Audience

- Intact teams
- Unaffiliated group
- Individual working with a coach

Facilitator Competencies

Advanced

Materials

- Emotions Affect Decision Making Handout

Time Matrix

Activity	Estimated Time
Discuss the effect of emotions on decision making	10 minutes
Distribute handout and review questions	5 minutes
In pairs, conduct the role play	15 minutes
Debrief	15 minutes
Total Time	**45 minutes**

Instructions

1. Discuss the effect emotions have on decision making using information such as the following:

    Well-known neuroscientist Antonio Damasio clarifies the interface between decision making and emotional intelligence in *Looking for Spinoza* (2003). He writes that emotions play a role in decision making in many ways, both subtle and more apparent, "practical and not so practical, all of which make emotions not merely a player in the process of reasoning, but an indispensable player" (p. 145).

    According to Damasio, "Every experience in our lives is accompanied by some degree of emotion and this is especially obvious in relation to important social and personal problems. Positive or negative emotions and their ensuing feelings become obligate components of our social experiences." As we accumulate experiences over our lives, we categorize the experience, including the outcome of the solution, in terms of emotion and feeling. We then draw on this database as we make decisions creating future outcomes.

Emotional Intelligence in Action

2. Ask the participants to share their thoughts and experiences regarding how their emotions affect their decision making. You are guiding them to build their personal awareness.
3. Give participants the Emotions Affect Decision Making Handout and review the key questions they are to follow in their role play.
4. Organize them in pairs with each person agreeing to play one of the roles. Give them six minutes, then have them shift roles and conduct the exercise again.
5. Bring the group together to debrief what they learned. Ask each of them to commit to a specific part of his or her life where he or she will use this process.

EMOTIONS AFFECT DECISION MAKING HANDOUT

In the following role play you will work in pairs to experience a problem scenario. The "leader" is aware of the impact that emotions have on effective decision making and that he or she is presenting a considerably emotional situation to the "senior supervisor." Therefore, the leader intends to ask questions that help the supervisor be aware of his or her emotions and to work through them to a positive outcome. At the same time, the leader knows he or she will have emotional responses as well during the discussion and intends to be aware of those emotions and manage them well throughout the discussion.

With this in mind, the leader will ask the following questions during the conversation. The first question in each pair is an internal one for the leader to ask him- or herself; the second question is to be asked directly to the supervisor. At some point in the discussion, show the supervisor this list and discuss the fact that you are using this list to have a more informed conversation.

- How am I feeling? / How are you feeling?

- Why am I feeling this way? / Why are you feeling this way?

- How do I want to feel? / How do I want you to feel?

- What can I do or say to reach my goals? / What can I do or say to help you reach your goals?

Any of these questions can be repeated throughout the process to improve success.

Role Play

Leader

As the team leader you have just learned that the project your team has been working on for the last two months has been reprioritized to the bottom of the list and your team will be starting a new effort from scratch as of right now. This new project seems to have less relevance, and it will be harder to measure success. You have scheduled a meeting with your most senior supervisor to give him/her the news and get things started in the new direction.

Senior Supervisor

As the most senior supervisor on a critical project your team has been working on for the last two months, you feel hopeful that in the meeting your boss has just requested you will finally get the scheduling data and specifications you have been asking for all week. When you arrive at the meeting, your boss actually has something different to discuss. Notice your feelings, how they change, how much they change, and whether or not you feel more or less encouraged as a result of the new information your team leader provides.

At one point your boss will show you a list of questions that he/she believes will help you and the team be more successful when you apply them. Explore whether there is a way you can use this model to help you, your team leader, and team work more effectively together.

Emotional Intelligence in Action, Second Edition. Copyright ©2012 by Marcia Hughes and James Bradford Terrell. Reproduced by permission of Pfeiffer, an Imprint of Wiley. www.pfeiffer.com

Problem Solving

Using the MasterSolve Model©
for Teams

PURPOSE

To give participants a real-life emotional intelligence problem-solving experience in which they receive real feedback about their success.

Thumbnail

65 to 85 minutes

A team will work with a sample problem taken from a situation they share. They will be required to put their differing information together to find the full nature of the problem and then to collaborate on the solutions.

Advanced Version: Facilitator introduces a new set of variables and changes that occur after the first solution has been implemented, and the team must craft a second response to the new problem. This can be repeated up to four times, continuing the fifteen-minute deadline for each new iteration.

Outcomes

- Experience a "real-life" problem-solving scenario and get "real" feedback

- Expand awareness of problem-solving capabilities
- Learn to combine the joint dynamics of considering the problem well while meeting a deadline
- Boost problem-solving skills

Audience

- Intact teams

Facilitator Competencies

Moderate to Advanced

Materials

- MasterSolve Model for Teams Handout
- Sample Scenario for facilitator
- Problem scenarios prepared for each participant (see Step 3 and Sample Scenario)
- Timer or clock
- Flip chart and colored markers

Time Matrix

Activity	Estimated Time—Group
Brief introduction to problem solving	5–10 minutes
Participants read and discuss the MasterSolve Model	10 minutes
Develop a general hypothesis on the nature of the problem	5–10 minutes
Read the case scenarios and collaboratively plug data into the problem-solving formula	20 minutes
Create response	15 minutes
Debrief	10–20 minutes
Total	**65 to 85 minutes**

Instructions

1. Give a brief introduction to problem solving.
2. Distribute the MasterSolve Model© for Teams Handout. Read and discuss the model.
3. Distribute the problem scenario sheets (prepared in advance by the facilitator). Each participant receives the same background statement and the unique information about the problem of which he or she alone is aware. This creates a puzzle effect, so the group has to work together to know the whole problem. If your group is too large for the situation, you can break into subgroups and have multiple groups solve the same scenario. The problem scenarios should be prepared in advance by the facilitator. A sample situation is included at the end of the instructions. Review it to ensure you understand the type of problem to which you will apply the process.
4. Instruct the participants to read their handouts; tell them that they will then be working together to solve the problem, given the information that they have. Instruct participants to develop a group hypothesis about the general nature of the problem.
5. Direct the group members to work collaboratively to plug all the facts into the MasterSolve formula to create a detailed model of the problem. Strictly enforce a twenty-minute deadline on this step.
6. Based on the model, have them create and report their potential solutions to you in fifteen minutes or less! Failing to respond in that amount of time results in a fatal crisis (created by the facilitator and relevant to the particular problem scenario developed for the team— the buyer withdraws the offer, the airplane departs without them, etc.). The solutions must directly reflect how they have used the steps of the model.
7. Debrief the process. Questions you might ask to get the discussion started include:
   - How well were you able to integrate all the facts to develop the whole picture of what is happening?
   - What was your process and experience as you applied Step 2 of the model to create awareness of the factors leading to a good solution?
   - What was the impact of the strict time rules? How is this like situations at work when it seems you are working on tight deadlines? How

would you suggest meeting those deadlines while staying creative and resourceful?

Sample Scenario

Note to Facilitator: When creating the problem sheets, the top part of each sheet should contain the same scenario. The bottom part of each sheet, however, should contain a different role so that only the person playing that role receives that information.

Success with this exercise requires that you use a factual situation similar to those your team struggles with. The following sample would work for a group of city or county employees. If your team is a different type of group, you will need to create a more relevant problem scenario.

In this example, the information under Cozy Coffee vs. National Biggie would appear on the top of each of the handouts that you create.

SAMPLE SCENARIO: COZY COFFEE VS. NATIONAL BIGGIE

Scenario: Your team works for the City of Hope and Well-Being. Despite your very positive name, which city leaders bestowed in a surge of zest and optimism, the city's tax base has been declining. Actually, it's an up-and-down affair. The city looks pretty good, but appearances can be deceiving. It's a struggle to keep up the good appearance. Now there's an opportunity to add a reliable storefront presence on Main Street, but there seem to be as many citizens against bringing in a national brand franchise coffee shop as there are for it. The city's team in the Planning and Zoning Department is convening to discuss the issue and attempt to provide leadership to turn dissension into a collaborative and positive result for the city.

Each staff member has focused on the dynamics and positions of one particular group (Cozy Coffee, National Biggie, neighborhood groups, college students, other downtown businesses, or the city council itself). Now you are coming together to understand the different perspectives and to problem solve so the city council can provide the leadership that is so important. National Biggie would like a zoning variance to remodel the store to meet its preferred format, but they could make it work without the variance. Therefore, the only explicit control the city has is in the decision, which will be made by the director of the department, is on whether or not to issue the variance the national chain franchise coffee shop has requested. The team includes the people from the planning department who have met with each of the different groups as described below.

....

Note to Facilitator: The bottom part of each sheet would then contain one of the following role descriptions, with each team member receiving a different sheet.

....

National Biggie

You have spoken with representatives from National Biggie and found them very eager to open a store in your downtown area. The location is selected, the franchise is ready to be signed. They think it should be a cakewalk for this to come to fruition. The citizen opposition is annoying, but they don't want to deal with it. After all, National Biggie is not inclined to take time building relationships with the community. You know this attitude will be at their peril, but you're not sure who to even talk to about the situation in this big, faceless corporation.

Cozy Coffee

Cozy Coffee has been a true neighborhood coffee shop and deli for thirty years. All the locals hang out there; the college kids love it and convene for late evening discussions; and you and your spouse drop by on Sunday mornings for the croissants and coffee while you read the paper. They've begun talking of expanding and adding an Internet café, but now their plans are on hold because they fear the influence of a large chain just down the block. They've heard about what happens to local businesses when a national chain comes in, and they're concerned that Cozy Coffee will be put out of business. They see it as the beginning of a negative trend, so they're certainly not in favor of allowing National Biggie to take over. Is there any leadership in this town to protect local charm and integrity? You are concerned about what you can raise on their behalf as a member of the local government planning team.

Neighborhood Groups

You have been contacted by a local neighborhood group, Vigorous Defense, which is up in arms about this potential insult to the charm and quaint aspects of your beautiful little town. They have asked you to fight this! They are sure you should help them as a part of your planning role. You want to be helpful but balanced. They argue that if this chain comes in, they are sure that many of the city's locally owned businesses are in peril, not just Cozy Coffee, and they are fighting this tooth and nail! You know they do have a good point.

College Students

Students at a nearby college tend to congregate at Cozy Coffee before, between, and after classes. They don't buy much, and may even be taking seats from paying customers. You have met with this group of enthusiastic students, and are concerned about whether they will be well organized or just introduce a chaotic element. However, your children both attended this college, and they have also protested to you that it's wrong to let a national chain take over what is one of the last sacred spaces on the planet. It's a cozy, beautiful community, and the students assure you that they are not going to sit idly by and see it destroyed. You have heard that the students are going to stage a protest at the council hearing and also attempt to fight the chain with a nationwide boycott. You know there's a lot of agitation on campus about this topic right now, and these small, private colleges do have many moneyed backers.

Downtown Businesses and the Chamber

Representatives of other downtown businesses and the Chamber of Commerce have bent your ear on this topic. They are a small but progressive group, determined to make sure the town turns into the city it's supposed to be. They are tired of the unreliable tax base and of businesses either closing or always being close to shutting their doors. They believe that the presence of a national chain is the beginning of good times. What's the fuss? Just let the coffee shop go in. Merchants you've spoken with want you to talk to the planning and zoning decision-maker and make sure the right decision is made. Progress is critical, they say, or the town may just whither and die.

City Manager

This is a tricky situation. The Council is split about whether the new coffee shop should go in or not. There are so many questions. About half the Council members want to build this community into a new progressive city. The other half wants the cozy community we've always had. Some of the Council members are confused about who should be making the decision. You will have to work with them to help them understand the limits of their authority.

Exercise 10.3. Problem Solving

329

MASTERSOLVE MODEL FOR TEAMS HANDOUT

The Collaborative Growth MasterSolve© Problem-Solving Model*

1. Construct your best understanding of the problem:
   - Decide what specifically you want to have happen
   - Observe in detail what is happening instead
   - Notice at what point(s) in the sequence does/did the problem appear
2. Concretize the solution in sensory based descriptions:
   - When the problem is completely resolved, what difference will people
     - See: (stable customer list, smiling faces, etc.)?
     - Hear: (familiar voices calling in regular orders, optimistic remarks and pleasant tonalities in the workplace)?
     - Feel: (safe and welcomed on arriving at work)?
     - Know: (interpersonal relationships are key to our productivity)?
3. Determine what is preventing the desired result from occurring now.
4. Brainstorm and record as many possible solutions as you can in an appropriately limited amount of time.
5. Analyze and test options to find the best one and rank order them, noting possible advantages and drawbacks for each one.
6. Confirm that the best one will produce the sensory-based results generated in Step 2; if not, make whatever adjustments are needed.
7. Enact the chosen solution and carefully monitor what happens.
8. Re-enter the new data into this process and run it again if the desired result hasn't yet been achieved.

---

*This exercise was created by and is used with the permission of Collaborative Growth, LLC.

Emotional Intelligence in Action, Second Edition. Copyright ©2012 by Marcia Hughes and James Bradford Terrell. Reproduced by permission of Pfeiffer, an Imprint of Wiley. www.pfeiffer.com

Problem Solving

Win-Win Negotiating

Purpose

To apply the key criteria for win-win negotiation that promote good problem solving.

Thumbnail

60 minutes

The team will explore four criteria that lead to win-win negotiation and practice them in a role play.

Outcomes

- Learn the four criteria for effective negotiation
- Recognize the many ways these can be used in effective problem solving, whether considered a negotiation or not

Audience

- Intact team
- Unaffiliated groups

Facilitator Competencies

Moderate

Materials

- Win-Win Negotiating Handout

Time Matrix

Activity	Estimated Time
Discuss connection between problem solving and negotiation and four key criteria	30 minutes
Role play application of the criteria	20 minutes
Debrief	10 minutes
Total	**60 minutes**

Instructions

1. Help the group understand that there is a close connection between problem solving and negotiation. Excellent examples of good problem-solving skills are those addressed by Fisher and Ury (1981) in *Getting to Yes*. The authors emphasize interest-based bargaining and break the key skills into four parts:
   - Separate the people from the problem
   - Focus on interests rather than positions
   - Expand options
   - Develop criteria

   Discuss these criteria with the group. Ask for an example of a good problem-resolution strategy. When has the strategy worked for them? When hasn't it? Does the strategy include the use of these skills?
2. Divide the group into pairs and distribute the Win-Win Negotiating Handout.

3. Have the pairs role play the problem scenario/negotiation in the Win-Win Negotiating Handout and use these four skills. You can change the scenario, if desirable, to a problem they are more likely to encounter.
4. Bring the group back together to discuss the role play and their application of the four criteria. Reflect on the value of following these options when they are problem solving.

WIN-WIN NEGOTIATING HANDOUT

In the following role play, do your best to apply the four criteria for problem solving as articulated by Fisher and Ury in *Getting to Yes* (1981):

1. Separate the people from the problem.
2. Focus on interests rather than positions.
3. Expand options.
4. Develop criteria.

Scenario

One of you is the boss, one an employee. The employee is asking for a 5 percent raise in salary. The boss would like to give the raise but is somewhat offended that the employee, not the boss, raised the issue and defensive and embarrassed that the profitability of the company just doesn't allow the raise at this time. The employee is aware that he or she has brought more customers in than anyone else in the last two years. The employee really likes the company, but his or her kids are going to college soon, and he or she just must have more money.

Both people would both like this to resolve well, but don't want to compromise, initially at least. They are hopeful and apprehensive at the same time.

REFERENCE

Fisher, R., & Ury, W. (1981). *Getting to yes: Reaching agreement without giving in.* Boston, MA: Houghton Mifflin.

Problem Solving

Let's Cover Our Bases

Purpose

To provide a logical problem-solving method that incorporates the four major thinking components.

Thumbnail

60 to 165 minutes

Using the Emergenetics® model, participants will solve a real-life problem with which they are struggling. (For more information on Emergenetics, see www.cgrowth.com; and www.emergenetics.com.)

Outcomes

- Expanded portfolio of problem-solving tools
- Increased confidence in problem-solving skills
- Better understanding of thinking styles

Audience

- Intact team
- Unaffiliated group
- Individual working with a coach

Facilitator Competencies

Moderate to Advanced

Materials

- Let's Cover Our Bases Handout
- Flip charts and markers

Time Matrix

Activity	Estimated Time
Define problem to be solved	20 minutes
Discuss Emergenetics model	10 minutes
Use the model to create solutions	15–120 minutes
Debrief	15 minutes
Total	**60 to 165 minutes**

Instructions

1. Ask participants to identify some problems they are having with the goals they need to achieve within their team or workplace. List these on a flip chart.
2. Have them select one from the list to work on in this session.
3. Ask, "How do we know it is a problem?" "What are the indicators?" Record their responses on the flip chart.
4. Distribute the Let's Cover Our Bases Handout and ask participants to read about the Emergenetics® Problem-Solving Model. Give them ten minutes.
5. Discuss the Emergenetics® Problem-Solving Model. (For background information on the model, refer to the websites referenced under the Thumbnail.)
   - Discuss the thinking modes—Conceptual, Analytical, Structural, and Social.

- Discuss how different behaviors can impact the group dynamics and task assignments.
6. Discuss solutions to the problem by examining the contributions of each aspect of the Thinking Attributes segment of the model in order—Conceptual (concepts and ideas), Analytical (logic, purpose, and strategy), Structural (control and status quo), and Social (people and relationships). Capture these ideas on the flip chart.
   - Ask the participants to use the Conceptual part of their brains to brainstorm solutions to fix the problem. Their behaviors will guide them in doing this.
   - Have them use the Analytical, Structural, and Social parts of their brains to evaluate the potential solutions.
   - Select the best solution and develop implementation steps.
7. In some cases, two sessions will be needed to complete the solution design, with an assignment to be completed by the participants between sessions. Here are some sample assignments:
   - Market research
   - Cost research
   - Find a politically well-placed champion for the solution. Assertiveness behavior influences how it will be done and by whom.
8. Debrief the process by asking questions such as:
   - What differences did you notice when you worked with the seven different parts of the model? Which ones did you relate to best?
   - Does the model address all aspects of solving a problem?
   - How can you incorporate the awareness of these seven components into your work or personal lives?
9. (*Optional*) In Step 4, with the entire group, use the Conceptual part of the model to brainstorm solutions to fix the problem. Then divide the group into three teams—Analytical, Structural, and Social—and ask each team to evaluate the potential solutions using their assigned attribute. Have each group prepare a flip-chart presentation to share its work with the group. Reconvene and have each team report back to the entire group. Select the best solution and develop implementation steps.

LET'S COVER OUR BASES HANDOUT

The Emergenetics® Problem-Solving Model*

This handout provides a summary of the seven components of the Emergenetics model:

Conceptual	Expressiveness
Structural	Flexibility
Analytical	Assertiveness\
Social	

Thinking Attributes

Conceptual—Concepts and Ideas (Brainstorm Solutions)

- What is the ideal vision of success for this situation?
- How can we not just fix the problem but improve the situation so the problem does not reoccur?
- What would we do if we were working with a clean slate with no restrictions or boundaries?

Analytical—Strategy and Logic (Evaluate Proposed Solutions)

- Will it resolve the problem?
- What is the strategic value?
- What are the benefits?
- What are the costs?
- How do we research this? What data do we gather?
- Have we analyzed it enough?

Structural—Control and Status Quo (Evaluate Proposed Solutions)

- Who will be in control?
- What's the timeline?
- Will it move us outside of our comfort zones?
- Will this be too much of a change for us?
- What are the rules and guidelines for what to include?
- What is the implementation process?

---

*This information is used with the permission of Morgan Browning, president, Emergenetics International.

Social—People and Relationships (Evaluate Proposed Solutions)
- Who will be involved?
- Are enough people involved?
- Are the right people involved?
- How will others be affected?

Behaving Attributes

Behavior attributes are expressed in terms of being in the first, second, or third segment of the behavioral continuum. The first third (1/3) means that a person demonstrates the behavior to a very small degree. The second third (2/3) indicates a moderate display of the behavior, and the third third (3/3) is a definite and strong manifestation of the behavior.

Expressiveness—The Amount of Social Interest People Show for Others and the World Around Them

1/3	quiet and reserved and may enjoy working with *things* more than with *people*
3/3	interacts easily with others and may easily express emotions

Assertiveness—Amount of Energy Invested in Expressing Thoughts, Feelings, and Beliefs

1/3	passive and accepting and may not want to express an opinion
3/3	likes a fast pace and may have a strong desire to convince others of a point of view

Flexibility—Willingness to Accommodate the Thoughts and Actions of Others

1/3	likes unchanging situations and may support the status quo
3/3	easily handles ambiguous situations and may be open to suggestions from others

Reality Testing

Political Savvy

Purpose

To build an understanding of what political savvy is, why it is important, and how to use it.

Thumbnail

40 minutes

Through a step-by-step process, participants define political savvy, build their awareness of why it is important to them, and select one situation in which they will apply political savvy.

Outcomes

- Understand what political savvy is and ways to use it
- Select a situation in which using these skills will help them now

Audience

- Intact teams
- Unaffiliated group
- Individual working with a coach

Facilitator Competencies

Moderate

Materials

- Flip-chart paper, easel, and markers
- Paper and pens

Time Matrix

Activity	Estimated Time
Define political savvy, explore where it is needed, what it is, and how to apply it	20 minutes
In pairs, discuss one application each will make, then debrief as a whole group	20 minutes
Total Time	**40 minutes**

Instructions

1. Ask what political savvy means to the participants and write key points on the flip chart. A good definition may be somewhat different for different people because of their unique situations. A sample definition from the Senior Executive Service of the U.S. Federal Government is:

   Political Savvy: Identifies the internal and external politics that impact the work of the organization. Perceives organizational and political reality and acts accordingly.

   This is a component of Competency Five: Building Coalitions, www .opm.gov/ses/recruitment/ecq.asp#ecq5.

2. Guide participants in recognizing that political savvy is a component of reality testing. In order to explain reality testing, refer to the description in Part Two on reality testing, including the statement that: reality testing determines how clearly we discern what is actually happening in the world around us. We have learned to interpret and color our objective experience with all sorts of desires, fears, and distortions. In order to avoid mistaking our overly negative or overly positive perceptions of

experience for reality, we must develop reliable processes for confirming the objective correspondence of our feelings, perceptions, and thoughts with the immediate situation.

When someone is applying sound reality testing he or she will be keeping a centered and grounded perspective on what is happening, noticing what is most important to do next and will be paying attention to the key individuals to work with for strategic success. These are the components of acting with political savvy.

3. Ask for examples of when participants need political savvy. Note that while it is thought of in workplace situations, it can be important in many other applications such as community projects like creating an Earth Day event, a fundraising walk, or a political rally. Write key ideas on the flip chart. Examples from the workplace could be developing relationships with peers, understanding why the boss is giving so much priority to a certain project, or recognizing the role of their organization in the community.

4. Hand out paper and ask each person to write three situations in which he or she needs to apply political savvy and to write about how he or she is or did go about using it.

5. Now explore what political savvy is. Ask participants to name components of political savvy. The list could include:

- Approaching problems with a clear perception of the multiple relevant considerations both from internal and external perspectives
- Seeking to understand what the underlying meaning of the matter is to key individuals or groups—remember that often what is first said is just the surface of what is really at stake
- Noticing alternative approaches to the desired outcome and factoring in possible consequences associated with the alternatives

6. Now ask participants to develop guidelines for applying political savvy. Example guidelines might include:

- Be mindful of using ethical practices.
- Ask questions and listen carefully to understand the actual desired outcome.
- Clarify the rules and expectations.
- Build coalitions to expand strength and capacity.
- Seek to de-politicize the matter rather than stir it up more.

- Build relationships with people who can mentor you and help you build connections.
- Consider the stakeholders in the matter and pay attention to their needs and influence.
- Watch for hot and cold buttons.

7. Ask participants to form pairs and to each identify one area in which each needs to apply his or her political savvy and describe how he or she will go about it. Bring everyone back to debrief the discussions and ask questions.

Reality Testing

Feel, Hear, See—Is It Reality?

Purpose

To help clarify how accurately we are assessing the correspondence between our experience and what exists objectively.

Thumbnail

60 minutes

Team members agree on one situation in the workplace that is challenging for all of them. Each person will write up an assessment of the problem, paying close attention to a list of specific factors. A group debriefing brings all the information together. Be certain to coach the participants in a manner that is highly accurate and descriptive rather than evaluative.

Outcomes

- Increase each participant's reality-testing skills
- Enhance team awareness of how they operate collectively

Audience

- Intact team
- Unaffiliated group

Facilitator Competencies

Moderate

Materials

- Feel, Here, See—Is It Reality? Handout
- Paper and pens

Time Matrix

Activity	Estimated Time
Analyze and write up assessment	15 minutes
Discuss in triads	20 minutes
Debrief in total group	25 minutes
Total	**60 minutes**

Instructions

1. Ask team members to agree on one situation in the workplace that is challenging for them.
2. Give each person paper, a pen, and a copy of the Feel, Hear, See—Is It Reality? Handout and ask them each to write up an assessment of the problem, paying specific attention to when it first began, identifying the initiating factors, how the players feel about the situation now, what it means to them, what the dangers and opportunities are, and so forth.
3. Tell the participants to form groups of three (if need be, there can be one pair) and to discuss their assessments.
4. Reconvene the full group to debrief. Sample questions you might start with include:
   - What kinds of situations will you address best if you do more concrete reality testing?
   - Do you have any other strategies you can share that promote effective reality testing for you?

FEEL, HEAR, SEE—IS IT REALITY? HANDOUT

Answer each question individually, and then move to group discussion as instructed.

1. Describe the problem that your team has agreed to investigate. When did you first become aware of the problem?

2. How did you first become aware of it? Was it a purely cognitive recognition, an emotional recognition, or some combination of the two?

3. What specifically did you see and hear that told you how big a problem others perceived it to be?

4. How did you feel about what you saw and heard?

5. Who, if anyone, has something to gain from the way this problem is resolved? Who has something to lose? What might be gained or lost, and how motivating will that be?

6. What proof do you have to offer in support of your analysis?

7. Is there any other logical way to explain this situation, whether it seems as likely or not?

8. Have there ever been any similar situations, either in this workplace or another, that you or other team members misperceived and/or incorrectly evaluated? What was the misperception? What was the actual situation? What was the outcome?

Reality Testing

Visit Their Reality

Purpose

To increase reality testing skills by learning how to view a situation through another person's eyes.

Thumbnail

40 to 45 minutes

Participants consider disagreements they are having with others in their lives (preferably something current) and explore how reality looks and works for the other person until they understand it well enough to argue the other person's side.

Outcomes

- Learn how to take someone else's point of view in order to test reality by looking at it from a different perspective
- Increase one's own empathy and negotiation skills at the same time

Audience

- Intact team
- Unaffiliated group
- Individual working with a coach

Facilitator Competencies ◯

Easy

Materials

- Visit Their Reality Handout
- Paper and pens

Time Matrix

Activity	Estimated Time
Complete worksheet	20 minutes
Practice with a partner being in the other person's shoes	10–15 minutes
Have the full group debrief the experience	10 minutes
Total	**40 to 45 minutes**

Instructions

1. Distribute the Visit Their Reality Handout and paper and pens.
2. Instruct participants to take up to twenty minutes completing the handout.
3. Have the group join in pairs and take turns so that each partner role plays being the other person in the disagreement.
4. Bring the whole group together to debrief the experience. Sample questions you might begin with include:
   - Has this process helped you expand your awareness of other perspectives?
   - Where else might this process be useful?
   - How will you help yourself remember to expand your understanding of other people's reality?

5. Illustrate the difference between positions and interests by describing the situation in which two people both want the same orange. That is their position. One wants it to eat, the other wants the rind to bake cookies. Those are their interests.*

---

*This is adapted from *Getting to Yes*. Fisher and Ury (1981).

VISIT THEIR REALITY HANDOUT

Think of a disagreement you have with someone in your life. It can be at work or with friends or family, but it should be something that you are currently experiencing. It might be longstanding and not very active now, but ready to flare up if the topic is raised. By now, something has probably already come to mind.

Make a list of the reasons that you are right about your position and a list of the reasons that the other person is wrong. Be as specific as possible.

Now make a list of why he or she would say that you are wrong and he or she is right. Be as accurate and thorough as possible.

Do your best to identify the interests, goals, desires, and perceived needs that motivate the other person. Interests are distinctly different from positions. Positions are the obvious solutions we insist we must have to be happy, while interests are the deeper needs that must be met in order to really resolve the core of the problem. People usually focus on their positions and may never truly understand their interests. However, people usually can recognize their interests with some work, although that often takes someone with an impartial point of view providing assistance.

Once you have identified the other person's interests and figured out what makes him or her "tick," take the other side of the disagreement and develop the best strategy for that position. Write down the best arguments you can construct against your own position and describe why they are valid, important, and merit your consideration.

Now go back and consider your own interests. There is probably a very direct but not necessarily obvious connection between the other person's interests and your own. What are the goals, desires, and perceived needs that are motivating you? Compare the list from your point of view with the list from the other person's point of view. Where is there common ground? Where is he or she being unrealistic? Where are you being unrealistic? How would a neutral third party observing this from the "outside" perceive the situation? How have you upgraded your perception of reality by doing this exercise?

Reality Testing

Using All Three of Your Minds

Purpose

To increase the effectiveness and accuracy of your reality testing by connecting with your head, heart, and gut.

Thumbnail

60 to 80 minutes

Working with a coach or in small groups, the individuals review past and present decision making to discover the value of conducting a reality check using all three "brains." Easy references for understanding this model are listed.

Outcomes

- Discuss the idea of having three different brains, one in the head, one in the heart, and one in the gut
- Consider how participants have made decisions in the past to assess whether they used information from all three brains to connect with the whole spectrum of reality
- Apply this to future decision making and reality testing

Audience

- Intact team
- Unaffiliated group
- Individual working with a coach

Facilitator Competencies

Moderate

Materials

- Using All Three of Your Minds Handout
- Flip chart and markers (optional)
- Pens

Time Matrix

Activity	Estimated Time
Discuss using all three brains	10–15 minutes
In pairs or threes talk about prior decision-making processes, then how to make a future decision and check reality using all three brains; write about learnings	30–40 minutes
Group discussion	10–15 minutes
Reflect	10 minutes
Total	**60 to 80 minutes**

Instructions

1. Discuss the importance of reality testing and that we obtain a great deal of information from all three of our brains—those located in our head, our heart, and our gut. (Many resources about the brain address this subject, for example, Childre and Martin's [1999] *The Heartmath Solution*, www.heartmath.com, and www.mindpub.com/art411.htm have good information about the heart brain. *The Other 90 Percent*, by Cooper [2001], has some good information on the gut brain.)

2. Distribute the handout and pens.
3. Work directly with your coaching client or organize your group in pairs (a group of three would be okay if there's an extra person) and have them follow the directions in the handout.
4. In the full group, have each person reflect on what he or she has gained from this exercise.

USING ALL THREE OF YOUR MINDS HANDOUT

In Pairs or Threes

1. Each of you tells the other(s) about a time when you made a difficult decision and what steps you took to determine what was really happening. Reflect on the details of *how* you made the decision. The issue itself is not important for this exercise, although you will discuss it some. What is important is your decision-making process. How long did you take to consider the matter? Why? How did you feel? What did you think about? Did you consider past and/or future events? Did you check in regarding each of these details with your head, heart, and gut before making a decision? If so, did you get different answers? If so, how did you decide what to do?

2. Having told each other your stories, take five minutes and make some notes for yourself about your observations.

3. In the same groups, have each person describe a pending problem that is important, but one for which no decision has yet been made. Ask yourselves all the questions discussed above. Notice what each of your brains is telling you. Answer the following:

Emotional Intelligence in Action

- My head is telling me (provide details):

- My heart is guiding me to:

- My gut let me know:

Now how do you bring these three parts of you together?

4. Take time for each person to answer these questions out loud, then take five minutes and make some notes for yourself about your observations.

In Group

Reflect on what you learned and how you will take time to incorporate the wisdom of all of your brainpower in your decision making so that you connect with the full picture of reality.

Impulse Control

Putting on the Brakes

Purpose

To learn what causes impulsiveness and learn a strategy for responding constructively under stress.

Thumbnail

20 minutes

This exercise provides a good understanding of why we react impulsively and gives a simple method for putting on the brakes when you feel your fuse is so short that you might boil over!

Outcomes

- Understand what causes impulsiveness
- Learn a practice for defusing impulsiveness

Audience

- Member of an intact team
- Member of an unaffiliated group
- Individual working with a coach

Facilitator Competencies ◯

Easy

Materials

- Putting on the Brakes Handout

Time Matrix

Activity	Estimated Time
Discuss impulse control	10 minutes
Practice three-step exercise	10 minutes
Total Time	**20 minutes**

Instructions

1. Distribute the Putting on the Brakes Handout and discuss impulse control with your participants. The first part of the handout will provide support.
2. Guide them to practice the three-step process presented in the handout.

PUTTING ON THE BRAKES HANDOUT

About Impulse Control

Impulse Control is sometimes called "the brakes" of emotional intelligence because it is a skill that helps us keep ourselves from doing things that we probably should not do. Understanding what motivates our behavior in the first place, however, is a critical component of being able to control it. At the most basic level of our humanness, the biological level, we operate very much like a computer. The physical body with all its various structures, types of tissues, and organ systems corresponds to the hardware. There are two kinds of software that run this unit. The operating system and boot disk instructions are more or less standardized for every individual, being hardwired in genetic memory as reflexes, instincts, and drives. Our eyes blink, our muscles contract, we gasp or cry out in pain, surprise, or fear, we shiver when we're cold. These are examples of reflexes. Instincts, or drives to satisfy biological and/or evolutionary needs, include the desire to eat, drink, stay warm, and procreate.

Our bodies are born with these instructions already operating or ready to go with our first breaths; however, then the far more complex and significant part of our programming begins. It's our own personal software development project called: *Learning How to Stay Alive!* Of course, this includes basics like learning to walk and talk, will but it also includes *learning what to value*, what to go after, what to avoid, and the appropriate kinds of behavior to use in our efforts to acquire and avoid. Remember that emotions are all about value, which is what they indicate and communicate. For young children, learning the value of sharing means controlling the impulse to take what you want when you want it so you can enjoy it right now! Some people never learn this.

Your Practice

This brief practice will help you clear your sensory system when you start to feel impulsive. When you notice the tension and stress building up that can cause you to react impulsively, do three things:

- First, take your own emotional pulse! Fill in the blanks with this language pattern: "I feel_____, because_____."

- Second, take a really deep breath of air through your nose and just let it rush out through your mouth. then keep exhaling through your mouth for as long as you possibly can. As you have less and less air in your lungs, it will take more intentional effort from your diaphragm to keep exhaling. That's okay. Keep on pressing gently until there is absolutely no more air left and you absolutely must inhale. Inhale through your nose and continue breathing freely and easily in whatever manner is comfortable.
- Third, ask yourself: "What is the very best possible outcome that can happen in this situation?" and see what occurs to you.

Taking your emotional pulse gives you some reality testing—you clarify what you're feeling and why you feel that way. Taking the very deep breath and exhaling it completely interrupts much of the physiological momentum that can build up and lead to an impulsive release. Thinking cognitively again takes your attention out of the emotional circuitry once more and helps you target the optimal outcome. Even though that best solution may not be available, it can help you see new options you are overlooking, and at least you'll be much less likely to react destructively than you were before.

Impulse Control

To Impulse or Not to Impulse

Purpose

To examine the impact of impulsiveness from a fresh perspective and to show how impulsive urges can have disastrous consequences.

Thumbnail

43 to 60 minutes

Group exercise uses Shakespeare's *King Lear* to illustrate the negative impact of impulsive behavior. Group members act out a portion of King Lear, Act 1, Scene 1. They identify and discuss the ramifications of impulsive behavior.

Outcomes

- New perspective on impulsiveness by looking at it through the lens of fictional history
- Increased awareness of the impacts of impulsiveness
- Utilize the learning to improve impulse control

Audience

- Intact team
- Unaffiliated group

Facilitator Competencies

Moderate to Advanced

Materials

- Facilitator Overview of *King Lear* (Step 2 of Instructions)
- Copies of *King Lear,* Act 1, Scene 1 Handout
  – OR –
- Film clip from *King Lear* showing the Earl of Kent stepping in to try to stop Lear from making a foolhardy decision regarding dividing his kingdom before his demise
- To Impulse or Not to Impulse Handout
- Pens

Time Matrix

Activity	Estimated Time
Provide overview of the scene	3-5 minutes
Read or show film clip of *King Lear,* Act 1, Scene 1, lines 36–188	15–20 minutes
Debrief	25–35 minutes
Total Time	**43 to 60 minutes**

Instructions

1. Assign six people to read *King Lear,* Act 1, Scene 1, lines 36 through line 188 (from Lear's first lines until Kent's farewell after being banished). There are three male roles—King Lear, the Earl of Kent, and Albany Cornwall—and three female roles—Goneril, Cordelia, and Regan.
   – OR –
   Set up film clip.
2. Provide the group with an overview of what happens in Act 1, Scene 1, of *King Lear,* as follows.

   - King Lear is in his eighties and appears to be in good health.
   - Knowing that at eighty he is "crawling toward death," he decides to divide his kingdom now to prevent disputes after his death.

- He has already decided to divide it into three parts, one for each daughter—Goneril, Regan, and Cordelia. King Lear has a map that divides the country into thirds, reflecting his decision.
- However, instead of sticking with his plan, he declares on the spot that whichever daughter professes to love him the most will receive the largest segment of his kingdom.
- He expects his youngest daughter Cordelia to win this contest.
- Cordelia has always been his favorite and she is completely devoted to her father.
- The other daughters are opportunistic and self-serving.
- His plan backfires.
  - The two older sisters flat-out lie. They profess profound love for their father.
  - Cordelia, disgusted by her sisters' hypocrisy, decides not to play this stupid game.
- Lear disinherits Cordelia and divides the kingdom between Goneril and Regan.
- The Earl of Kent, Lear's trusted advisor, loves the king and is completely loyal to him.
- Kent tries to intervene by telling Lear that he's engaging in "hideous rashness."
- For his insubordination, Lear banishes Kent from the kingdom.
- Lear should have listened to Kent's advice.
  - "By disinheriting Cordelia, Lear sets his tragedy in motion: the daughters who pledged their undying love turn on him, take away his authority, and drive his entourage from the palace and he goes mad. By the end of the play all Lear has left is Cordelia's love. And Kent's love." (Whitney & Packer, 2001, p. 81)

3. Distribute the *King Lear*, Act 1, Scene 1, Handout and have the role players read their parts.
4. Debrief, making the following points and asking the following questions:
   - Lear was in a very emotional state. He was upset about Cordelia's response. Kent was very emotional about Lear's actions.
   - Did Lear act impulsively?

- **Answer:** Yes, by devising that "stupid parlor trick" as the basis for dividing the kingdom and also by deciding to ignore his original plan to divide the kingdom into thirds.
- Was Cordelia's decision to basically ignore her father's request a question of impulsiveness (the impulse to be in stark contrast to her sisters)?
  - This is a tricky question to raise because the group may veer off into questions of ethics. Some may think Cordelia's decision to sparingly respond to Lear's request was a matter of ethics: (a) she did not want to support her sisters' hypocrisy by acting as if their statements had any validity or (b) she did not want to support their rash, and maybe unethical, behavior by participating in the charade.
- Were Kent's comments to the King measured or rash?
  - **Answer:** Rash—he called the king's actions "hideous rashness." He did not speak to Lear in a measured way. He responded emotionally and used potentially incendiary language.
- Was Kent acting impulsively by intervening at that moment in the way in which he did?
  - **Answer:** Many scholars and management consultants believe he acted impulsively.
- How would you have advised Kent to respond? When should he do it? What should he say?

5. Ask group members to share examples from their lives when they reacted impulsively and would have benefited from a more thoughtful and strategically sound approach.

6. Ask the group what lessons are to be learned from both Lear's and Kent's behavior.

7. Give everyone a pen and a copy of the To Impulse or Not to Impulse Handout. Ask them to respond to the questions and to record the lessons and insights that resonate with their own behavior.

KING LEAR, ACT 1, SCENE 1, HANDOUT

By William Shakespeare
> (Lines 37 to 188)

King Lear

> Meantime we shall express our darker purpose.
> Give me the map there. Know that we have divided
> In three our kingdom: and 'tis our fast intent
> To shake all cares and business from our age;
> Conferring them on younger strengths, while we
> Unburthen'd crawl toward death. Our son of Cornwall,
> And you, our no less loving son of Albany,
> We have this hour a constant will to publish
> Our daughters' several dowers, that future strife
> May be prevented now. The princes, France and Burgundy,
> Great rivals in our youngest daughter's love,
> Long in our court have made their amorous sojourn,
> And here are to be answer'd. Tell me, my daughters,
> Since now we will divest us both of rule,
> Interest of territory, cares of state,
> Which of you shall we say doth love us most?
> That we our largest bounty may extend
> Where nature doth with merit challenge. Goneril,
> Our eldest-born, speak first.

Goneril

> Sir, I love you more than words can wield the matter;
> Dearer than eyesight, space, and liberty;
> Beyond what can be valued, rich or rare;
> No less than life, with grace, health, beauty, honour;
> As much as child e'er loved, or father found;
> A love that makes breath poor, and speech unable;
> Beyond all manner of so much I love you.

Exercise 12.2. Impulse Control

Cordelia

> [Aside] What shall Cordelia do?
> Love, and be silent.

Lear

> Of all these bounds, even from this line to this,
> With shadowy forests and with champains rich'd,
> With plenteous rivers and wide-skirted meads,
> We make thee lady: to thine and Albany's issue
> Be this perpetual. What says our second daughter,
> Our dearest Regan, wife to Cornwall? Speak.

Regan

> Sir, I am made
> Of the self-same metal that my sister is,
> And prize me at her worth. In my true heart
> I find she names my very deed of love;
> Only she comes too short: that I profess
> Myself an enemy to all other joys,
> Which the most precious square of sense possesses;
> And find I am alone felicitate
> In your dear highness' love.

Cordelia

> [Aside] Then poor Cordelia!
> And yet not so; since, I am sure, my love's
> More richer than my tongue.

King Lear

> To thee and thine hereditary ever
> Remain this ample third of our fair kingdom;
> No less in space, validity, and pleasure,
> Than that conferr'd on Goneril. Now, our joy,
> Although the last, not least; to whose young love
> The vines of France and milk of Burgundy
> Strive to be interess'd; what can you say to draw
> A third more opulent than your sisters? Speak.

Emotional Intelligence in Action

Cordelia

Nothing, my lord.

King Lear

Nothing!

Cordelia

Nothing.

King Lear

Nothing will come of nothing; speak again.

Cordelia

Unhappy that I am, I cannot heave
My heart into my mouth: I love your majesty
According to my bond; nor more nor less.

King Lear

How, how, Cordelia! mend your speech a little,
Lest it may mar your fortunes.

Cordelia

Good my lord,
You have begot me, bred me, loved me: I
Return those duties back as are right fit,
Obey you, love you, and most honour you.
Why have my sisters husbands, if they say
They love you all? Haply, when I shall wed,
That lord whose hand must take my plight shall carry
Half my love with him, half my care and duty:
Sure, I shall never marry like my sisters,
To love my father all.

King Lear

But goes thy heart with this?

Exercise 12.2. Impulse Control

Cordelia

Ay, good my lord.

King Lear

So young, and so untender?

Cordelia

So young, my lord, and true.

King Lear

Let it be so; thy truth, then, be thy dower:
For, by the sacred radiance of the sun,
The mysteries of Hecate, and the night;
By all the operation of the orbs
From whom we do exist, and cease to be;
Here I disclaim all my paternal care,
Propinquity and property of blood,
And as a stranger to my heart and me
Hold thee, from this, for ever. The barbarous Scythian,
Or he that makes his generation messes
To gorge his appetite, shall to my bosom
Be as well neighbour'd, pitied, and relieved,
As thou my sometime daughter.

Kent

Good my liege—

King Lear

Peace, Kent!
Come not between the dragon and his wrath.
I loved her most, and thought to set my rest
On her kind nursery. Hence, and avoid my sight!
So be my grave my peace, as here I give
Her father's heart from her! Call France; who stirs?
Call Burgundy. Cornwall and Albany,
With my two daughters' dowers digest this third:
Let pride, which she calls plainness, marry her.

Emotional Intelligence in Action

I do invest you jointly with my power,
Pre-eminence, and all the large effects
That troop with majesty. Ourself, by monthly course,
With reservation of an hundred knights,
By you to be sustain'd, shall our abode
Make with you by due turns. Only we still retain
The name, and all the additions to a king;
The sway, revenue, execution of the rest,
Beloved sons, be yours: which to confirm,
This coronet part betwixt you.
[Giving the crown]

Kent

Royal Lear,
Whom I have ever honour'd as my king,
Loved as my father, as my master follow'd,
As my great patron thought on in my prayers,—

King Lear

The bow is bent and drawn, make from the shaft.

Kent

Let it fall rather, though the fork invade
The region of my heart: be Kent unmannerly,
When Lear is mad. What wilt thou do, old man?
Think'st thou that duty shall have dread to speak,
When power to flattery bows? To plainness honour's bound,
When majesty stoops to folly. Reverse thy doom;
And, in thy best consideration, cheque
This hideous rashness: answer my life my judgment,
Thy youngest daughter does not love thee least;
Nor are those empty-hearted whose low sound
Reverbs no hollowness.

King Lear

Kent, on thy life, no more.

Kent

> My life I never held but as a pawn
> To wage against thy enemies; nor fear to lose it,
> Thy safety being the motive.

King Lear

> Out of my sight!

Kent

> See better, Lear; and let me still remain
> The true blank of thine eye.

King Lear

> Now, by Apollo,—

Kent

> Now, by Apollo, king,
> Thou swear'st thy gods in vain.

King Lear

> O, vassal! miscreant![Laying his hand on his sword]

Albany/Cornwall

> Dear sir, forbear.

Kent

> Do:
> Kill thy physician, and the fee bestow
> Upon thy foul disease. Revoke thy doom;
> Or, whilst I can vent clamour from my throat,
> I'll tell thee thou dost evil.

King Lear

> Hear me, recreant!
> On thine allegiance, hear me!
> Since thou hast sought to make us break our vow,

Emotional Intelligence in Action

Which we durst never yet, and with strain'd pride
To come between our sentence and our power,
Which nor our nature nor our place can bear,
Our potency made good, take thy reward.
Five days we do allot thee, for provision
To shield thee from diseases of the world;
And on the sixth to turn thy hated back
Upon our kingdom: if, on the tenth day following,
Thy banish'd trunk be found in our dominions,
The moment is thy death. Away! by Jupiter,
This shall not be revoked.

Kent

Fare thee well, king: sith thus thou wilt appear,
Freedom lives hence, and banishment is here.
[To Cordelia]
The gods to their dear shelter take thee, maid,
That justly think'st, and hast most rightly said!
[To Regan and Goneril]
And your large speeches may your deeds approve,
That good effects may spring from words of love.
Thus Kent, O princes, bids you all adieu;
He'll shape his old course in a country new.
[Exit]

Emotional Intelligence in Action, Second Edition. Copyright ©2012 by Marcia Hughes and James Bradford Terrell. Reproduced by permission of Pfeiffer, an Imprint of Wiley. www.pfeiffer.com

Exercise 12.2. Impulse Control

TO IMPULSE OR NOT TO IMPULSE HANDOUT

1. What are the lessons learned from the play *King Lear*?

   - From King Lear the man?

   - From the Earl of Kent?

2. Briefly describe a time when you spoke before thinking.

3. What triggered your impulsive behavior? Is that part of a pattern for you? What could you do in the future to manage your impulsiveness?

Impulse Control

The Urge to Splurge

Purpose

To explore the motivation and results of the participants' impulsive behavior, and to chart a new path.

Thumbnail

35 to 55 minutes

Participants closely scrutinize their impulses by identifying when they are impulsive, why they are impulsive, what desired and undesired results accrue, and how they can behave differently in the future.

Outcomes

- Heightened awareness due to an in-depth examination of one's own behavior
- Increased commitment to develop better impulse control
- Newly available behavioral alternatives

Audience

- Intact team
- Unaffiliated group
- Individual working with a coach

Facilitator Competencies

Moderate

Materials

- The Urge to Splurge Handout
- Pens

Time Matrix

Activity	Estimated Time
Introduce concept and exercise	5 minutes
Complete PCG ChangeNow™ steps	15–20 minutes
Debrief	15–30 minutes
Total Time	**35 to 55 minutes**

Instructions

1. Briefly introduce the concept of impulse control. Ask the individual or group for examples of helpful impulsive behaviors:
   - Sample answer: Expressing anger (appropriately) instead of stuffing it
   - Sample answer: Impulse to flee from a dangerous situation

   Ask for negative examples of impulsiveness.
   - Sample answer: Confronting someone at work about an issue publicly, when it would be better to wait until a more appropriate time
   - Sample answer: Shopping for clothes when you have scores of items in your closet you have never worn
   - Sample answer: Gaining weight due to overeating
2. Explain that this exercise will help them identify their counterproductive impulsive behavior and devise alternatives.
3. Distribute The Urge to Splurge Handout and pens and then review the PCG ChangeNow™ Model. The model explores an area in which participants are getting suboptimal results due to impulsive behavior. It asks them to analyze the circumstances in which the behavior occurs, discuss how the behavior is serving them, and identify unintended consequences.

The model then asks them to focus on desired results, brainstorm new behaviors that would help them achieve the desired results, surface barriers that might inhibit success, and develop strategies to overcome the barriers.

4. After reviewing the model, ask the participants to complete the handout.
5. Debrief by asking the following:
   - How did it feel to examine this behavior?
   - Were you able to identify the benefits you derive?
   - How did you feel about those benefits?
   - Did the benefits outweigh the undesired outcomes, or vice versa?
   - Were you able to move beyond the undesirable condition and achieve your desired results?
   - What alternatives to the impulsive behavior did you find?
   - Think ahead about what barriers you might encounter. What will you do when you encounter those barriers?
6. If they want to develop their skills in this area, have them notice and record their encounters with impulsiveness for one week.
   - Each day record the times you felt impulsive and how you responded.
   - During the day, catch yourself doing something right, and reward your successes with a proven stress-buster like congratulatory self-talk ("I said I was going to do it and I really did! I'm strong, I'm disciplined! I'm awesome!"), step outside for a breath of fresh air, or take a brisk walk.

THE URGE TO SPLURGE HANDOUT

PCG ChangeNow™ Model*

Current Results

1. List the areas in your life where impulsiveness is producing suboptimal results such as anxiety, unhappiness, arguments, avoidance, and so on.

Factors

2. Write down which specific impulsive behaviors are causing those results.

3. Analyze the circumstances that give rise to the impulsive behavior
   - Are the impulses localized in key areas of your life or paired with specific situations?
   - Are you operating at a generally high level of free-floating hostility that is ever-poised for an opportunity to express itself?

---

*This exercise was created by and used with the permission of Polaris Consulting Group.

Benefits of Current Behavior

4. Determine how the impulsive behavior is serving you.
   - What do you get out of it?
   - What needs, desires, or habits does it satisfy?

Undesired Outcomes of Current Behavior

5. Subsequent to the initial satisfaction, what negative results do you experience?

Desired Results

6. What are the outcomes you really DO want to have—short term and long term?

Emotional Intelligence in Action, Second Edition. Copyright ©2012 by Marcia Hughes and James Bradford Terrell. Reproduced by permission of Pfeiffer, an Imprint of Wiley. www.pfeiffer.com

Create New Approach

7. Brainstorm new behaviors that will satisfy both the positive intentions of your current approach and achieve the desired results you have not attained yet. The approaches may need to be different for each type of situation or impulse.

Barriers to Implementing Your New Approach

8. What old habits, behaviors, and unexpected conditions might highjack your new efforts and allow your previous strategies to re-assert themselves?

Strategies to Overcome Barriers

9. What will you do to overcome the barriers and resist the pull of impulsiveness?

Impulse Control

Hot Buttons

Purpose

To help people notice and modify how they respond when their self-control is starting to lose ground to their impulsiveness.

Thumbnail

60 minutes

Participants will determine whether they are triggered more easily by approach impulses or by avoidance impulses. They will learn to notice their automatic behaviors and discuss how to change them. The exercise is written so that participants can choose to improve their control over both kinds of impulses— those situations that tempt them and those situations that make them angry.

Outcomes

- Be able to anticipate and counter the effects of unconscious response patterns
- Understand the dynamics of the "move toward" and "move away from" responses

Audience

- Intact team
- Unaffiliated group
- Individual working with a coach

Facilitator Competencies

Advanced

Materials

- Hot Buttons Handout
- Paper and pens

Time Matrix

Activity	Estimated Time
Read the handout and think about how impulsiveness shows up in your life	5 minutes
Work with partner in decoding a specific impulse-control pattern in your life you'd like to change	20 minutes
Develop impulse-control plan and practice using it while partner attempts to trigger the old pattern	20 minutes
Group discussion of what people learned	15 minutes
Total Time	**60 minutes**

Instructions

1. Distribute pens, paper, and the Hot Buttons Handout.
2. Ask participants to form pairs for this exercise.
3. Ask them to read the handout all the way through on their own, and then follow the directions together.
4. After twenty minutes remind them they should now begin developing their impulse-control strategy.
5. After fifteen more minutes, give them a five-minute warning.
6. In five minutes begin a debriefing with questions such as, "What has changed about the way you understand your impulses now?"

Emotional Intelligence in Action

HOT BUTTONS HANDOUT

Consider for a moment which type of impulses are the hardest for you to control—those that move you toward something you desire (food, shopping, alcohol, and other forms of gratification) or those that move you away from something you reject (behavior that makes you angry, kinds of people and remarks that put you off).

Once you have identified which impulses are most difficult, choose a specific example you can share with your partner in which you tried your best to consciously restrain what you said and/or did, but ended up behaving impulsively anyway. Try to identify what was happening when you first felt the impulse and, second, when your resistance was finally losing out and you actually acted on the impulse.

Carefully describe the situation to your partner, being very specific about the sequence of events that led you to start. Pay particular attention to your three most commonly used senses—sight, sound, and touch. Tell your partner what you were seeing, hearing, and feeling as well as what you were saying to yourself as the specific impulse started.

Once your partner understands the pattern that initiates the sequence of impulsive behavior in this kind of situation, he or she can "argue on behalf of your impulse" by reminding you of your responses to the various environmental stimuli. For example:

> Partner: "You are seeing the beautiful coat on the rack in the store and start to feel excited as you move toward it."

Notice how your *body* responds to this description! If you are tracking down the sequence of responses of a "move toward" impulse, they may be significantly different from those that are associated with a "move away from" impulse. Eyes dilating, temperature increase, salivation, and such are common for "move toward." Tension in the face, jaws, stomach, and hands are common responses for "move away." Self-talk is typical for each type of behavior, while increased heart rate and flushing can be common responses for *both* kinds of impulses.

Now have your partner remind you of the cues that occurred at the second stage as the impulse was escalating and you were about to act. For example:

Exercise 12.4. Impulse Control

Partner: "You are seeing the beautiful color of the fabric and feeling how smooth and silky it is while you remember the fancy party you attended and hear yourself saying 'I look like a million bucks!,' and you feel that buying this coat might make everything that wonderful once again."

Notice how your *body* responds to this description! Meanwhile, practice your new strategy for resisting this impulse by seeing your credit card bill and feeling worried that you can't pay the bill, while you see all the clothes already hanging in your closet and you say to yourself, "Wait, I'm happy with who I am, not because of what I have!"

In the space below list the cues that trigger impulsiveness and the resourceful behaviors you have learned in this exercise as reminders you can use to help you notice and interrupt destructive impulse patterns in the future. Then you will be able to choose more constructive ones that serve your true goals. Use the back side of this paper if you need more space.

Flexibility

The Highly Flexible Team

Purpose

To help team members clarify their workflow process, including what the specific roles, contributions, and interfaces of each member are.

Thumbnail

60 minutes

The combined flexibility of all the members delivers a critical strength and durability to teamwork. Conversely, if this is an area for which improvement is necessary, lack of flexibility can actually be a serious bottleneck. Your team can learn how well it performs in flexibility from your team identity and positive mood scores in the TESI. Teams follow an eight-step process to explore their current process in detail to gain the information for places where flexibility can be added.

Outcomes

- Familiarize entire team with all the steps of its workflow process, including where it is the strongest and where the process can be improved
- Help all members understand what each member specifically contributes to the process

Audience

- Intact teams

Facilitator Competencies

Advanced

Materials

- The Highly Flexible Team Handout
- Flip-chart paper, easel, and markers
- Paper and pens
- The ability to order pizza or another treat if you choose to do so

Time Matrix

Activity	Estimated Time
Discuss and work through the eight-step process with an intact team	60 minutes
Total Time	**60 minutes**

Instructions

1. Follow the steps in The Highly Flexible Team Handout. Your discussion will be much more successful if you remind team members or group participants to always engage each other with respect and to speak more descriptively than evaluatively through Step 7. In Step 8 more evaluative kinds of comments can then be made productively. *Note:* If you have time constraints, you could have the team focus on one key aspect of its work instead of all the key demands they face.
2. Remember to order or make reservations for the pizza! You may choose to let participants know or use pizza as a surprise reward for their hard work.

THE HIGHLY FLEXIBLE TEAM HANDOUT

Flexibility is the skill that helps us adapt to change we cannot predict or control; it is also what allows us to accommodate the needs of other people, even when they may encroach on our own. Too much flexibility means we end up doing other people's work; too little flexibility means we may live in a familiar if not comfortable rut and that may make it frustrating for others to interact with us, especially in times of change.

A major component of team flexibility comes from everyone understanding and appreciating the roles of all the team's members. With a firm basis of understanding the roles and responsibilities, the team then has the information it needs to build in flexible practices. The following exercise is designed to facilitate team flexibility with a new level of awareness by consciously exploring what is generally only assumed about team roles and functions. Everyone on the team needs to be present for this to work!

1. With all team members including the leader present, begin the exercise by choosing two people to alternate as scribes. First, create a statement that comprehensively explains key actions your team is responsible for. Everyone has to sign off on this statement, which should be simplified as much is possible without losing necessary details.

2. Now that you have explicitly described just what it is your team does, get a feel for the specific sequence of the process. Discuss items such as where your work assignments come from. Do they come directly from your final customer or from another team within your organization? How are the expectations/requirements for success presented? Does the team or leader have any input? If not, should this change? Can it?

3. Once the work has been assigned, who needs to do what first? Every team member may start working on some aspect right away, but how do the different processes and tasks fit together?

4. Now that you have developed a general outline of the process your team uses, each team member is to describe in detail what it is he/she does. If the process is clear-cut and sequential, then follow the process in your discussions as closely as possible. If that is a less dominant feature of the workflow, team members can just take turns as they feel works the best. This does not have to be highly structured and should allow for plenty of discussion.

5. Within the team there may be individuals who collaborate to a high degree with each other; give them a chance now to discuss their relationship and how their relationship interfaces with other relationships on the team or on other teams if that is the case.

6. Most work begins with gathering things and/or data (such as raw materials or subassemblies). What needs to be gathered for your team to do its work? Where does it come from and how easy is it to obtain? When there are problems, what are they typically? How does the work your team does change the data and/or things to add value?

7. How do you know when you are finished? Where does your work product go when your team has finished its contribution to the process? How does the team know how successful efforts were? What is the feedback loop? Does it need to be improved?

8. Now that your team has done most of the work to trace the structure and process of the interdependent relationships within the team, ask for feedback about where the various processes and interfaces can be improved. This may be an animated, even heated discussion, but if conducted respectfully the material you have already generated will provide strong support. It will also generally have taken long enough that people will be ready to make specific observations and requests to expand the flexibility of the team engagement and process (especially if they know that everyone's going out for pizza soon)!

Flexibility

No More Shutdowns

Purpose

To discover how to be more productive, flexible, and resilient by using positive statements to counter destructive self-talk and free our attention from disturbing, negative thoughts.

Thumbnail

32 to 42 minutes

Individuals and team members will practice observing their negative, limiting thoughts and learn to substitute more positive ones. As they notice the difference from using the more flexible statement, they will be motivated to give themselves the type of messages that will increase their flexibility. Team members will observe how negative self-talk influences others, thus decreasing flexibility and the power to deal effectively with change. They will list the negative, fearful messages they hear themselves saying and will practice countering them by substituting more positive phrases.

Outcomes

- Learn how the way we think about an issue impacts us, and particularly focus on the consequences of flexible thinking
- Discover the value of clarifying statements and requests before jumping to *"No!"* or *"It won't work!"* and similar comments that shutdown options for resourceful responses

Audience

- Intact team
- Unaffiliated group
- Individual working with a coach

Facilitator Competencies

Moderate

Materials

- List of negative thoughts and positive counters. You may use the No More Shutdowns Handout or create your own list to meet the specifics of your individual's or team's situation
- Paper and pens

Time Matrix

Activity	Estimated Time
Brief introduction of flexibility	5 minutes
Participants read and discuss the concept of positive "can do" thoughts; make a commitment to change	7 minutes
Individually, or in pairs, practice the different negative messages followed by the positive messages	10–15 minutes
Discuss and apply to real-life examples	10–15 minutes
(Optional) Set a strategy for repeating the process on their own and then reporting back if possible	Up to the discretion of the trainer
Total Time	**32 to 42 minutes**

Instructions

1. Give a brief introduction to the topic of flexibility. Refer to the discussion in Part Two of this book on flexibility for guidance.
2. Distribute the No More Shutdowns Handout (or your own list) and pens. Explain that the participants will be working with the statements in the handout, first making a negative comment that will then be followed by a positive comment intended to open up possibilities.
3. Ask the participants to form pairs.
4. Tell participants to begin practicing the statements with their partners, noticing how they feel when they say or receive shutdown statements, as compared to opening statements of possibilities.
5. After ten to fifteen minutes, reconvene the entire group and debrief with a focus on what occurred and why. Notice multiple areas of response. How did it feel to say no, or to hear no? How did it feel when new possibilities were invited using the positive statement? Connect feelings with the meanings.
6. Lead the group or individual in a discussion about how to apply this learning in the workplace.

NO MORE SHUTDOWNS HANDOUT

Moving from Shutdown (SD) to Possibility (P)

Four areas of comments are listed in the following chart. Expand the categories or add new ones as meets your needs.

Change

SD	I've always done it this way and it keeps me safe. I don't want to change.
(Shutdown)	
P	I think I'll explore how well this is thought out. Perhaps I should give it a chance.
(Possibility)	
SD	Every reorganization we've tried has been meaningless. This will be just the same, so I'm not going to try.
P	I know they have worked hard on this reorganization, so, while I'm skeptical, I'll give it a chance. (Bonus: I'll help them be successful by using my skills.)

About Me

SD	It seems like I never finish my work as it is; there's no way I can join the office softball team.
P	I've heard that getting exercise helps people do their work faster. I'll join the team for the six-week season and give it a try.

Others

SD	Sally is always making big changes; she must never get her work done.
P	I'm curious about all those changes Sally makes. I'm going to ask her how that helps her get her work done.

Work

SD	When I go to work, I have to follow my routine to get my work done. Otherwise, I'm derailed and the day is pointless.

Emotional Intelligence in Action

P	I like to follow my routine at work. But some of what is on my plate just isn't getting done. I need some new tools or strategies. What have I got to lose looking in a new direction?
SD	All these changes hurt my friends; no one is looking after their interests.
P	I wonder what these changes will mean for my friends and others here? I'm going to help everyone consider what is happening very seriously.
SD	I just know they haven't considered all the facts in developing this new plan. I oppose it.
P	I'll give this a chance and along the way find out what data they have looked at. Maybe I can help them consider all the critical factors.

Flexibility

Yes, No, Maybe So

Purpose

To recognize the value of flexibility in responding to life's endless challenges. To note how our choices relate to other emotional intelligence skills such as reality testing and stress tolerance.

Thumbnail

40 minutes

Participants discuss what it means to be flexible and recognize that judgment is required for effective application of this skill. They also discuss the rich connection to other emotional intelligence factors in determining the consequences of their flexibility.

Outcomes

- Gain awareness of the value of flexibility and of specific applications in our lives
- Recognize that using flexibility requires judgment; it is not a black-and-white world

Audience

- Intact team
- Unaffiliated group
- Individual working with a coach

Facilitator Competencies ◯ ◑

Easy to Moderate

Materials

- Yes, No, Maybe So Handout
- Flip chart and markers
- Range of Response Continuum (see Step 2 in instructions)
- Pens

Time Matrix

Activity	Estimated Time
Discuss pros and cons of flexibility	5 minutes
Review a range of responses to challenges	5 minutes
Discuss scenarios	20 minutes
Pull together with a list of key points	10 minutes
Total Time	**40 minutes**

Instructions

1. Review the reasons why we tend to be inflexible. Notice that there are many personal differences. Some seem to go with the flow; others want it just so. Each can have strengths at different times. However, we know that our world is dramatically impacted by continuous changes and we can't fight against too many of them and still survive. Note the need to pull in additional emotional intelligence elements in determining how to respond to many situations. Reality testing is often key: "Is this worth resisting?" Optimism can be critical: "Even though this seems like a setback, we know we can find a good solution. We just don't know it *yet*."

2. In order to gain perspective, instruct the individual you are coaching or your group to consider the following range of responses to opportunities to use their flexibility. (The following range should be on a flip chart to which you can point.)

Don't Change	Moderate Change	Go for It

3. Ask what pros and cons they see to the different responses. Then lead the group in a discussion of how to choose and how to be flexible in degrees. Can they say yes to aspects of a change and help find win/win answers? Record key strategic points they make in the discussion.
4. Distribute the Yes, No, Maybe So Handout and pens and ask participants to read through the scenarios. If you wish, supplement this list with examples of your own choosing or actual examples from participants' experiences.
5. As a group, discuss a variety of responses, noting the ways to build flexibility. Help them grow to understand the value of flexibility in their lives and to recognize that it's not about giving up values. Show them that there are times to say "Yes!" and times to say "No!" and times to say, "Maybe, let's see."
6. To conclude, have participants list the key points they have discovered. Then have each take a few minutes to think of a recent time in his or her life when he or she would have benefited by being more flexible.

YES, NO, MAYBE SO HANDOUT

1. Your assistant has just made a passionate presentation on the value of changing your computers from PCs to Mac's. It's the first thing he's ever really advocated, and he spent a lot of time researching this proposal, although you had no idea he was working on such a plan. Your whole office uses PCs, and you've never touched a Mac.

2. Your boss wants you to give up flex hours. She says it's just too confusing and reduces productivity to not have a five-day work week. Currently you work ten hours a day for four days. This fits your childcare needs perfectly.

3. You manage a section with fifty people and have four direct-report first-tier supervisors. They're begging you to moderate your highly flexible strategy with the staff. You allow people to set their own hours and trust that they worked those hours if they accomplish their goals.

4. Your colleague keeps a messy office and seems to love it that way. He says he can find things and he loves to have lots going at once. You strongly prefer a neat, orderly office. Your files are put away at the end of the day. (His never are!) You work best on one project at a time. The two of you have started getting on one another's nerves because you work in close quarters and share data. It's becoming a stressor for everyone so you have both agreed to discuss your different styles and see whether you can find a way to reduce the tension.

5. Your daughter just took up drums and practices religiously for an hour, starting just when you get home from work and need quiet time.

6. You have been working diligently to get a favorite project done; however, every time you take it to the review committee, they ask for more changes.

7. The City just added a turn light at the intersection near your home. It seems like it takes forever to go through it and get home.

8. Getting through security at the airport takes three times as long as it used to, and you just don't have that much time.

Flexibility

Flex Time

Purpose

To begin the process of increasing flexibility by committing to do at least one flexibility enhancing activity.

Thumbnail

30 to 35 minutes

Participants or individuals discuss the negative impacts of not being flexible. They brainstorm to create a list of things they can do to increase flexibility. Each person selects one or two activities to do in the next week. If they are meeting in an ongoing forum, they report back to the group at the next meeting and share their experiences.

Outcomes

- List of activities to develop flexibility
- Commitment to use at least one tool to increase flexibility and report back to group or coach

Audience

- Intact team
- Unaffiliated group
- Individual working with a coach

Facilitator Competencies ◯

Easy

Materials

- Flip chart and markers
- 3 x 5 cards
- Pens

Time Matrix

Activity	Estimated Time
Discuss impacts of lack of flexibility	10 minutes
Develop list of activities	10 minutes
Create pocket card	10–15 minutes
Total Time	**30 to 35 minutes**

Instructions

1. Ask the participants to think of recent situations in which they believe they should have been more flexible.
2. Ask the group to share negative impacts of not being more flexible, and capture the responses on a flip chart.
3. Say to the group, "What could you have done to be more flexible? One of the biggest obstacles to increasing our flexibility is that we don't want to!" Have the group list three reasons that people don't want to be more flexible; discuss why and what we can do about it. Capture the information on a flip chart.

Emotional Intelligence in Action

4. Next, ask participants to develop a list of things they can do differently that would require them to be more flexible. Record the list on a flip chart. If the group has trouble getting started, use items from the following list to jumpstart the process:
   - Eat a kind of food you've never eaten before
   - Drive a different route to work
   - Listen to a different type of music
   - Read something outside of your usual area—biography, mystery, history, art, science
5. Tell participants to select at least one or two of these specific changes to incorporate into their lives and to make a written commitment to do so—including when and how.
6. Distribute the 3 x 5 cards and pens. Tell participants that they will be creating pocket cards.
   - On one side, they are to list the specific behavior to change.
   - On the reverse side, they should write why it is important to be more flexible and list the specific times of day and the number of days they will refer to the card to reinforce the commitment.
7. (*Optional*) In the next meeting or coaching session, share experiences and select another activity to increase flexibility.

Stress Tolerance

The EZ Stress Buster

Purpose

To give people a simple but more thorough understanding of stress and an easy practice for managing stress

Thumbnail

30 minutes

Stress concepts are explained, and participants put easy steps into practice with movement, drinking water, and telling jokes.

Outcome

- To help people improve their stress management and have fun

Audience

- Intact team
- Unaffiliated group
- Individual working with a coach

Facilitator Competencies ◯

Easy

Materials

- EZ Stress Buster Handout
- Access to hall, sidewalk, and/or stairway
- A glass of water for each participant
- Prepared jokes

Time Matrix

Activity	Estimated Time
Distribute handout, discuss, climb stairs, or otherwise move	20 minutes
Discuss and commit to practice	10 minutes
Total Time	**30 minutes**

Instructions

1. Distribute the EZ Stress Buster Handout and ask everyone to read it. Discuss. Practice. Send everyone out to climb two flights of stairs or walk around the block; just use what's naturally available. When they come back, have a glass of water at each place and instruct them to drink it. Then ask for people to tell (clean) jokes they know. As a back-up plan, have some jokes available and distribute copies for people to take turns reading.
2. Have fun! Ask for commitments to put the concepts into practice.

EZ STRESS BUSTER HANDOUT

What is stress? Stress is the numb sensation in your lips and face from drinking out of a fire hose all week (all month? all year?). It is the hair trigger on your temper that everyone you work with understands but your four- and six-year-olds are completely oblivious to . . . even when you do your best to give fair warning!

Stress is the exhaustion of the physiological systems that we use to pay attention, gather enough data, gather the right data, analyze it correctly, find the loopholes, plug the loopholes, make decisions, monitor their effectiveness, do it again, deal with an unforeseeable crisis, start a new project, do it again, 24/7/365. These kinds of expectations are completely unrealistic, and human beings are not built for this kind of a race. We are, in fact, racing against our own technology, against machines that do not need to eat or sleep or throw a graduation party or visit parents in a nursing home or love up the four- and six-year-old little rascals we think we're doing all this for.

Under conditions such as these, there are only three things you can do. Well, four if you count collapse. You can use Reality Testing externally to challenge the expectations of the people whose unrealistic assessment of what's valuable and what's possible is causing the problem. If you are successful you may well help create a more sustainable workplace in which people and profits can *both* thrive. This is often a bit of a long shot, because usually those people have invested heavily in the belief system that happiness is the result of consuming the things that money can buy . . . and its really scary to call that—and consequently all of our popular media—into question. But it's usually hard to get their attention anyway, because they are just about to succeed and finally prove for certain that they're right . . . or they're desperately scrambling to avoid some kind of catastrophe.

If you don't succeed in your challenge, you may be fired, or sidelined and abused more than before, but then you can apply Option 2 and use your Reality Testing *internally* to reprioritize your values and adjust your behavior and your daily and weekly and yearly schedules to align with them. You should be warned in advance that reassessing what your core values are at *any* point in your life may be a little disruptive and stressful in and of itself;

however, the net result of such an extreme makeover will be exceptionally worthwhile and may save you X number of additional years of suffering your way down a path you really don't want to be on.

Option 3 is that you can GET STRONG! At the physiological level, stress tolerance results from a balance that allows us to shift between tension and relaxation in a sustainable rhythm so that our nerves and muscles and life-support systems can rest, recharge, and provide resources for our bodies to deal with the typical postmodern demands to process large amounts of complex data while under a great deal of pressure to decode the meaning accurately, and then persuade other people who are similarly stressed to do whatever it is we need them to do.

Stress impacts our muscle tension, connective tissue, skeletal structure, circulation, respiration, nervous fatigue, and neurotransmitter balance, as well as more obvious things like how we smell and how much fun we are to be with. The chemical byproducts of stress such as cortisol and the catecholamines can build up to toxic levels that make it as uncomfortable inside our bodies as the high-pressure situations we're confronting on the outside. If they could be eliminated directly through the urinary system we could just drink several beers, and that would be that—but no such luck! It requires the significantly increased oxygen levels and increased circulation that can only come from increased physical exertion.

That brings us to the real title of this exercise, "Stair Therapy." Now don't start whining and act all discouraged. This is still an easy stress buster. It turns out that if you work in an office with more than one floor, it's actually a world-class Olympic training facility in disguise—or at least a way you can easily take a big bite out of stress on a several-times-a-day basis. It's really not that hard; in fact it soon becomes enjoyable, and every little bit helps!

If you're really serious about feeling better and living longer, here's all you need: nothing. Just go climb two or three flights of stairs halfway between when you arrive in the morning and when you go for lunch, and then again halfway between lunch and when you leave at night. Amen! Easy shmeazy! All done, no excuses!

That's the bare-bones version of the stress buster, but if you are a more self-aware individual who wants something a little more sophisticated, for the intermediate level you need two additional things: a glass of water to

Emotional Intelligence in Action

drink when you're done and a joke book. Seriously, obtain a joke book—we suggest a clean joke book because those writers have to understand the more complex aspects of human nature better, so consequently they're often funnier, but that's up to you. Basically, you need to laugh more. Laughter helps reduce cortisol and, much more importantly, it makes life more enjoyable! So climb your two or three flights of stairs and drink your water while you read five or ten jokes a couple times a day. They won't all be funny, but some will be, and the neurotransmitters that you release while laughing will help reset your synaptic potential so your nerves can fire harder and faster and longer than they ever did before!

That's a joke. We personally have little or no idea what you're neurotransmitters will do, but we do know that laughter is good for you and bad for stress, so find a joke book or find some clean jokes online, climb some stairs, and have a drink (of water!).

The advanced level includes all the intermediate steps plus this ancient dietary secret from our Tibetan guru. *Eat more fresh fruit and vegetables and less junk!* That's not a joke! Eat them raw, because chewing crunchy stuff reduces stress. If you don't believe us, then you're clearly not ready for the advanced level or, if you want to try to prove us wrong, just try chewing celery and carrots and red bell pepper slices and cucumbers and see! One day we watched our guru chewing and chewing a single bite for what seemed like half an hour. Finally, we asked him what he was chewing. He spit out a mouthful of something. "Sand," he said, wiping his beard.

"But why are you chewing sand, Master?" we asked him. He looked at us sternly and said quietly, "To practice chewing."

Maybe we missed something by not trying that practice (maybe even enlightenment!), but since we didn't try it, we can't and don't recommend it. Actually it was Gil, our alternative health professional, who gave us the very best advice for stress tolerance, and it kind of sounds like the way a guru would talk: Eat less, move more!

Now get out there and bust some stress!

Emotional Intelligence in Action, Second Edition. Copyright ©2012 by Marcia Hughes and James Bradford Terrell. Reproduced by permission of Pfeiffer, an Imprint of Wiley. www.pfeiffer.com

Stress Tolerance

'Cause You've Got Personality

Purpose

To identify whether participants have personality types that tends to be stressed out. To explore their reactions and select an intervening response.

Thumbnail

19 to 28 minutes

This exercise is specifically helpful for people or groups where there is a lot of highly charged, rather aggressive behavior (Type A). Participants take a personality quiz that highlights Type A behaviors. They reflect on a recent situation in which they exhibited Type A behaviors and explore how they felt and what they were thinking. They select strategies to help them calm down in those situations.

Outcomes

- Heightened awareness of reactions
- Proactive commitment to calm down and be less harsh with others, starting with using the techniques they select in the exercise

411

Audience

- Intact team
- Unaffiliated group
- Individual working with a coach

Facilitator Competencies

Moderate

Materials

- Personality Quiz Handout
- 'Cause You've Got Personality Handout
- Flip chart and markers
- Pens

Time Matrix

Activity	Estimated Time
Personality Type Quiz	3–5 minutes
Explanation of personality types	3 minutes
Group discussion	5–10 minutes
Calming exercise	5 minutes
Debrief	3–5 minutes
Total Time	**19 to 28 minutes**

Instructions

1. Distribute copies of the Personality Quiz Handout and pens. Ask the participants to complete the quiz.
2. After everyone has completed the quiz, review the scoring instructions on the second page.
3. Provide the group with an overview of the various types of behavior.

Emotional Intelligence in Action

Type A Individuals

Tend to be impatient, aggressive, competitive and multi-tasking, with a high need for advancement and achievement. They are often described as hard-driving. Although they are often successful in their careers, they are never satisfied. Some extreme Type A's experience "free-floating" (ever-present) hostility and frequently react with anger. The risk of heart disease may be high for Type A personalities. This is a generalized description, but you get the point. Several of these characteristics are likely to be manifested, at least to some degree.

Type B Individuals

Tend to be noncompetitive, consciously control anger, and express emotions appropriately. They are often described as easygoing. Although they are not driven over-achievers, they are often as successful in their professions as Type A's. This also is a generalized description. Several of these characteristics are likely to be manifested, at least to some degree.

Type C Individuals

Tend to be passive and self-sacrificing, denying their own needs. They suppress anger and appease others. They are often described as bland. Extreme Type C's, not most of them, can have a profound sense of hopelessness and despair. The risk of cancer may be high for Type C personalities. This also is a generalized description. Several of these characteristics are likely to be manifested, at least to some degree.

4. Lead participants in a discussion about how their bodies feel and what they are thinking when they experience the types of situations referenced in the test.
5. Ask them whether they would like to be completely laid back, noncompetitive, and passive (extreme Type C). They will probably say no because they see that as being weak and not having gumption.
6. Ask them whether they can see a middle ground between where they are now, especially if that is between Type A and extreme Type C behavior. Work with the group to develop a list of more helpful alternative behavioral characteristics (Type B). Record these on the flip chart.
7. Distribute the 'Cause You've Got Personality Handout and ask participants to complete it.

8. Debrief by:
   - Asking whether they would like to share the stress reduction responses they selected in Item 6 of the 'Cause You've Got Personality Handout.
   - Asking them to choose specific times in their daily lives that they will commit to practice.
9. For an immediate experience of stress reduction that your participants can later utilize as a reference, have everyone practice a calming experience such as those listed in Item 6 of the handout.

PERSONALITY QUIZ HANDOUT

Complete the following statements by indicating whether they are true (always or usually) or false (rarely or never) for you.

Statement	True	False
1. I see myself as competitive and driving.	_____	_____
2. I hate to wait.	_____	_____
3. I work best when I'm up against a deadline.	_____	_____
4. I prefer to do more than one thing at a time.	_____	_____
5. I am often angry with others, even though it may not show.	_____	_____
6. I become irritated with people who make mistakes	_____	_____
7. I often feel I'm in a race against time.	_____	_____
8. I set very high goals for myself, but I still get angry when I don't meet my goals.	_____	_____

Emotional Intelligence in Action, Second Edition. Copyright ©2012 by Marcia Hughes and James Bradford Terrell. Reproduced by permission of Pfeiffer, an Imprint of Wiley. www.pfeiffer.com

SCORING SHEET

- If you have six to eight true answers, you may exhibit the behaviors of a Type A personality.
- If you have four or five true answers, you are probably more prone to Type B behavior that is balanced between the extremes of Type A and Type C.
- If you have one to three true answers, you may be rather passive and tend toward Type C behavior.

'CAUSE YOU'VE GOT PERSONALITY HANDOUT

Think of a recent interaction with others in which you felt upset, impatient, or angry. Answer the following questions about that experience.

1. How did your body feel?

2. If you felt any of the following symptoms, circle them: heart racing, sweating, twitching, breathing hard, clenching your jaw or other part of body. Did you experience other symptoms?

3. How would you characterize your thoughts about the situation? Rank them on a scale from 1 to 10, where 1 is the most forgiving and 10 is the most judgmental.

4. How did the situation work out? Were you able to reach a mutually agreeable solution?

5. Did your responses increase or decrease the level of stress in that situation?

6. Select and practice one of the following methods for calming down and relieving the pressure. Rehearse it several times in neutral situations with the intention to apply it the next time you find yourself in a stressful situation:

   - Take a deep-breathing break to release the impatience and anger. Clear your mind and concentrate fully on your breathing. Inhale through your nose slowly and deeply to a count of ten, expanding your lungs. Exhale through your nose, slowly and completely to a count of ten, contracting your chest.
   - Even it you don't feel it at the moment, act as if you have high regard for the others involved in the situation. Behave as if you want to resolve the issue *while* treating the person with respect and dignity. Call him or her by name, and make frequent eye contact.
   - Follow another method of your own design.

7. Practice the behavior at least once and preferably twice a day for several minutes and for several days to develop the habit and perfect the technique.

Stress Tolerance

Water Off a Duck's Back

Purpose

To manage stress by anticipating issues and having coping mechanisms in place.

Thumbnail

30 to 50 minutes

Participants list activities that are stressful to them and itemize the specific stressful aspects. For each aspect of the situation, they develop strategies to mitigate the stress.

Outcomes

- Enhanced ability to avoid or reduce stress through effective management
- Greater awareness of the power of planning for stressful situations

Audience

- Intact team
- Unaffiliated group
- Individual working with a coach

Facilitator Competencies ◯

Easy

Materials

- Paper and pens

Time Matrix

Activity	Estimated Time
List and select stressful activities	5–10 minutes
Outline stressful aspects	5–10 minutes
Identify stress mitigation strategies	5–10 minutes
Share with partner	10 minutes
Debrief group	5–10 minutes
Total Time	**30 to 50 minutes**

Instructions

1. Distribute paper and pens to all participants.
2. Ask individuals to list the three most stressful activities or situations they face on a regular basis—making a presentation, confronting a co-worker, getting through traffic, managing a heavy workload, dating someone new, attending or hosting a family gathering, and so on.
3. Ask each of them to select one from the list to work on. Encourage them to pick one they will be dealing with in the near future.
4. Have participants notice and write down the sequence of symptoms that indicate the onset of stress.
5. Ask participants to write down one thing they can do to mitigate or alleviate each symptom of stress that arises in the problematic situation. The following examples may be helpful:
   - Have conversations with key people about the situation. The discussion should cover everyone's expectations and commitment.
   - Climb a flight or two of stairs, taking deep breaths all the way up and back.

　　　　　　　　　　　　　Emotional Intelligence in Action

- Schedule extra time for unforeseen contingencies.
- Seek assistance from a friend.
- Hire a service provider to help.
- Redirect all of your attention from the external world and focus on the internal rhythm of your breath or heartbeat.

6. Divide teams into pairs; individuals continue to work with their coaches. Ask the pairs to share their situations, including which aspects are stressors, and to ask their partners for ideas on some ways they would attempt to mitigate the stressors. Take up to ten minutes gathering this information.

7. Debrief the group. Ask what sorts of suggestions they heard and liked, but had not come up with on their own.

Stress Tolerance

Deep Center Breathing

Purpose

To provide simple instructions in a stress reduction technique that will enable people to get in touch with the tension they are holding in their bodies and release it.

Thumbnail

13 to 18 minutes

This exercise is primarily for individuals and can be done in any comfortable location that is quiet and where one will be undisturbed. If a group of individuals wishes to undertake the experience simultaneously, there should be private or silent space available for each individual. The participant(s) practice deep breathing. The most significant competency needed in this exercise will be the facilitator's familiarity with the power and rhythms of his or her own breathing. It is recommended that the facilitator practice for two or three consecutive days before attempting to coach others. The facilitator needs to have direct experience of the value this process provides in order to help the participant(s) slow down and appreciate something as intangible as breath.

Outcome

Each person who practices the Deep Center Breathing exercise will gain a greater appreciation for the power of his or her breathing, the rhythms of the body, and the amount of stress that is stored in the body.

Audience

- Intact team
- Unaffiliated group
- Individual working with a coach

Facilitator Competencies

Moderate

Materials

- Deep Center Breathing Handout

Time Matrix

Activity	Estimated Time
Sit comfortably in a quiet place, begin relaxing	2 minutes
Read and practice the instructions	3–5 minutes
Practice one or two rounds of the breathing exercise	6–8 minutes
Experiment with the advanced method	2–3 minutes
Total Time	**13 to 18 minutes**

Instructions

1. Invite participants to sit comfortably in a quiet place, relaxing to the best of their ability. Provide the participants with the handout.
2. Emphasizing that each individual's experience of breathing is as unique as his or her fingerprints in its depth, rhythm, frequency, tension, and

cycle (and that it is regularly changing), encourage the participants to first discover just how they happen to be breathing right now.

3. After several minutes, invite them to read the handout and practice the breathing exercises.

DEEP CENTER BREATHING HANDOUT

According to Candace Pert (2000), a leading neuroscience researcher, people who have lived in the developed world all their lives have over ninety industrial chemicals present in their bodies. Over 70 percent of our bodies' waste by-products are eliminated through our breathing and our skin. Blood, which is fully oxygenated, removes more toxins from our bodies at the cellular level and makes it more difficult for viruses and bacteria to grow in our bodies.

Deep Center Breathing is a powerful stress reduction technique that supports muscle growth and supplies the brain and body the energy they need. It can also help to relieve muscular tension and alleviate stress. Although it is simple, its value should not be underestimated! Patterns of shallow or incomplete breathing do not give the body enough oxygen, which in itself can cause stress and fatigue due to the toxic build-up of carbon dioxide. These kinds of breathing patterns are often learned and repeated unconsciously. Until some sort of conscious breathing technique such as Deep Center Breathing is employed, most people never discover the natural power of their breath. So enjoy!

Deep Center Breathing

Sitting comfortably in your chair; observe your breathing. Notice which parts of your body move with your breath; notice how often you inhale, and how deeply.

Now spread your hands across your stomach, with your thumbs just under your ribs.

Shift your breathing out of your chest down and into your belly.

Feel your lower abdomen swell as the air inflates your lungs. As you exhale, feel your abdomen shrink and grow softer.

Now draw in your abdominal muscles and empty the remaining air from your lungs. Again, feel the difference.

Now breathe in this fashion for the next three minutes, inhaling slowly to a count of four and then slowly exhaling to the same count. After you have the hang of it, just let your hands relax comfortably in your lap. Notice what happens to your heart rate. How is it different when you inhale compared to when you exhale? After three minutes, return to normal breathing. Notice what you're thinking. Notice what you're feeling.

Do this exercise two or three times throughout the day, especially when you feel tired, or spacey, or upset. You can also do a longer version in which you build up time gradually by adding another minute every day until you reach fifteen or twenty minutes. For an additional stretch, try holding your breath for four counts when your lungs are full and again for four counts when they are empty, creating a four-part breathing pattern.

REFERENCE

Pert, C. (2000). *Your body is your subconscious mind.* Boulder, CO: Sounds True.

Optimism

Optimistic Self-Talk and Behavior

Purpose

To increase optimism through coordinating self talk with optimistic behaviors.

Thumbnail

40 minutes

What many people do not recognize or acknowledge about optimism is that it is not so much a gift that one is born with as it is an attitudinal commitment that is nurtured and developed. This exercise provides instructions for a practice that will help participants develop a more optimistic attitude and more effective emotional results.

Outcomes

- Understand the conscious and unconscious components of developing optimistic self talk
- Set up a specific daily practice

Audience

- Members of intact teams
- Members of an unaffiliated group
- Individual working with a coach

Facilitator Competencies

Moderate

Materials

- Optimistic Self-Talk and Behavior Handout
- Sticky notes
- Paper and pens

Time Matrix

Activity	Estimated Time
Discuss points from first part of handout	10 minutes
Review the four steps and discuss	10 minutes
Implement the four steps, with Step 3 being conducted in pairs	10 minutes
Debrief as a whole group	10 minutes
Total Time	**40 minutes**

Instructions

1. Distribute the Optimistic Self-Talk and Behavior Handout and sticky notes for later use. Read the handout either directly with the participants or ask them to read it and then discuss it as a group. Stop at the point where the four-step practice begins.
2. Ask participants to review the four steps of the optimism practice and carefully consider implementing this strategy and then invite questions.
3. Guide your participants to follow the four-step process. Ask each person to choose two active, positive emotional energies that he or she

wants to be able to feel on a regular basis and to write notes as directed in Step 3.

4. Then ask participants to form pairs, choose one of their energies, and take turns fully expressing it as called for in Step 3.

5. Finally, they should write their sticky notes as called for in Step 4.

6. Bring everyone together and debrief their experience, using questions like:

- How did it feel when you practiced one of your preferred energies?
- What key strategy can you commit to in order to tap into this energy more?
- What gets in your way of using that energy now?

OPTIMISTIC SELF-TALK AND BEHAVIOR HANDOUT

The collective unconscious of humanity is filled with every kind of thought and attitude imaginable, from murder and mayhem to the most devoted altruism. If we wander out into all that commotion without setting our intentions for the quality of day we want to have, we can find our feelings resonating with the craziest kinds of thoughts *and thinking that they're really ours!*

In fact it is pretty difficult to start one's day without some kind of desire structure informing it. Most people unconsciously go with something from the generic set: "I will succeed by getting important things done." "I will do better than everyone else." "I will stay safe." "I will get what I want." "I will receive friendly, approving responses from others."

Here's the problem. While we are asserting these kinds of thoughts at one level, at another level we are actually seeking to counter our fears that we won't get important things done, that others may do better than we do, that we won't be safe, or get what we want, or be accepted. And there are thousands of other people out there whose fears are aligning with ours, and they will scare us plenty if we mistakenly identify with them.

Here's a way to bypass most of that kind of internal conflict. Start the day with some *choices* about *what kind of person you want to be*, **not** what kind of results you would like but haven't achieved yet. The second approach entails looking for effects in the world outside of ourselves rather than "being the change we want to see in the world" (to echo a popular observation by Mahatma Gandhi).

But how do we "be" that? First, choose the feelings you want to feel inside yourself, for instance, excited, alert, persistent, strong, flexible, assertive, relaxed, grateful, confident, resourceful, happy, playful, or committed. Believe it or not, we have the internal ability to generate these emotions regardless of what's going on in the environment. We do it by remembering a specific time when we felt excited or grateful or confident, and so on, in great detail.

While you are remembering, notice your physiology in that situation. What is your posture? How are you standing or sitting? How are you breathing? How focused are your eyes? How does your face look? What are you saying to yourself? These are the keys that unlock your access to the kinds of energy you need to be able to generate intentionally to succeed in the social world.

This exercise is designed to help you feel optimistic that you can generate the kinds of emotional states and energies you need throughout the day, *but it is a **practice** not a realization!* It's not like, "Oh I get it. That's why emotionally intelligent communication makes teams work together more efficiently." Rather, it's like, "Well, I've written a good speech here, so now I'm going to present it in front of the mirror and videotape myself at a podium and record my voice on a CD I can listen to it in the car. I'm going to try it in front of a few friends and absorb all the feedback I can. I'll experiment with different timing and different emphasis until I know I'm going to nail it!"

With this background, now we will work with the four-step process. Stop reading at this point and wait for further instructions.

Four-Step Practice

Step One

To design your own optimism practice, choose two active, positive emotional energies that you want to be able to feel on a regular basis. Yes, we often need tolerance, patience, forbearance, and so forth, but for this exercise pick something more active and generative (and fun!). Choose the kind of energy that you can intentionally radiate into the environment, like commitment, playfulness, excitement, gratitude, or confidence.

Step Two

Write down several details from two or more specific situations in which you clearly recall experiencing each of these emotional energies. (This will help you remember and re-access them.) Pick whichever emotional energy you want to start with, then vividly replay the first situation in which you felt it, seeing how everything looked, hearing the sounds and/or voices that were present, feeling all the physical sensations and emotions you felt at the time. After you have reabsorbed the energy from this situation, do the same for your second emotional energy.

Step Three

Now BREATHE that energy while you're moving purposefully—jog in your living room, climb a flight or two of stairs, walk briskly down the sidewalk or through a hallway thinking "Confidence!" while you inhale, perhaps even speaking softly as you exhale. You are imbibing the energy of confidence from the strength of your intention. Visualize yourself standing confidently, speaking confidently. Hear how your voice sounds internally, then speak that way out loud! The extra oxygen will give you more physical energy; the dramatic behavior will definitely get your subconscious mind's attention—"Hey! What's going on? This must be really important! S/he must need me—I'd better get in the game and see what's cooking!" Bringing your subconscious mind online is one of the most powerful support systems you can engage when you need to feel optimistic.

Step Four

Now get three sticky notes and write on them something like this:

> **I'm Optimistic I can feel more *playful* and *committed* from this practice!** (Fill in the blanks with the two words that you have chosen.)

Put one sticky note on your bathroom mirror, one on the dashboard of your car (or somewhere you will see it en route to work), and the third in your workspace on the job. The one on the mirror will help you set your intentions for the day early and remind you to start by enjoying the energetic feeling states you want to access. It will also help you revisit those positive feelings just before bed. (This timing helps a great deal in engaging your subconscious mind's cooperation.) The note on your dashboard will remind you to practice on the way to work *and* on the way home (where you also want to have these positive emotional energies available!). And the note at work will remind you to energize as many situations as you can with your optimism and positive emotions. Use the Goldilocks approach (not too much, not too little), and you'll be surprised at how the other people in interaction with you will appreciate your contributions.

Do this for a week and you will definitely increase your ability to access the emotional energies that you have chosen. Do it for two weeks and your positive responses will start to become automatic. Do it for four weeks and you will not only have programmed an automatically resourceful response, you will have developed a new habit of rehearsing positive feelings throughout the day and you will be able to plug in new emotional resources that you want to develop until you master them as well!

Optimism

Be Solution-Focused

Purpose

Individuals and teams will learn the benefits of being solution-focused and expressing positive messages rather than staying stuck in the problem.

Thumbnail

17 to 25 minutes

Participants working in pairs, or individuals working with a coach, will read the problem scenarios and seek to fully focus on the problem (*not* on the solution). Then they will shift to a solution-focused approach using positive statements to stimulate a hopeful, optimistic attitude. This helps the participants directly experience the difference between the two styles.

Outcome

To recognize the power of beginning the decision-making process with an upbeat, solution-focused approach, as it supports better decisions and generally leads to making them more quickly.

Audience

- Intact team
- Unaffiliated group
- Individual working with a coach

Facilitator Competencies

Moderate

Materials

- Be Solution-Focused Handout or design scenarios to meet your specific situation

Time Matrix

Activity	Estimated Time
Review the practice scenarios focusing on the problem	3–4 minutes
Discuss how participants feel when their attention is fully on a problem	3–4 minutes
Repeat both steps above and discuss, this time with a focus on the solution	6–7 minutes
Facilitator presents a brief discussion on optimism, linking it to solution-focused thinking and behavior	5–10 minutes
Total	**17 to 25 minutes**

Instructions

1. Distribute copies of the Be Solution-Focused Handout and ask the participants to form pairs. If appropriate, develop an alternative list of scenarios to the ones provided here that better match the circumstances facing your individual or group.
2. Tell participants to review the practice scenarios with a focus that emphasizes the problem. Participants are *not* to solve the problem, but rather to figure out all the issues and just how difficult they are.

3. Next ask participants to discuss how they are feeling when the focus is fully on the problem. This may be done in pairs or as a group.
4. Repeat Steps 2 and 3 with a focus on the solution and follow with group discussion. Encourage the group to notice any negative expectations and to set them aside in a willingness to generate more open, "can do" responses.
5. Present a brief discussion on optimism, linking it to solution-focused thinking and behavior. Take questions from the participants.

BE SOLUTION-FOCUSED HANDOUT

Sample Problem Scenarios

With your partner, discuss how to solve the following scenarios using a strategy that focuses intensely, if not exclusively, on the problem, making sure to notice all the issues and just how difficult they are.

1. You work in an organization where you provide assistance to several "bosses." Boss A asks you to complete an assignment in two weeks, and you say, "No problem." Then another assignment comes in from Boss B that is due in twelve days. It is much more interesting than the first assignment, and the deadline is much more solid; the first one could be extended. However, it is just about impossible to get them both done. Boss A is out of town until the day the assignment is due. What do you do?

2. Jamie needs a ride to soccer at the same time that Terry needs a ride to dance lessons. They cannot take a bus and there is no other family member to help out.

3. You're really tired of working on the weekends and committed to balancing your life better, but you also have a creative project under way that you have wanted to do for many years. It's finally started up. The best way to get time for the project—which is work, just more creative—is to get caught up on work so you can work on the project, but that requires working on the weekends. What do you do?

4. You will have a lot less stress in your life if you have your bills paid off, but you really want to help your son and daughter go to college. Paying for college will only increase your debt, but. . . .

5. You have four managers reporting to you. Only one is a woman and she is convinced that you put her down. The last survey from her staff is reflecting increasing disgruntlement with her, and her productivity is down. She reports that she's doing more than ever and thinks her staff highly respects her. What do you do?

After some discussion, you will repeat this activity when the facilitator instructs you to do so. You will be given new directions.

Optimism

See a Positive Resolution

Purpose

To learn how vividly imagining a problem as well-resolved generates the positive energy to help us move more rapidly toward an effective resolution.

Thumbnail

50 minutes

Discussion of how our beliefs affect our optimism and why it's valuable, and then some reflective time to allow new associations to surface. Next a discussion of an issue in each person's life that doesn't have a readily apparent answer and pairs work to imagine the details of a positive result.

Outcomes

- Expand awareness of the consequences of thinking pessimistically, as contrasted with thinking positively
- Make a commitment to guide thinking for more positive results

Audience

- Intact team
- Unaffiliated group
- Individual working with a coach

Facilitator Competencies ◯ ◑

Easy to Moderate

Materials

- None needed

Time Matrix

Activity	Estimated Time
Discuss connection between optimism, values, and beliefs	10 minutes
In pairs, or with coach, discuss value of optimism	10 minutes
Take some quiet, reflective time to allow new associations to develop	5 minutes
In pairs, discuss an issue in each person's life that doesn't have an answer and then imagine a positive result	5 minutes
Learn the details of the resolution	10 minutes
Discuss learnings and set commitments for practicing optimism	10 minutes
Total	**50 minutes**

Instructions

1. Discuss the relationship between optimism and the belief in positive outcomes. What we believe will happen has a powerful effect on the outcomes we experience. One example of this result is that optimistic salespeople are the most effective at their jobs. New salesmen at MetLife who scored high on a test of "learned optimism" sold 37 percent more life insurance in their first two years than did pessimists (Seligman, 1990); also cited by the Consortium for Research on Emotional

Emothional Intelligence in Action

Intelligence in Organizations at www.eiconsortium.org/reports/business_case_for_ei.html.

2. Ask the individual you are coaching or the team members to discuss their perceptions of the value of optimism in their lives with partners. Then discuss the topic as a group. Ask how much value optimism contributes to their lives.

3. Ask people to share what they do when they find themselves in a pessimistic state. How soon do they notice? Does it creep up on them so they don't even notice when they are feeling fairly depressed and discouraged?

4. One way to counter the pessimism is to change thoughts such as: "I am overwhelmed and don't think this can work out well" to "I know there's a good result to this concern; I just don't understand what it is *yet*."

5. Have participants choose partners to work with and announce that the first step in the following learning process is to remain silent for four minutes. Acknowledge that it may seem like a long time, but that you will watch the clock carefully and tell them as soon as the time's up. Ask them to sit comfortably, breathe deeply, and let their minds rest. When thoughts come up, they will just let them go and redirect their attention to the sound of their breathing or the sensations they feel in their bodies.

6. At the end of the time, ask them to bring their attention back into focus in the room and to turn to their partners. One person will go first and tell the other about a situation that he or she believes won't work out well and over which he or she feels a lack of power. (*Note:* Guide the level of difficulty of the issue you raise based on your familiarity and expertise in expanding emotional intelligence skills and the nature and skills of your group or the individual with whom you are working. You can keep this simple by instructing participants to think of a meaningful but moderate challenge. This skill can be expanded as they take on new issues, having mastered the process at less challenging levels.)

   - Now that the first person has described the situation, the other should be instructed to say: "I understand that you don't know the answer yet, but let's work together to imagine that somehow a miracle happened, and the issue is now completely resolved. Notice everything that is different. What do you feel, what do you see, what do you hear? What else do you know now that this change has occurred?"

- The person in the listening role works with the other for four or five minutes to develop as detailed a positive resolution as possible.
- Tell them to reflect with their partners about the difference between feeling like they don't have the answer yet, but recognizing that it will appear at some time, and just feeling powerless because they don't know the answer.
- Ask the pairs to switch roles and repeat the process.

7. Reconvene the entire group and discuss the activity. Ask participants to commit to practicing optimism by remembering this day and this group and this process when a new problem arises, and to remind themselves in such situations: "I just don't know the answer *YET*." Questions you might ask in debriefing include:
- What do you feel in your body when you are feeling pessimistic as compared to when you are feeling optimistic?
- On a scale of 1 to 10, how important is optimism to you?
- How might you influence others to be more optimistic?

Optimism

The Optimistic Explanation

Purpose

To help participants explore the way they explain the events that happen to them in life and to understand how that dynamic affects their optimism and, ultimately, their success.

Thumbnail

25 to 30 minutes

Each participant will read the brief scenarios in the hand-out and do his or her best to imagine that what happened in the vignette actually happened. Participants will then write explanations of why each point in the story occurred the way it did and be given a key for analyzing the significance of their responses.

Outcome

This exercise will teach participants how their explanatory styles influence their optimism and how they can modify their styles to change the results they get in the world.

Audience

- Intact team
- Unaffiliated group
- Individual working with a coach

Facilitator Competencies

Moderate

Materials

- The Optimistic Explanation Handout
- Paper and pens

Time Matrix

Activity	Estimated Time
Explain optimism using handout	5 minutes
Scenario One	5 minutes
Scenario Two	5 minutes
Group discussion or individual reflection	10–15 minutes
Total	**25 to 30 minutes**

Instructions

1. Provide participants with paper, pens, and The Optimistic Explanation Handout.
2. Explain optimism, drawing on the explanation in Part Two of this book and the analysis section of the handout.
3. Instruct the participants to read the two scenarios and write their explanations of what caused the events as if they really happened to them.
4. Convene the full group to debrief the experience. Sample questions you might begin with include:
   - What was your experience as you worked with the two scenarios?
   - What did you learn that would benefit your work and life as a whole?
   - Do you find that, when you're more optimistic, it is easier to solve problems?

THE OPTIMISTIC EXPLANATION HANDOUT

Analysis

The explanations of causality that we offer hinge on three critical dynamics, and these ultimately determine how optimistic or pessimistic a person is. This concept is discussed by Martin Seligman (1990) in *Learned Optimism*. We explain these three concepts as follows:

1. *Permanence*—We perceive the causes of events in our lives to either be *temporary* or *permanent*. "I never remember to fill my gas tank" is permanent. "I forgot to fill my tank yesterday" is a temporary explanation.
2. *Pervasiveness*—"People who make *universal* explanations for their failures give up on everything when a failure strikes in one area. People who make *specific* explanations may become helpless in that one part of their lives, yet march stalwartly on in the others" (Seligman, 1990, p. 46).
3. *Personalization*—When bad things happen, humans either attribute the cause to other people or to circumstances (externalization) or we attribute it to ourselves (internalization). When we blame ourselves, it tends to erode our self-esteem. When we blame others or external circumstances, we don't lose self-esteem, but persistent blaming of others can become problematic in itself because it is inherently disempowering, and other people will begin to reject us if we never take responsibility for the effects we cause. Appropriate reality testing is an excellent tool for helping maintain the desired balance.

Here is the formula for optimism: When you are explaining *positive* events, you want them to be permanent, universal, and internal. For example, "*All* the good things that happen in my life are *always* a result of *my faith* (internal) in our Creator." When you are explaining *negative* events you want them to be temporary, specific, and external. For example, "The flat tire I had *today* (specific) was the result of some *nails that were spilled on the highway* (external)." Contrast that with, "I *always* (permanent) get flat tires because *I* (internal) can *never* (permanent) avoid all the road hazards out there."

How do these kinds of explanations compare with the ones you usually use to explain what happens in your life? If you want to be more optimistic, and hence more successful, practice changing the way you use these three dynamics when you explain the causes of both the positive and negative events in your life.

Read the two scenarios that follow and explain the causes that contributed to each step in the story as if they happened to you. Apply the three dynamics of optimism you just reviewed as you make up your explanations.

Scenario One

1. You are reading an article in the newspaper and see a display ad that says "Wanted . . . Good Problem Solvers."
2. Although you already have a job, you call them, and they sound like they are interested in you right away.
3. You schedule an interview and find the office where you apply to be friendly, well-appointed, and easy to get to. When you find out what kind of work they do, it's almost like a dream come true!
4. The pay is significantly better than your current job, so you accept the position and begin to have the best work experience of your entire life.

Make up an explanation of why each step happened the way it did as if this story actually happened to you. In Number 1, for example, you might write: "I've always been a curious person who follows up on unusual things that catch my eye . . . like an ad for "Good Problem Solvers." Write your answers below.

1.

2.

3.

4.

15.4. Optimism

Scenario Two

1. You are on the way to meet someone you're really interested in for a date, and your car runs out of gas.
2. You manage to get a ride to a gas station and call the restaurant, leaving a message that you will be about half an hour late. It takes a long time to get back to your car and it's closer to an hour when you finally arrive.
3. Your date is still there, but obviously not too happy. The conversation drags and you can't seem to stop apologizing.
4. When the check comes, you insist on paying as the least you can do, and your date finally chuckles and seems to lighten up.
5. Unfortunately, the waiter returns saying your credit card has been declined and their policy, as the signs clearly state, is "Absolutely no checks!" You have only $3 in cash, and your date ends up paying the bill.

Make up an explanation of why each step happened the way it did as if this story actually happened to you.

1.

Emotional Intelligence in Action

2.

3.

4.

Emotional Intelligence in Action, Second Edition. Copyright ©2012 by Marcia Hughes and James Bradford Terrell. Reproduced by permission of Pfeiffer, an Imprint of Wiley. www.pfeiffer.com

15.4. Optimism

Examine the explanations that you made for the causes of each event in the two scenarios. Were they permanent or temporary? Universal or specific? Internal or external? Do you feel more optimistic?

REFERENCE

Seligman, M. (1990). *Learned optimism.* New York: Pocket Books.

Happiness/Well-Being

Beyond Personal Silos

Purpose

To understand happiness and well-being as a multi-dimensional part of life that benefits from integration.

Thumbnail

45 minutes

Participants discuss the concept of well-being and how happiness is deeply affected by the application of other skills, such as self-regard. Participants explore how they live their lives in silos (such as work, family and community) and discuss the value of an integrated approach.

Outcomes

- Expand awareness of personal happiness and well-being
- Explore the ways that silo, or compartmentalized, thinking about one's life leads to frustration and develop an integrated approach

Audience

- Intact teams
- Unaffiliated group
- Individual working with a coach

Facilitator Competencies ◯

Easy

Materials

- Beyond Personal Silos Handout
- Flip chart paper, easel, and markers

Time Matrix

Activity	Estimated Time
Discuss well-being	10 minutes
Explore the consequences of silo thinking	5 minutes
Write individually; in pairs discuss integrating their lives	20 minutes
Discuss as a whole	10 minutes
Total Time	**45 minutes**

Instructions

1. Discuss the concept of well-being. Note that this is highlighted in the EQ-i$^{2.0}$ with the well-being indicator, which gives a score for happiness and then highlights the relationship of happiness with four other key skills: self-regard, optimism, interpersonal relationships, and self-actualization. Team well-being is also one of the target goals of working with the TESI. Ask some or all of the following questions and write key points on the flip chart.
   - What do you gauge your current level of happiness to be?
   - What is well-being? How are the two related?

- How important is it to you to be happy?
- Do you think that every decision you make is in some way designed to help you be happy? If so why do you feel dissatisfied some of the time?

2. Explore the role that conflicting goals has in contributing to personal happiness as well as to frustration. Ask participants to take a look at their lives and explore how much they think of their lives in silos, such as one part is work, one part is family, one part is community involvement, and so on. Write key points on the flip chart.

3. Tell them the concept of silos is looking at one's life in fragments and is usually divided functionally so they might think of their silos as being work, family, community, and fun. Ask what other silos they think of for their lives and ask them to make a list of the silos of their lives.

4. Distribute the Beyond Personal Silos Handout and ask participants to write about their lives first from a silo perspective and second from an integrated perspective, which could be defined as one life with overlapping needs, skills, interactions that co-influence to one integrated life. After fifteen minutes, ask them to form small groups of three or four and discuss what they wrote and their preferences and strategies for how to integrate their lives.

5. Bring the group back together and discuss strategies for viewing and living an integrated life.

BEYOND PERSONAL SILOS HANDOUT

My Life from a Silo Perspective

List the ways you think of your life: the work part, the family part, the community part, and so on. How does this view of your life serve you?

How does it interrupt the natural flow of your life and lead to frustration?

My Life from an Integrated Perspective

List the ways you think of your life as a whole with flow from one part to another and considerable overlap. How does this view of your life serve you?

How does it interrupt the organization of your life and lead to frustration?

Happiness/Well-Being

Growing My Happiness

Purpose

For participants to notice how happy they are, how happy they would like to be, and develop a strategy to get there.

Thumbnail

35 to 45 minutes

Participants assess their current level of happiness, connect that level with circumstances in their lives, and then develop action plans to live with the level of happiness they prefer. The total time could be expanded in order to have an advanced version.

Outcomes

- Increased understanding of some of the attitudes and conditions in life that influence one's happiness
- Enhanced ability and willingness to influence how happy one is

Audience

- Intact team
- Unaffiliated group
- Individual working with a coach

Facilitator Competencies

Moderate

Materials

- Growing My Happiness Handout
- Paper (could be a journal) and pens

Time Matrix

Activity	Estimated Time
Introduce the topic and exercise	5 minutes
Each individuals write in response to provided questions	5 minutes
With coach or in groups of two or three, discuss what was written	10 minutes
Conduct individual assessment and write action plans	5–10 minutes
With coach or in small groups, discuss the plan and commit to implementation	5 minutes
Debrief group	5–10 minutes
Total	**35 to 45 minutes**

Instructions

1. Distribute paper and a pen to each participant.
2. Discuss what happiness means. You can draw on the material in Part Two of this book on happiness for information.

3. Each participant, or the coaching client, should develop a list of responses to the following statements:
   - I'm content about:
   - I'm worried/frustrated about:
4. Now instruct each participant to write a few paragraphs observing and connecting these two factors as they are currently playing out in the participants' lives.
5. If working with a team, have them get together in groups of two or three and discuss what they wrote. Each person should take three to four minutes. Individuals should discuss their responses with their coach.
6. Distribute the Growing My Happiness Handout and instruct participants to use the handout to assess their current levels of happiness and then develop action plans.
7. Discuss what participants wrote in their small groups or with their coaches and make a commitment to follow through with improving their happiness through heightened awareness and commitment.
8. Debrief as a group. Potential questions you might ask include:
   - Who are some of the happiest people you know? Do you want to be like them?
   - What does happiness mean to you?
   - How important is happiness in your life?
9. *Advanced Version:* Take more time and be more comprehensive with each step. For example, for Step 2, participants could do a comprehensive inventory of the positive and negative life conditions affecting their lives. Expand each of the other steps accordingly. Meet again to follow through with a discussion on complying with commitments.

GROWING MY HAPPINESS HANDOUT

Personal Assessment

This is similar to the Fordyce Emotions Questionnaire discussed in Seligman (2002, p. 15).

_____ 1. On a scale of 1 to 10 (10 is highest), how happy am I?

_____ 2. On the same scale, how unhappy am I?

_____ 3. On the same scale, how neutral or checked out am I?

_____ 4. How happy would I like to be? (Make it an amount you are willing to strive toward accomplishing in your life.)

My Happiness Action Plan

In order to accomplish my intention and heartfelt desire to be happy at a . . . level, I commit to take the following actions. Be specific so you can measure your success. (*Note:* Use the information from your reflections at the beginning of this exercise so that you connect with your current state of happiness. You may find a need to add much more information about your current life conditions to fully develop this action plan. You are encouraged to add in further reflections as you have more time.)

REFERENCE

Seligman, M. (2002). *Authentic happiness.* New York: The Free Press.

Emotional Intelligence in Action

Happiness/Well-Being

Pay It Forward with Gratitude

Purpose

To recognize that gratitude is contagious, feels good, and expands our resourcefulness.

Thumbnail

50 minutes (can be expanded or contracted)

After discussing the power of gratitude, individuals working with a coach and teams or groups working in pairs review five or more items for which they are grateful. They develop a commitment to pay it forward so when they receive a statement of gratefulness, they reach out to expand the attitude.

Outcomes

- Feel happier
- Know how to keep and increase happiness, even with just one strategy
- Recognize that there are many more great ways to enhance happiness

Audience

- Intact team
- Unaffiliated group
- Individual working with a coach

Facilitator Competencies

Easy to Moderate

Materials

- None needed

Time Matrix

Activity	Estimated Time
Discuss research on the power of gratitude	10 minutes
In pairs, take turns reviewing five things for which each person is grateful; the other listens attentively	15 minutes
As a whole group, discuss what they have recognized	10 minutes
Group discussion to increase awareness	10 minutes
Develop commitment to pay it forward	5 minutes
Total	**50 minutes**

Instructions

1. Discuss with the group, or the person you are coaching, that there is now research on the power of gratitude. Refer them to www .authentichappiness.com to take the gratitude questionnaire and learn more about how gratitude works in their lives. (*Note:* This can also be an assignment before the group or individual comes to this session. If so, have them print out and bring their results.)
2. Say to the group, "Fortunately, the benefits of gratitude are becoming well-recognized. The *New York Times Sunday Magazine* included Seligman's

'Gratitude Visit' in its annual list of '100 Great Ideas.' The strategy is described as follows:

> "You think of a person in your life who has been kind to you but whom you've never properly thanked. You write a detailed 'gratitude letter' to that person, explaining in concrete terms why you're grateful. Then you visit that person and read the testimony aloud. According to Seligman, the ritual is powerful. 'Everyone cries when you do a gratitude visit,' he says. 'It's very moving for both people.'" (Pink, 2004, pp. 2–3)

Ask your participants whether any have done a gratitude visit. Recommend that it can serve them well.

3. For this exercise, have each person pair with someone else and tell him or her five things for which he or she is grateful. If you are coaching, the individual will tell you. The coach/listener should listen attentively and then ask questions. Help the individual become clear about why he or she is grateful. Then switch and the coach/listener will identify about five items for which he or she is grateful and tell the partner, who will help to clarify why the person feels grateful.

4. As a group, or with your client, discuss what you experienced during this process. If you are working with a group, time permitting, ask for people to move and create new pairs and repeat the process. You can repeat this as often as fits your group and the time available.

5. Conclude with everyone discussing how they are feeling having just spent this time on gratitude. Apply this awareness to work. Ask:
   - What happens when someone genuinely thanks you?
   - How do you feel?
   - How do you engage with your work when you return to it?

6. Take gratitude a step further by building in a pay-it-forward commitment. The gratitude visit, Seligman believes, can be an effective way to "increase the intensity, duration, and frequency of positive memory" (p. 3). We can expand this benefit by returning gratitude every time someone expresses gratitude to us, but only if we truly received his or her gift first.

7. Ask the partners to commit to pay gratitude forward at least twice a day for one week. Then have the pairs agree to commit to a time when they will get together at the end of that week to revisit their commitment

and discuss how it is working. Hopefully, they will agree to renew the commitment for another week. Emphasize that change happens only with practice; therefore, the amount of diligence they give this benefit will have a direct impact on their success.

REFERENCE

Pink, D. (2004, January 24). The AHC gratitude visits. *New York Times* Sunday magazine's 100 great ideas. *Authentic Happiness Coaching Newsletter, 2*(1).

Happiness/Well-Being

Attitude of Gratitude

Purpose

To experience how an attitude of gratitude and expectation expands the palette of possibilities for creating hope and happiness.

Thumbnail

30 to 50 minutes

The team or individual focuses on what he or she is good at and what has been done successfully. Participants "dream" of what they can do to build on what they've done well. (*Note:* It will be helpful if the facilitator has an awareness of the appreciative inquiry process.)

Outcomes

- Greater self-appreciation
- Increased confidence
- Expanded happiness

Audience

- Intact team
- Unaffiliated group
- Individual working with a coach

Facilitator Competencies

Easy to Moderate

Materials

- (Team) Flip chart and colored markers
- (Individual) Paper and pens

Time Matrix

Activity	Estimated Time
Discuss concept of an appreciative approach	5–10 minutes
Share occurrences of excellence	5 minutes
Envision future	5 minutes
Discuss how they feel	5–10 minutes
Reconvene and debrief (team only)	5–10 minutes
Actions after session and wrap-up	5–10 minutes
Total	**30 to 50 minutes**

Instructions

1. This exercise is based on appreciation, as understood through the appreciative inquiry process. Discuss with the group the power of focusing on the positive. Discuss these points:
   - When the focus is on problems—"Where do they exist?" and "How many are there?" and "How do we fix them?," you will always find

Emotional Intelligence in Action

problems. In fact, you find more and more of them. The focus on problems can exacerbate them or make them seem more dire.

- Appreciative inquiry research has shown that highlighting and sharing instances of excellence ignites its proliferation. (Refer to the article "What Is Appreciative Inquiry?" www.thinbook.com/chap11fromle.html for more information.)

2. Hand out paper and pens. Ask participants to remain silent for three minutes and think in detail about:
   - (For a team) When the team or organization was at its best.
   - (For an individual) When he or she was at his or her best.

3. Ask the group or individual to share the information. Record the details about what was excellent about the situation in terms of what event or behavior made it significant. Discuss the impact and the meaning. How did it look? How did it feel? What were people saying? Record their responses on the flip chart.

4. Ask them to envision a positive future based on past or current successes. Record responses.

Team Questions

- What would the organization be like if the type of peak moments we just discussed were the norm instead of the exception?
- How would it look different?
- What would it mean to be part of it?
- What would people be saying?
- How would you feel being part of that organization?
- How would you behave in that organization?

Individual Questions

- What would it mean if peak moments were regular daily occurrences in your life?
- How would it look different?
- What would it mean to be part of it?
- What would people be saying?
- How would you feel about your life?
- How would you behave differently in the workplace? At home with family or friends?

5. Work with the individual or divide the team into groups of two to five to discuss how they feel. Have them respond to these questions:
   - Did focusing on the valuable things that have already been done make you feel more hopeful? Why or why not?
   - Did you feel happier knowing that greatness is present now and ready to manifest in you, the team, or the organization? Why do you think you felt that way?
6. If working with a team, reconvene and debrief. Ask them to share what they discussed. Capture responses. If working with an individual, capture responses as part of Step 5.
7. Ask what they can do beyond this session to expand their focus on creating more positive situations and outcomes and minimize emphasis on looking for and fixing problems. For example, when a problem surfaces, ask, "When has the organization done this correctly and what were the conditions of that positive situation?" Or, if working with an individual, ask, "When have you done this correctly and what were the conditions of that positive situation?"
8. Gain commitment from the individual or team to experiment further with this positive approach.

Resources

Authors' Consulting Services

Collaborative Growth
Marcia Hughes, President
James Terrell, Vice President
P.O. Box 17509
Golden, CO 80402
303.271.0021
connect@cgrowth.com
www.cgrowth.com
www.EITeams.com

Assessments

The following is contact information for the four assessments covered in this book:

EQ-i$^{2.0®}$
EQ360®
Multi-Health Systems, Inc.
P.O. Box 950
North Tonawanda, NY 14120–0950
800.456.3003
customerservice@mhs.com
www.mhs.com

MSCEIT™
Multi-Health Systems, Inc.
P.O. Box 950
North Tonawanda, NY 14120–0950
800.456.3003
  customerservice@mhs.com
  www.mhs.com

TESI®
Collaborative Growth
P.O. Box 17509
Golden, CO 80402
303.271.0021
  contact@cgrowth.com
  www.cgrowth.com

TESI® Short
Pfeiffer, an Imprint of Wiley
866.888.5159; 317.572.3517
  www.pfeiffer.com

Emotional Intelligence Skills Assessment (EISA)
Pfeiffer, an Imprint of Wiley
866.888.5159; 317.572.3517
  www.pfeiffer.com

References

Books and Articles

American Psychological Association. (1997). "Learned optimism" yields health results. Available: http://health.discovery.com/centers/ mental/articles/optimism/optimism.html.

Angelo, M. (1978). *And still I rise*. New York: Random House.

Angier, N. (1995, May 14). Society's glue: Science explains empathy's role for man, beast. *Denver Post*.

Ashkanasay, N.M., Hartel, C.E.J., &. Serbe. W.J. (2000). *Emotions in the workplace: Research, theory, and practice*. Westport, CT: Quorum Books.

Bar-On, R. (2000). Emotional and social intelligence: insights from the emotional quotient inventory. In R. Bar-On & J.D.A. Parker (Eds.), *The handbook of emotional intelligence*. San Francisco: Jossey-Bass.

Bar-On, R. (2001). EI and self-actualization. In J. Ciarrochi, J. Forgas, & J. Mayer (Eds.), *Emotional intelligence in everyday life*. New York: Psychology Press.

Bar-On, R. (2002). *Bar-On emotional quotient inventory (EQ-i) technical manual*. Toronto, Ontario: Multi-Health Systems, Inc.

Bar-On, R.,& Handley, R. (1999). *Optimizing people: A practical guide for applying EQ to improve personal and organizational effectiveness*. New Braunfels, TX: Pro-Philes Press.

Bennett-Goldman, T. (2001). *Emotional alchemy*. New York: Three Rivers Press.

Caruso, D.R., & Salovey, P. (2004). *The emotionally intelligent manager*. San Francisco: Jossey-Bass.

Chang, P.P., Ford, D.E., Meoni, L.A., Wang, N., & Klag, M.J. (2002). Anger in young men and subsequent premature cardiovascular disease. In *Archives of internal medicine*. Available: http:// archinte.ama-assn.org.

Cherniss, C., & Adler, M. (2000). *Promoting emotional intelligence in organizations.* Alexandria, VA: American Society for Training & Development.

Cherniss, C., & Goleman, D. (2001). *The emotionally intelligent workplace.* San Francisco: Jossey-Bass.

Childre, D. (1994). *One minute stress management freeze frame.* Boulder Creek, CA: Planetary Publications.

Childre, D., & Martin, H. (1999). *The heartmath solution.* San Francisco: Harper.

Ciarrochi, J., Forgas, J.P., & Mayer, J.D. (2001). *Emotional intelligence in everyday life.* London, England: Taylor and Francis.

Collaborative Growth's EQ Symposium. (2004). *Power tools: Connecting theory and action.* www.cgrowth.com

Cooper, R. (2001). *The other 90 percent.* New York: Three Rivers Press.

Cooper, R., & Q-Metrics. (1996). *The EQ map interpretation guide.* San Francisco: AIT and Essi Systems, Inc.

Crum, T. (1987). *The magic of conflict.* New York: Simon & Schuster.

The Dalai Lama & Cutler, H. (1998). *The art of happiness.* New York: Riverhead Books.

Damasio, A. (2003). *Looking for Spinoza.* Orlando, FL: Harcourt.

Dennison, P.E., & Dennison, G.E. (2010). *Brain gym* (teacher's ed. rev.) Ventura, CA: Edu-Kinesthetics, Inc.

Eisaguirre, L. (2002). *The power of a good fight.* Indianapolis, IN: Alpha.

Eliot, T. (1968). *Collected poems.* New York: Harcourt Press.

Eliot, T. (1968). *Four quartets.* Orlando, FL: Mariner Books.

Feldman, D.A. (1999). *The handbook of emotionally intelligent leadership: Inspiring others to achieve results.* Falls Church, VA: Leadership Performance Solutions Press.

Fisher, R., & Ury, W. (1981). *Getting to yes: Reaching agreement without giving in.* Boston: Houghton Mifflin.

Flury, J., & Ickes, W. (2001). Emotional intelligence and empathic accuracy. In J. Ciarrochi, J. Forgas, & J. Mayer (Eds.), *Emotional intelligence in everyday life.* New York: Psychology Press.

Foundation for Inner Peace. (1975). *A course in miracles.* Tiburon, CA: Foundation for Inner Peace.

Frankl, V. (2000). *Man's search for meaning.* Boston: Beacon Press.

Goleman, D. (1995). *Emotional intelligence: Why it can matter more than IQ.* New York: Bantam.

Goleman D. (1998). *Working with emotional intelligence.* New York: Bantam.

Goleman D., Boyatzis, R., & McKee, A. (2002). *Primal leadership: Realizing the power of emotional intelligence.* Cambridge, MA: Harvard Business School Press.

Gowing, M.K. (2001). Measurement of individual emotional competence. In C. Cherniss & D. Goleman (Eds.), *The emotionally intelligent workplace.* San Francisco: Jossey-Bass.

Government of India. (1987, March). *Gandhi's life in 5000 words.* Available: www.mkgandhi.org/bio5000/bio5index.htm.

Hargie, O., & Dickson, D. (2004). *Skilled interpersonal communications*. New York: Routledge.

Hughes, M. (2009). Building your team's conflict-resolution skills with emotional and social intelligence. In M. Hughes, H.L. Thompson, & J.B. Terrell (Eds.), *The handbook for developing emotional and social intelligence: Best practices, case studies and strategies*. San Francisco: Pfeiffer.

Hughes, M. (2006). *Life's 2% solution*. Boston: Nicholas Brealey.

Hughes, M. (2004). *Success and EQ*. www.cgrowth.com.

Hughes, M., & Terrell, J.B. (2007). *The emotionally intelligent team*. San Francisco: Jossey-Bass.

Hughes, M., & Terrell, J.B. (2009). *Team emotional and social intelligence (TESI short): Facilitator's guide*. San Francisco: Pfeiffer.

Jenkins, M. (2003, August). The hard way: Aaron Ralston—between a rock and the hardest place. *Outside Magazine, 28*(8).

Kapadia, M. (2004). *Emotional intelligence: A workbook for beginners*. New Delhi: BPI PVT LTD.

The King Center. (2003). *Biographical outline of Dr. Martin Luther King, Jr.* Available: www.thekingcenter.com/mlk/bio.html.

Lane, R.D. (2000). Levels of emotional awareness: Neurological, psychological and social perspectives. In R. Bar-On & J.D.A. Parker (Eds.), *The handbook of emotional intelligence*. San Francisco: Jossey-Bass

Maslow, A. (1970). *Motivation and personality* (2nd ed.). New York: Harper & Row.

Mayer, J.D., Salovey, P., & Caruso, D.R. (2000). Emotional intelligence as zeitgeist, as personality, and as a mental ability. In R. Bar-On & J.D.A. Parker (Eds.), *The handbook of emotional intelligence*. San Francisco: Jossey-Bass.

Mayer, J.D., Salovey, P., &. Caruso, D.R. (2001). *MSCEIT™ personal summary report*. New York & Toronto: Multi-Health Systems, Inc.

Mayer, J.D., Salovey, P., &. Caruso, D.R. (2002). *MSCEIT™ users manual*. New York & Toronto: Multi-Health Systems, Inc.

Neff, K.D., Rude, S., & Kirkpatrick, K.L. (2007). An examination of self-compassion in relation to positive psychological functioning and personality traits. *Journal of Research in Personality, 41*, 908–916.

Orme, G. (2001). *Emotionally intelligent living*. Glasgow, Scotland: Crown House.

Pearman, R. (2009). Personality type and emotional intelligence: Pragmatic tools for the effective practitioner. In M. Hughes, H.L. Thompson, & J.B. Terrell (Eds.), *The handbook for developing emotional and social intelligence: Best practices, case studies, and strategies*. San Francisco: Pfeiffer.

Pert, C. (1997). *Molecules of emotion*. New York: Simon & Schuster.

Pert, C. (2000). *Your body is your subconscious mind*. Boulder, CO: Sounds True.

Pink, D. (2004, January 24). The AHC gratitude visits. *New York Times* Sunday magazine's 100 great ideas. *Authentic Happiness Coaching Newsletter, 2*(1).

Salovey, P., & Sluyter, D. (1997). *Emotional development and emotional intelligence.* New York: Basic Books.

Seligman, M. (1990). *Learned optimism.* New York: Pocket Books.

Seligman, M. (2002). *Authentic happiness.* New York: The Free Press.

Seligman, M. (2011). *Flourish.* New York: The Free Press.

Shakespeare, W. *King Lear.* Available: www-tech.mit.edu/Shakespeare/works.html.

Stein, S., & Book, H. (2011). *The EQ edge: Emotional intelligence and your success* (3rd ed.). San Francisco: Jossey-Bass.

Turow, J. (1997). *Breaking up America: Advertisers and the new-media world.* Chicago: University of Chicago Press.

Ury, W. (2000). *The third side: Why we fight and how we can stop.* New York: Penguin Books.

Various Artists. (1987). *Largo.* San Francisco: LIND Institute. Available: www.relaxwiththeclassics.com/pages/ordering.htm.

Webster's third international new dictionary. (1993). Springfield, MO: Merriam-Webster, Inc.

Weisinger, H. (1998). *Emotional intelligence at work.* San Francisco: Jossey-Bass.

Whitney, J., & Packer, T. (2001). *Power plays.* New York: Simon & Schuster.

WEBSITES

www.authentichappiness.org

www.cgrowth.com

www.christianethicstoday.com

www.eiconsortium.org

www.eiconsortium.org/reports/business_case_for_ei.html

www.EITeams.com

www.emergenetics.com

www.heartmath.com

www.MayoClinic.com or www.TheMayoClinic.com

www.mhs.com

www.mindpub.com/art411.htm

www.MKGandhi.com

www.newworldrecords.org

www.pfeiffer.com/go/Hughes/EIAction2

www.positivepsychology.org

www.opm.gov/ses/recruitment/ecq.asp#ecq5

www.thinbook.com

About the Authors

Marcia Hughes, J.D., M.A., is president of Collaborative Growth®, L.L.C., and serves as a strategic communications partner for teams and their leaders in organizations that value high performers. She weaves her expertise in emotional intelligence throughout her consulting work, facilitation, team building, and workshops to help people motivate themselves and communicate more effectively with others. Her keynotes are built around powerful stories of how success can grow when people work collaboratively. Marcia and her partner, James Terrell, are authors of The Team Emotional and Social Intelligence Survey® (TESI® and TESI® Short), an online team assessment. She is co-editor of *The Handbook for Developing Emotional Intelligence* (2009), co-author of *Developing Emotional Intelligence: Exercises for Leaders and Teams* (2010), *A Facilitator's Guide to Team Emotional and Social Intelligence,* (2009), *A Coach's Guide for Emotional Intelligence* (2008), *The Emotionally Intelligent Team* (2007), *Emotional Intelligence in Action* (2005), and author of *Life's 2% Solution* (2006). Marcia works with many diverse clients, including American Express, Medtronic, the World Bank, the Office of Personnel Management, and the Department of Agriculture.

Marcia is a certified trainer in the TESI®, and the EQ-I$^{2.0®}$ and EQ360®. She provides train-the-trainer training and coaching in powerful EI delivery. Her efforts to improve productivity in the workplace through strategic communication grew out of a distinguished career in law, where her firm specialized in complex public policy matters. She also served as an assistant attorney general and clerked on the 10th Circuit Court of Appeals for the Honorable William E. Doyle.

James Bradford Terrell is vice president of Collaborative Growth, where he applies his expertise in interpersonal communication to help a variety of public- and private-sector clients anticipate change and respond resiliently. Co-author of the Team Emotional and Social Intelligence Survey®, (TESI®), *Emotional Intelligence in Action, The Emotionally Intelligent Team*, and *A Coaches Guide to Emotional Intelligence*, he coaches leaders, teams in transition, and senior management, using the EQ-i®, the EQ360®, the TESI®, Emergenetics®, and other assessments.

He worked as a psychotherapist in private practice for many years, seeing primarily clients who were seeking to resolve conflict in relationships—with their spouses, children, parents, employers, and/or co-workers. For three years, he was executive director of the Syntropy Institute, a not-for-profit research organization investigating how communication training impacts human effectiveness. He also served as the director of training for the Metro-Denver Mutual Housing Association, an early developer of cooperative housing.

In a previous life, he was the owner/operator of Integrity Building Systems, a construction company specializing in residential and commercial renovation and served as a project coordinator on a wide variety of projects, including Denver International Airport and the National Digital Cable Television Center.

Index

Page references followed by *fig* indicate an illustrated figure; followed by *t* indicate a table.

Emotional expression handouts: Expressing Emotions in Social Media, 210; Expressing Resistance, 197–198; Say It Nonverbally!, 28*t*, 201–202

Emotional intelligence skill building: be informed for, 117; change required for, 119–120; using the exercises for, 120; facilitator skills for, 118–119

Emotional power development, 15–16

Emotional self-awareness: EQ-i$^{2.0}$ on, 18, 19*fig*, 20; exercises and handouts on, 28*t*, 171–194; *Frost/Nixon* reel performer of, 36*t*, 50–51; how we can build, 49; Maya Angelou star performer of, 36*t*, 49–50; transitional benefits of, 49; why we should care about, 48–49

Emotional self-awareness exercises: Are You in Touch?, 28*t*, 175–178; Expanding Your Uncommon Awareness, 28*t*, 171–172; It Just Bubbles Up, 28*t*, 181–183; Moving Toward and Moving Away, 28*t*, 187–189

Emotional self-awareness handouts: Are You in Touch?, 179; Expanding Your Uncommon Awareness, 173–174; It Just Bubbles Up, 184–185; Moving Toward and Moving Away, 190–194

Emotions: biochemistry roots of, 10; the brain and, 13; description of, 12; examining meaning and nature of, 10–11; expressing in social media, 207–210; the heart and, 13–14; how we develop, 48; identity and, 14–15

Emotions Affect Decision Making Exercise, 31*t*, 317–319

Emotions Affect Decision Making Handout, 320–321

Empathy: definition of, 71–72; EQ-i$^{2.0}$ on, 19*fig*, 20; exercises and handouts on, 30*t*, 269–288; how to build, 73–74; learning to read body language and, 74; Mother Teresa star performer of, 36*t*, 74–75; *Terms of Endearment* reel performer of, 36*t*, 75; transformational benefits of, 74; why we should care about, 72–73

Empathy exercises: Connect Feeling with Meaning, 30*t*, 273–275; Do as the Empathic Do, 30*t*, 285–287; Mixed Emotions, 30*t*, 277–279; Recipe for Influence: Curiosity and Compassion, 30*t*, 269–272

Empathy handouts: Do as the Empathic Do, 288; Mixed Emotions, 280–284

The EQ Edge (Stein & Book), 21, 43, 110, 156

EQ (emotional quotient): description of, 11; examining four measures of, 2–3

EQ-i, 18, 53

EQ-i$^{2.0}$: Cross-Reference Matrix to use with, 27*t*–34*t*; elegance of the, 21; Happiness/Well-Being Indicator in, 19*fig*, 21, 113–116, 453–470; intro to scales and skills defined by the, 18–20; introduction to, 18–21; learning how to use the, 15–16; skilled interpretation of, 20

EQ-i$^{2.0}$ scales: intro to Decision Making scale, 19*fig*, 20; intro to Interpersonal scale, 19*fig*, 20; intro to Self-Expression scale, 19*fig*, 20; intro to Self-Perception scale, 18–19*fig*, 20; intro to Stress Management scale, 19*fig*, 20, 21. *See also specific scale*

EQ Symposium (Collaborative Growth), 2

EQ360: Cross-Reference Matrix to use with, 27t–34t; description of, 18; elegance of the, 21

"An Examination of Self-Compassion in Relation to Positive Psychological Functioning and Personality Traits" (Neff, Rude, and Kirkpatrick), 122

Exercise handouts: assertiveness, 214–216, 222, 226, 229–230; emotional expression, 197–198, 201–202, 210; emotional self-awareness, 173–174, 179, 184–185, 190–194; empathy, 280–284, 288; flexibility, 389–390, 394–395, 400; Happiness/Well-Being Indicator, 456–457, 462; icon indicating downloadable copies of, 5; impulse control, 363–364, 376, 380–382, 385–386; independence, 234–235, 240, 244, 248; interpersonal relations, 257, 261–263; optimism, 434–436, 440, 447–452; Personality Quiz, 415–416; problem solving, 313–315, 320–321, 330, 334, 338–339; reality testing, 352–353, 358–360; reproducing exercise, 120; self-actualization, 142–144, 149–153, 158–161, 166–169; self-regard, 124, 128, 132–134, 138; social responsibility, 295–297, 301–303; stress tolerance, 415–419, 428–429

Exercises: assertiveness, 29t, 211–230; building emotional intelligence skills by using the, 120; Cross-Reference Matrix on, 26, 27t–34t; debriefing and reflection section of, 6; emotional expression, 28t, 195–210; emotional self-awareness, 28t, 171–194; empathy, 30t, 269–288; facilitator skills and best practices for, 118–119; flexibility, 33t, 387–403;

Happiness/Well-Being Indicator, 34t, 453–470; impulse control, 32t–33t, 361–386; independence, 29t, 231–248; interpersonal relations, 29t–30t, 249–267; "materials" section of each, 6; optimism, 34t, 431–452; problem solving, 31t–32t, 309–339; using the Purpose, Thumbnail, and Outcomes sections of, 120; reality testing, 32t, 341–360; recommendations prior to using the, 117; selection of specific, 6; self-actualization, 27t, 139–169; self-regard, 27t, 121–138; social responsibility, 31t, 289–307; stress tolerance, 33t–34t, 411–429. *See also* EI (emotional intelligence)

Expanding Your Uncommon Awareness Exercise, 28t, 171–172

Expanding Your Uncommon Awareness Handout, 173–174

Expressing Emotions in Social Media Exercise, 28t, 207–209

Expressing Emotions in Social Media Handout, 210

Expressing Resistance Exercise, 28t, 195–196

Expressing Resistance Handout, 197–198

EZ Stress Buster Exercise, 33t, 405–406

EZ Stress Buster Handout, 407–409

F

Facilitator guidelines: debriefing and reflection, 6; materials, 6; preparation, 5–6; recommended for exercises, 118–119; selection, 6

Facilitators: using the exercises in for individual and team coaching, 4; guidelines for, 5–6; Ramp It Up role-play template instructions for, 221;